THE LAST GREAT APE

THE LAST GREAT APE

A Journey Through Africa and a
Fight for the Heart of the Continent

OFIR DRORI and DAVID McDANNALD

PEGASUS BOOKS
NEW YORK

THE LAST GREAT APE

Pegasus Books LLC
80 Broad Street, 5th Floor
New York, NY 10004

First Pegasus Books cloth edition 2012

Interior design by Maria Fernandez

All photographs © Ofir Drori

ISBN: 978-1-60598-327-1

10 9 8 7 6 5 4 3 2 1

Printed in the United States of America
Distributed by W. W. Norton & Company, Inc.

If you set out on a journey pray that the road is long
a wandering without apparent aim a blind groping
so you come to know earth's harshness not just by sight but by touch
so that you measure yourself against the world with your whole skin

When you come to know don't speak of knowing
learn the world again like an Ionian philosopher
know the taste of water and fire of air and earth
for they will remain when all has passed away

So if there is a journey pray that it be long
a true journey from which you do not return
a copying of the world an elemental journey
a dialogue with nature an unanswered question
a pact forced after a battle

from "Journey"
by Zbigniew Herbert

KITA

The cinderblock wall glowed green in the light, as if the house were underwater. A metal bowl sat on the clay near a plastic bucket for washing clothes. In the outdoor kitchen were enough plates and pans to serve a village, and standing next to the mud-splattered wall was a young chimpanzee. She walked forward on her hind legs and extended a hand toward an old man, Christopher.

"How's it going?" Christopher said in French, as if the chimp were greeting him.

When she reached the end of her chain, she jerked and lowered an arm to the ground to regain her balance. The chimp was a year and a half to two years old and no doubt a survivor of the slaughter of her family by poachers.

"Leave it. Leave it," said the dealer. "Hey, Kita!"

"You call her how?" Christopher said.

"Kita. Kita, leave it!"

She grew panicked and scared as Christopher followed the big-bellied dealer away from her, toward the road. Kita whined, "Ooh ooh ooh ooh." And Christopher mumbled something I couldn't understand;

he was difficult to understand in person, let alone on the recording of a hidden camera.

I rewound the tape.

On the video recorder's tiny screen I watched the footage again.

The shoulder bag Christopher had just carried from his meeting with the dealer sat at my feet. Stuck to the bag as a distraction from the button-sized eye of the hidden camera was a yellow Guinness pin, now covered with bugs that had crawled out of the grass. The camera contraption inside the bag was held together by duct tape, our near budget-less improvisations never ceasing to amaze me for working. Christopher was a retired military adjutant in his mid-fifties and one of my undercover agents, and we stood together, hiding behind luxurious Hotel Azur in Bastos, Yaoundé's richest neighborhood.

I touched Christopher's shoulder, and he moved off toward the hotel entrance to wait. The dealer Tonye Nken had set the price of the chimpanzee at 150,000 francs, around $250. And if what Nken had said was true, he was now on his way to the hotel to finalize the sale to Christopher.

I pushed the rifle barrel of one of the men down toward the grass. Four armed policemen stood around me with an officer from the Ministry of Environment and Forestry (MINEF). I felt the inevitable fear of violence that accompanied the necessary deterrent of guns.

"Temgoua, do you understand we need to do it quick?" said our lead police officer, Julius, who wore an olive green uniform.

"Yes, of course," said Temgoua the MINEF official as he adjusted his beret.

"Not like at the market with those ladies selling elephant meat," Julius said. "We don't want luck to be the reason we get out of here. You explain the law and we take him. He doesn't need a lecture about animals."

Julius' forearms were roped with veins, his bearing that of a man twice his size. Quiet Temgoua spent a decent portion of his MINEF salary on cable television so he could watch nature films.

"Again," I said, "if a car comes with the dealer but no chimp, no one moves."

"Mmm," Julius and Temgoua hummed in accord.

"If that happens, Christopher calls me from his mobile, and I give him new instructions. If the dealer plays it smart and sends someone in his place to deliver the chimp, no one moves. To keep the dealer from escaping we have to get him away from his vehicle."

I rushed around the building when a car drove up, but Christopher waved me off. I could smell the tropical stink of my underarms. The pipes in my house had been dry for days and I was even dirtier than when I'd slept in the bottom of a canoe on the Niger; rivers had long been better habitats for me than towns. The police officers blotted their foreheads with their sleeves. Ignatius, a man along to film the arrest, had helped to recruit Julius to the team. We made a suspicious gang lurking behind the hotel with a video camera and assault rifles and we could only hope no one spotted us.

At 1:20 P.M., twenty minutes past the meeting time, I crept along the flowerbeds between the hotel and its high outer wall. The equatorial sun was radiating off the driveway, the place as hot as cleared jungle. Christopher leaned against an empty concrete guardhouse at the hotel entrance. He wore a light blue administrative suit with a short-sleeve coat and he'd lowered his top hat over his eyes like an old-time detective.

"Call him, Christopher. Ask if he's on his way. We don't care much about his answer. Just listen if you can hear a car engine in the background."

Christopher moved off toward the hotel lobby, swinging his limbs in slow motion as if parodying a spy film, as if such a gait made him invisible. I was anxious, squeezing the bridge of my nose, marveling at the potential catastrophes I managed to invent. We'd picked Bastos for the arrest, a place packed with embassies and non-governmental organizations (NGOs) where empty streets offered safety from mobs we'd faced in recent operations, some of them so chaotic I'd rushed to erase our video footage to avoid losing the support of anyone who saw it.

Christopher had searched Yaoundé the past week for dealers, inquired in the markets, posed as the cook of a white man interested in having a pet chimp. A number of recent leads on apes had turned out to be monkeys unprotected by law, and I was skeptical when Christopher told me he had the phone number of a man trying to sell a chimpanzee. Twice Christopher had visited the dealer's house in Chapelle Simeon. He told the dealer, "The white man won't come to you, and I'm not going to handle this wild animal. You come with it, eh? He gives you the money direct." For every live orphaned ape outside the jungle, it was estimated that there were nine other apes who'd been shot in the hunt. The illegal commercial trade for ape meat and for pets, not subsistence-level hunting or habitat loss, was driving chimps and gorillas toward extinction. Jane Goodall had estimated that, if the well-organized trade was not stopped, apes in the wild would be gone in fewer than twenty years.

Outside the hotel lobby, a Cameroonian driver leaned against a Mercedes, another against a 4×4, their patrons likely dining inside or attending the seminar advertised in French on a sign by the front steps: "Poverty Alleviation—Phase II Workshop." Decades of meetings and strategy papers had left Central Africa even poorer, lagging behind in indicators ranging from education to health; the international community and the aid business did not deal with the primary obstacle to both development and conservation: corruption. I'd recently founded my NGO with the aim of bringing new ways to an old system. Fighting for animals, I hoped, was just the beginning.

Christopher slid into view, walked across the parking lot and whispered to me, "The dealer is coming now. Yes." He lowered his top hat and sidled toward the guardhouse. I dashed past the flowerbeds and the finely clipped cone-shaped trees and ducked around the back of the hotel where our tiny army was waiting. For a few seconds my mind went to Rachel, the woman I loved and could not stop loving, the woman I'd lived with in Tel Aviv, who I'd neither seen nor spoken to in the months since I'd told her I had to return to Africa.

A car clanked up the road. Stopped. I peeked out from behind the hotel. Christopher stepped back and lifted his arm in a gesture lacking even a hint of subtlety.

"We move! He's here," I said to the team. "Go! Go! Go!"

I sprinted toward the gate. Julius shot past me with the policemen, their rifles raised. The dealer looked up as we rushed into the road and swarmed him and a younger man. It seemed not to have occurred to them to flee. The dealer Tonye Nken was slumped at the shoulders, his striped red and brown shirt tucked in around his gut, kempt with unkempt. The chimp, hugging the young man, was redolent with a sour, oily smell I'd come to love.

"The wildlife law of 1994, article 158," Temgoua said, "states that any person caught with a class A endangered species, living or dead, whole or in part, is subject to a maximum of three years in prison."

Kita spun out of her handler's arms and sat between his feet, looking up at him.

"I'm the son of a chief," the dealer said in French, likely thinking he could threaten or bribe his way out of the problem; in Cameroon, police harassment was as ordinary as eating, and the culture of corruption rendered many laws useless.

Temgoua was mumbling again about animals. "Who is the owner?" I said.

"I am," the dealer said, patting his chest and then motioning toward the young man holding Kita. "I'm his father."

"You came here to sell it?" I said.

"Yes." He pointed at Christopher. "Ask him."

Christopher held up his arms as if a pistol had been jammed against his ribs.

"He's just working for me," I said. "He didn't know I was coming for you."

A waitress yelled from the hotel driveway. Passing taxis stopped in the road to watch. The stressed, mustard-eyed chimp pursed her lips. An officer swung toward the hotel with his gun when a man in a suit sprinted toward us, his shoes slapping the hotel driveway. The man said, "I want to see your IDs! You can't do this at my hotel! There are customers here. Who is your boss?"

"Come, come, we go. Let's move!" Julius said and ushered the dealer toward one of our waiting taxis. Julius pushed him into the backseat and climbed in with the officers, and they headed for the station.

Not wanting to shock the baby chimp by separating her from her handler, I asked the dealer's son to accompany me to my house on the edge of Yaoundé, where the city gave way to rainforest. Scowling and quiet, the thick-shouldered boy sat beside me in the cab, watching Yaoundé pass beyond the window. He wore blue jeans. He was around eighteen years old. I was twenty-six.

"I think your father will be locked tonight in jail. Tomorrow the state council will decide if the case moves forward to trial. You can see your father tonight if you want. Tomorrow, too. In the end, it's the judge who decides what happens."

The chimp grabbed at the window. A naked man may have seemed just as out of place in a cab as Kita. She pressed her nose to the boy's neck.

"I see she loves you very much," I said. "You must be treating her well."

The boy's angst broke with a smile.

"Kita will stay with me," I said. "For one month, two months, until we find her a place in the forest with other chimpanzees.

"To get this law applied and to make sure no one bribes the police, lawyers, or judge—this is my work." I pulled a business card from my pocket and put it in the boy's hand. "My phone number is written there. My name is there. It's Ofir. If your mother has questions or if you want to know what's happening with your father, call me. Or she can. And I'll explain more."

I didn't tell him that if his father was sentenced for trafficking in an endangered species, it would be a victory over corruption and likely the first prosecution for wildlife crime in all of West and Central Africa. I didn't tell the boy that while I felt for his father, I planned to battle with all I had to put the man in prison.

And to prison he would go. My path to activism and my arrival to this moment, at the birth of the Last Great Ape Organization, had led across the continent, from the savannah to warzones, to rivers, rebels, and back. Without intense experiences spread across eight years, I would never have learned how to begin my fight.

1994

KENYA

WILD CONQUEROR

Nairobi was cold as morning desert. The savannah stretched into the bluish haze beyond the airport like an image I'd carried in childhood. The sun peeked over the horizon, and light moved through branches of the acacia trees, through the grass, until the scene was beautiful enough for elephants.

I descended stairs parked against the jet and scampered up the runway behind other passengers, my pack wobbling on my back. I approached a stranger in the terminal and asked him to share a taxi into the city. Swahili sounded from the cab's stereo as the car creaked away from the airport like a swing on a playground. The driver accelerated. Kenya rushed at me as we swerved between potholes and minivans jammed with passengers. A broken traffic light was bent over, on the verge of toppling into an intersection. A man in a rancid T-shirt pushed a cart but turned before I could see his face. A boy, even skinnier than I, sold wrenches. Women strolled with pots balanced on their heads. An advertisement on a crumbling wall of a fat woman drinking Coke. A median strung with barbed wire, cracked, disintegrating pavement, businessmen in suits standing in the dirt.

There was too much to follow, all at once everything new. And gray.
A world filled with trash unlike the Africa I knew from books, magazines, and films. I became conscious of my breath: winded, breathing
through my mouth. Was I wrong to have come?

Nearly from the time I could talk, I'd planned to travel to Africa,
a place as different as I wanted to think I was. My parents had
ordained my love of the continent, perhaps, by naming me after an
ancient and unknown African land mentioned in the bible. *Hiram's
fleet brought gold from Ophir.* My mother had stoked my wildness.
She took me to a junkyard to play with glass so I would experience
being cut as a three year old. She brought home bags of shredded
paper and styrofoam and said, "Swim in this." When I was four,
she sent me off to buy milk for my younger sister, and a neighbor
found me trying to cross the highway two kilometers away. Mom,
an Arabic teacher, scoured bookshops for Tarzan comics by Edgar
Rice Burroughs: "Tarzan, King of the Apes," "Tarzan, the Wild
Conqueror," "Tarzan and the Treasures of Ofir." I roamed the neighborhood through first grade in underwear, climbing and falling
and swinging from trees, my mother criticized then for how she
raised me and criticized now for allowing me at the age of eighteen
to travel to Africa alone.

The cabdriver stopped at a *matatu* station, a chaos of minibuses
and bodies in a swirl of dust. The man in the front seat spoke with
the driver, both of them bungling their English. I gripped the door
handle but couldn't see the faces of those standing around the cab.
My glasses slipped down my nose. I checked my pocket notebook
again, which I'd filled with photocopied maps and details from
Lonely Planet about safaris and hotels. I could hear my father's
voice: *You have your backpack? Your passport? The money didn't fall
out of your pocket? Check the seat. Okay. You just need a hotel room.
It's as simple as you planned.* I opened the door when the other
man did and stepped outside, smelling wood smoke and tar. The
air was colder than in Israel. "Hell Raider" was painted on the side
of a *matatu*. I spun around. Men were shouting. At me? I scurried
through a cloud of truck exhaust toward the sign for Hotel Iqbal.
A street tout stood on shattered pavement near the front doors, and
he said, "Want to go on safari? Let's go." As he led me up the road, I

stumbled because I was looking back at the hotel, wondering if my father would say I was stupid for allowing the plan to change.

Skyscrapers gave way to metal shacks and then to savannah, and I motored with seven other travelers in a minivan toward the Maasai Mara, saying little, anxious I'd become passive, for participation grew harder the longer it was absent. A Frenchman in a khaki adventure vest talked to a cute Israeli girl. Two Brits in the back spoke to each other, though if they were a couple it didn't count that they were talking. Had the Mexican spoken more than I? His cheeks were so dry and cracked, it seemed he'd been buried in the desert for decades. He probably thought I was a child. Why hadn't I spoken at the beginning when it was easy?

Three Thomson's gazelles leapt from the edge of the highway. *Eudorcas thomsonii*! Just beside the road! And we weren't even in a park! Their white tails bobbed as they darted off, and I turned consciously to watch them as we passed, in part because it made sense not to talk when fascinated. The grasslands were endless, so vast that they seemed already to belong to a different year than the quick morning in Nairobi.

A thousand afternoons I'd spent barefoot in the field near our three-room flat in Tel Aviv, often with my sister, Mor. We overturned rocks in search of lizards, hedgehogs, and snakes and one winter carried home a viper and called up to Dad. "Don't worry, Dad!" I said. "It's cold; she's not moving!" And he descended the stairs and photographed eight-year-old Mor holding the viper up by the tail.

Alarmed neighbors more than once called wildlife control.

From fifth through ninth grade, I attended Teva, a shoeless, gradeless experimental school where knowledge became an identity and I grew to believe that gathering knowledge was life's highest calling. Dad, an electrical engineer who wore a thick beard, helped in every pursuit I dreamed up. He brought home a thermostat from work so I could regulate the temperature of snake eggs in my living room aquariums. He helped me build a camera trap using a car battery, a mechanical arm and a beam and reflector from an elevator. I extracted venom from scorpions, dissected snakes and whitened their bones with chlorine. Dead geckos I dried and I stored their skeletons in

bubblegum boxes and memorized the Latin names of the bones. I'd left Israel just once in my life, on a family bus trip to Egypt, the gift I'd wanted for my *bar mitzvah*. Now, I had three weeks in Kenya and then three years of drudgery in the army.

The tourists grumbled about the dust and the potholes, about creeping toward the Maasai Mara to the detriment of daylight, about rushing away from the curio stands. The Mexican held up the plastic handle he spun to rewind his cassette tape without using batteries. "These will do so much for the human race," he said with great seriousness. "They're from Mexico." I pretended to rewind his voice back into his throat.

Beyond the town of Narok we sliced across plains where zebras stood in high grass. Hills flared in all directions. Red-robed men grazed cattle on distant ridges—Maasai. The farther we traveled, the less likely it seemed we would ever happen upon another town, and I was struck by the power over the psyche of a place so far from home.

The Maasai Mara was orange in the late-day sun. We stopped within a herd of buffalo. The driver slid back the roof. And everyone climbed onto the seats, our heads sprouting above the truck like giant warts. Behind the buffalo were more buffalo and zebras and gazelles stretching forever in a shifting, uncountable herd, like a massive, singular life form claiming the land—the world before Nairobi, before Tel Aviv in a wetter time. Elephants crossed the road without even glancing at us. I hadn't understood why my friends had flown off to Disneyland and Pisa in our break between secondary school and the army, and I understood it even less now.

The next afternoon we stopped at the "lunch station," an island of dirt marked off under an acacia tree like some magical safe zone. The tourists huddled with their food near the vans as if from fear of being run down by cheetahs. A blond four-year-old girl explored among the trucks, dashing around the African drivers, touching them and laughing. The girl balanced barefoot on one of the boundary poles lying flat in the grass, then hopped and sprinted away. I caught my reflection in the side mirror of the safari truck. I was gangly, in bottle

cap glasses with gold frames and huge square lenses that made my nose look thin as a guitar pick. I thought of my army interview two months earlier when I'd sat at the desk of a beautiful woman. She'd said, "I notice you have a gray tooth. Does it disturb you?" This was as close as I'd come in the last year to a date.

I shifted from foot to foot, starved for sugar, regretting I'd brought no chocolate, not knowing whom to talk to and sure I looked as awkward as I felt. The Mexican, who had a masters in biology, was the easiest of the tourists to approach. He nodded and touched my shoulder as I told him that after the army I planned to devote my life to the academy as a biologist or physicist. I told him I'd volunteered in the zoological gardens of Tel Aviv University where I managed a hundred aquariums and assisted a scientist in his research on water snakes. I said, "I studied the social life of the common lizard at fourteen and I think the agamidae and iguana families arose, not through convergent evolution, as believed, but *divergent* evolution, and we must do more research on their thyroid bones!"

The light brought such texture to the clouds that the sky seemed full of faces. Clouds over Israel now seem by comparison to be flat. I gazed across the Mara and imagined that beyond the hills lived isolated tribes, who were herding cattle, hunting, guarding themselves—from us, from me. After Teva, I'd enrolled in an everyday high school and then woken each morning and decided whether to go to class. Often I went instead to Tel Aviv University and rode the elevator up to the library to read textbooks in English. My mother was always thrilled to write "my child was sick" notes. By eleventh grade, I had earned the ire of most of my teachers. *Oh, yeah, Ofir is sick again.* Near the start of twelfth grade, while driving the family car, I listened to Metallica's "Jump in the Fire" over and over again to build the courage to cut the safety rope to the education system. I registered as an independent with the Ministry of Education so they would send me exams directly, gambling that I could teach myself as well as my disgruntled teachers. Then I went to the head teacher and said, "I'm not continuing at your high school."

Hovering in front of the safari van was a creature shaped like the letter T, a giant black T, like a flying top children spin from their palms. We drove closer. It was a bird! Its long tail hung down like a ribbon as it flew. I stood on the seat alone and snapped a photograph. We found another animal of impossible proportions later in Amboseli, a giraffe gazelle or *swala twiga*, whose ears stuck out like an alien's and whose neck was so long in proportion to his body, he seemed to have been assembled by children. Why were animals so interesting not taught in school? How in all the books I'd read had I never learned of a *swala twiga*? I looked back at the travelers. Only the British girl showed any interest. The animals were as bored of us as the tourists were of anything but the Big Five. We followed the ant trails and worked our way through a traffic jam of a dozen safari vans to a leopard.

"It looks like it's made of rubber and nailed to the tree," the Frenchman said.

The Brits pontificated as to why the leopard or some lion wouldn't just attack us—fear of the truck, fear of the scent of gasoline, fear of our collective size. The driver put an end to their talk when he said, "No, no, the only thing scaring a lion is the red *shuka* of a Maasai."

"Whoever wants to pay three hundred shillings extra can see the nice village, a Maasai *boma*," said the driver as he flung open the van door.

We were just outside the Mara.

Encircling the village was a mud wall built and shaped by hands, and around the wall was a thorn bush fence. A man in a *shuka* chatted with the driver in Swahili as we walked toward the village entrance. Heavy earrings pulled the man's earlobes to his neck as if his ears were tuned to something I couldn't hear.

Inside the fence, women in blue checkered capes hurried over in a buzz of shouting. "Hello. Hello. You like?" Jewelry hung from the hands and arms of the chattering, jittery Maasai. People charged from all directions with carvings, knives, necklaces, as if they'd just raided the inner sanctum of a temple. I searched through the mayhem for the village, wanting my bearings in the swarm of hands. Dust. Necklaces. Flies landed on my lips. Sour cow dung roasted in the sun. I wiped sweat from my face and slid through a gap in the throng. Rectangular mud huts with flat roofs faced inward onto a courtyard. The Mexican, bartering for a bow and arrow, said, "I'll give you 150 shillings. Not more." A man thrusting circular knives up to my face spoke in a language I didn't understand.

Jewelry, on black sheets of plastic, lay on the ground in swirls of color beside cheap daggers with cowskin sheaths. People shouted around the Frenchman. A camera flashed. Women on tiny stools watched as I picked up an earring as big and beautiful as a butterfly's wing. I caught my breath and let myself imagine that the earring's beads were from old times, traded perhaps for spices or ivory. I flipped the earring over and found that half of it was made of plastic, yellow lettered plastic that I traced to the margarine tubs where the women stashed their money.

An old woman pushed armloads of necklaces up to my eyes.

"Thank you. I don't need this," I said as gently as I could.

I stuck my hand out, and she finally lowered the jewelry so I could see. The world fell away as the old Maasai looked at me in silence. Her eyes were moist. She seemed to be thinking of something—a calf, I imagined, a calf that needed tending. And her face! It was entirely wrinkled, with lines cutting through wrinkles, wrinkles within wrinkles, as though her skin had been cut by water. She wore on her face an entire lifetime of living outside and a map of what her people were.

The jewelry swung from her forearms as she hobbled toward the Mexican.

I scanned the periphery. Goats milled near the entrance. Children dashed, disappeared into a hut. A breeze carried the sharp odor of goat dung. And the soil was dung, old dung, with a consistency of dry broken dirt. Shouting villagers behind me went silent. In a ring of Maasai, the Frenchman performed a magic trick with a stick that spurred the men to drop their goods and search the ground for sticks of their own. In one small gesture he transformed the selling into conversation and laughter.

"We can see a *manyatta* now, a hut," the driver said. "You'll want to take pictures."

A Maasai led us deeper into the *boma*. Children peeked out from doorways. Bowlegged, uncircumcised boys waddled around their grandmother's knees. A girl darted into a hut. The goats are real, I said to myself. The wrinkles and smells and children are real. We stopped at the door of a mud hut. The red-caped man turned and called to someone. A woman stepped forward, wearing one red and one blue *shuka*. Her head was shaved. Encircling her neck were necklaces, different from those I'd seen for sale, the patterns of the beads encoded, our driver had said, with her story, age group, family, and who she'd married. She found a rope among the beads and slipped it off her head. On the rope was a brass key. The Maasai man worked the key into a padlock on the door.

I closed my eyes. How could a traditional hut be locked? Wasn't a village supposed to be a family? I stepped inside the *manyatta* with my expectations churning in my stomach like soured food. Ashes, a recent fire; people did live here. But they'd made their home into an exhibit, just another part of the market. I walked out by myself; whatever was real within the village I could not touch.

HELL'S GATE

Naivasha seemed as arbitrarily located as a *matatu* stand, a town built around a place in the dirt where vehicles stopped. Kenyans strolled the unpaved roads, the men in Western clothes, their belts pulled tight as balloon knots, the women in colorful, puffy-shouldered dresses, kicking along in high heels too small for their feet. Shops were made of concrete and sheet metal, the businesses within revealed by the murals that adorned them: on the *Duka ya Dawa* was a painting of cough syrup pouring into a teaspoon, on the *Kinyozi* a mural of scissors and a man with a triangular hairdo.

It was my sixth day in Kenya, and I'd begun my journey again, by *matatu*. I was headed for the wilds alone. I sat on the public bus waiting for empty seats to fill and thumbing through my pocket notebook to where I'd written the names of safari and rafting companies. I drew an X across the page. I drew an X over information on jeep rentals, an X across the location in Nairobi of the Thorn Tree where travelers clipped notes for each other, for the safari had revealed how far greater were the freedoms I sought. I left my bag on the seat and climbed off the bus, which looked like one of the wrecked lorries along the Jerusalem highway dating to the war of '48.

A man smiled at me as a truck stormed up the road.

"*Jambo*," I said, greeting him.

Swahili raced out of his mouth like a rabbit shooting through the grass.

I said, "I'm just learning."

"Where do you come from?" he said in English. "What are you doing?"

Two more men stopped to talk and teach me lines of Swahili. I skipped to a grocery shack made from rough-cut boards and bought a deck of cards and a packet of balloons while thinking of how the Frenchman had disarmed and charmed the Maasai sellers with his magic trick. Back in the bus, I played cards with a Kenyan guy my age, and within minutes I learned to count in Swahili and was laughing at the vocabulary words I'd cut from *Lonely Planet* and glued into my notebook, the Swahili for *custard apple, guyaba, squid*. X. When the bus was full of Africans, a woman climbed on with a baby and a piece of luggage that was a white grain sack. I gave her my seat; participate, I told myself. And I leapt down to the road. Two ladders ran up the back of the bus, and a boy scurried up and down one of them, loading luggage onto the roof, shouting what had to be the names of villages around Lake Naivasha. I climbed midway up the second ladder. The boy and I slapped hands. He banged the roof with his palm. And the bus puttered out of the station, the ladder trying to pull free from my grip as we accelerated up the road. Air rushed into my open mouth, because I couldn't stop smiling for the joy of having finally arrived in Africa.

I slept at Fisherman's Camp on the lake and trekked alone to the boundaries of Hell's Gate National Park. I had my tent. I'd brought food—Nice biscuits, buns, and a dozen Cadbury chocolate bars. The landscape beyond the park entrance was so gray and barren compared to the Mara, that I was surprised to see gazelles. They were watching me. When I realized there was no reason not to, I veered off the gravel road toward them. I paused and pretended to graze, then rotated my head. The gazelles were delicate and nervous, with curious black eyes. Their ears twinkled. And they ran.

I tiptoed toward a warthog with tusks jutting from his mouth like the legs of a half-swallowed frog. I crept up to a hartebeest, his horns black and crooked as daggers ruined by fire. He glanced up, put his nose down, then looked over again, as though torn between fear and flirtation. Dik-diks, antelope, and ostriches came toward me, not like images from a textbook, but like characters, like individuals. Elated, I bounded from tree to rock to animal, zigzagging away from the road until I lost all sense of where I was, the landscape more wondrous with each hour I roamed.

A black ridge stretched into the distance like a wall protecting some older world. I scrambled up loose shale on the pathless mountain, through rock and brush, feeling the constant urge to laugh as animals shrank below me on the plains. Wind shot up the cliff wall, caught my backpack and twisted me. I pressed my stomach to the rock and waited for the updraft to blow itself out. An eagle circled against the moon, which lay on its curve like a half-closed eye. The wind brought a sense of isolation that engulfed all but the sound of my climb—rocks clinking, tumbling down, my boots sliding in the gravel as if they were too big for my feet. I reached the flat mountaintop with the ascent burning in my lungs and I lay on my stomach, eyes over the cliff edge. Giraffes below were barely more than motionless dots, and the landscape swept into the distance and disappeared into a haze of sandy air. I was amazed at the thought of who in the past had seen the same. And I was amazed at how much world there was beyond Israel. Our culture was so strongly rooted—who were we? We were Israeli and we were Jewish. It was a religion, a nationality, and a place of birth. This was old skin and I wanted to slough it off.

I bent the stems of my glasses around my ears to keep them from slipping down my nose. The entire face of the ridge, with its bald rock and pitches of gravel, was a blind spot, and I couldn't see how to get down. Panic tightened in my throat as I circled and searched. An hour passed. Whatever I'd noticed on the way up I couldn't remember. I didn't even know which *side* of the ridge I'd climbed. The wind was raw and uncontained, hissing with the sound of a great emptiness. The sun was dropping, my breathing fast, nausea as sharp as the realization that I hadn't been ready for this, that my boy-ness could not so easily die. I tightened the backpack straps, swallowed, and descended into the dead space, my body sideways, gravity pulling me, the ground slowly slipping away.

A head-size boulder broke free and vanished below.

I scuttled back to the ridge top, panting. An updraft, like an insult, slung sand into my face. I gripped a boulder and closed my eyes. One innocent step after another and the buses, gravel roads, and towns beside the lake had disappeared. *Let me down!* I wanted to say to Hell's Gate. *I was just following interesting things.*

Heels dug into the gravel, my right hand bleeding, I descended again. An antelope stood below me in the flats. I gripped shrubs, grass, rock. The mountain held the afternoon's heat, and I thought of the warm Shabbat plate on which my father cooked his weekly *Jachnun.* I looked down again at the antelope that was not an antelope but a man, and where the slope finally flattened I barreled toward him.

There were two Africans in the khaki uniforms of park rangers.

"*Habari yacko, rafiki?*" one of them said, calmly, smiling. How are you, friend?

"*Mzuri sana,*" I said. "*Habari za leo?*" Very fine. How are you today?

I dropped my pack. My legs were trembling, sweat dripping in my eyes. They asked in English what I was doing in Kenya and in the park, and when I described my trouble descending from the peak, it was clear they saw me, not as a lost boy looking for help, but as a man who'd walked off a mountain.

Instantly, they gave me back my breath.

"Can I just put my tent here?" I said. "With the animals?"

One ranger shrugged as if no one had ever asked.

"Ehh, I think so," said the other ranger. "Why not?"

I said good-bye and walked on and realized I'd forgotten to ask them where I was.

A rain shower swept in without warning. I yanked my tent from its cinch sack, snapped the poles straight and fed them crosswise through the seams of the silver nylon. The ground was rocky, dotted with shrubs. A grass as tough as *agropyron elongatum* pierced the tent floor with its blades. Rain drummed on my twenty-dollar supermarket tent, which shuddered with me inside it. A rumble followed the shower into the distance and was gone.

The sun fell behind the mountains, prolonging dusk, and a chill seeped out of the shadows. I wrote a postcard to my grandfather Moshe and ate a chocolate bar, my bare feet sticking out of the tent, the soil broken and cool under my heels. The sense of remoteness, both magical and frightening, which had been contained in the wind on the mountaintop, settled over the plains.

The darkness began to sing, screeching, cooing, clicking. A short cry—from a small-lunged animal. A rasping—likely an insect. A bird whistled overhead. A voice seemed to call to me. Close, now farther away, now on the opposite side. One creature moving in circles or several. A cry, distressed—infant or animal. The night grew massive around the tent. I climbed out and fanned the flashlight, shaking, scanning the brush for eyes. The screeching and clacking continued as though I didn't exist, the thorny terrain nearly as brutal on my feet as a field of glass. Littering the bare ground were acacia roots and dust-filled fragments of wood that might have come from trees fifty years dead. I lined branches around the tent, a perimeter of loose wood to knock together under a predator's paws.

A scream. A hyena? I leapt into the tent. Or my body leapt. Chills washed over me. I pulled my legs against my chest and zipped the tent door. My heart thumped against my knees as I jammed the flashlight against the fabric wall and stared out through the insect screen. I knew the technical terms for the ways adrenaline worked, how in stress mode blood rushed from the digestive tract to the survival systems, how the pupils dilated and hair stood on end. But reading it in books was nothing compared to the power, in a single second, of actually *feeling* my body seized by fear.

How naïve I'd been to confuse knowledge and experience.

A screech.

I bounded out *because* I was scared, shined the flashlight in an arc, securing the space again from the nothingness. The beam shook in my sweaty hand. You interacted with these animals during the day. Wait, those animals were diurnal. Break it down, break it into parts, quantify it. The rangers wouldn't have let me pitch the tent if there were lions in the park. Or had they not really given me permission? Or had they assumed I knew what to do in this place?

I picked up a sharp rock and found enough comfort to tilt back my head and gaze at the sky. I thought, *I'm too fond of stars to be fearful of the night*. There were more stars than I'd ever seen, clouds of stars that reached clear to the horizon, as at a planetarium. What had been the point of making grids to learn the constellations? Of memorizing the Latin names of lizards' bones? Nothing I'd learned had gotten me a millimeter closer to understanding what was out in the darkness.

A LION'S CLAWS

All eyes were on me when I unzipped the tent the next morning—a horizon of animals framed by the mountains. Warthogs shot into the grass. A zebra stared, then buried his head in the herd. Neurotic gazelles all pointed one way like weathervanes. I peeled back the tent door for a wider view, and a gazelle leapt sideways and all the gazelles leapt, as if connected by string. Layers of animals filled the savannah in the daily ritual of traveling to drink, to find good grass, half of them staring at my silver tent, which may have looked to them as odd against the landscape as it would have to me just days before.

I packed and walked, the gazelles slashing across the flats, zebras trotting. Insipid wildebeest squeezed against each other in the distance like a shoal of fish. My destination, again, was no more than the sum of a thousand random steps. Though I was making an effort to keep the black mountain ridge on my right.

Hours passed. Acacia trees sprouted from the plains. A giraffe browsed in a treetop and I sneaked toward him in the shadows. The bottom of his white orange stomach towered overhead like the belly of a god. When he spotted me through the leaves, he jerked upward, ripping loose from the ground. I fell backwards as the giraffe wheeled like scaffolding in slow motion, his legs lifting high over the savannah as he ran.

All my life, I thought, I've been touching things through gloves.

When the grass grew thick farther on, it occurred to me I might have crossed beyond the park's borders. I stopped, listened. The brush whispered in the breeze. I stopped again when the clank of goods in my pack and the rocks grinding under my boot soles overwhelmed whatever I should have been listening for. The land looked like a place in the Mara only Maasai dared walk, where the grass was high enough to conceal a lion's head. A pair of baboons glided parallel to my path. They'd been watching me. The juvenile crept close, his feet turning inward in his pigeon-toed walk.

From my backpack, I tore out two buns. The juvenile lunged, seized the bread and sprinted off. A clan of baboons had been shadowing me in the brush. A female appeared, her sharp snout making her seem a cousin to wolves. I jumped; a male had crept around and touched my hand. The female moved closer. Dozens of baboons marched into the open. Some, like scouts, sat to watch, forearms resting on their knees, the land revealing that it could select out the weak. In the Tel Aviv University Library, I'd studied the behavior of baboons, who had highly developed social structures that helped them defend their groups. And helped them attack. And they closed ranks around me.

I stomped my boots. Baboons scurried behind boulders like fleeing mice. Then returned. A male jumped forward as if to test how close he could get without inciting a response. So much intelligence showed in his eyes and expressions. Was I as alert? When he looked toward the others, I picked up a rock, yelled, smashed it down. They scuttled away in a dust cloud, their asses pink as though diseased. They crept back into formation. When I began to walk, they walked. *Does he mean it when he scares us?* they seemed to think. *We'll find out.*

"Bah!" I smashed rocks and waved my arms and they melted away into the brush.

I was dehydrated and nearly out of water when I spotted, tiny in the distance, the red of his *shuka* bright against the brown valley, a Maasai warrior.

"*Jambo!*" I shouted and the distance swallowed the word. "*Habari!*" I ran, the bag rattling and hopping on my back. The soil was packed hard, petrified by the sun. Spastic and shouting and out of control, I stomped and sprinted down the side of the valley into the creek bed to a trail where I stopped in front of the Maasai.

He was smiling, leaning against a spear, one leg crossed behind the other. Wind blew through the landscape as though we were the only men left on earth.

He reached out and touched the side of my face with the back of his hand.

The Maasai, forty or fifty years old, watched me in a way that seemed to say we had all the time in the world. Here, he was saying, we are not in a hurry. I felt ridiculous for running, for shouting as though he might have fled, for carrying a massive backpack when all he needed was a spear.

I reached out and touched the side of his face with the back of my hand.

The Maasai stood motionless. He was tall and thin, mostly hidden under his red cape, his sandals cut from old tires.

"*Ninaitwa Ofir. Ninatoka Israel.*" I'd been practicing my opening statements. "*Unaitwa nani?*" What's your name?

Another minute of silence and he began to speak, not KiSwahili, but KiMaasai, which was full of hard K's and rolling R's and quick, almost hidden syllables. Swahili was softer, closer in sound to Arabic. That I did not and could not answer did not stop the Maasai from talking on and on.

"*Kijiji ni wapi?*" I said in Swahili; I needed far more to drink than the sips I'd been saving. The village is where?

With a patience that was almost holy, he continued in KiMaasai.

I pointed in different directions, said, "*Kijiji? Kijiji?*" Village?

He smelled of cooking fires and cattle.

"*Kijiji?*" I said and, as his monologue continued, I reached across his field of vision and pointed. "*Kijiji?*" I pointed as if a brush fire were roaring toward us through the valley. "*Kijiji!*" I said, "*Wewe kulala wapi?*" You sleep where? In dozens of variations and tones, miming and pointing in all direction, I uttered a dozen *kijijis* in hopes of hitting the magical combination that would mean, *Let's go!*

"Ah, *kijiji*," the Maasai said and nodded.

But didn't move. Before we lost our iota of understanding, I gave one final *kijiji* and started up the path. He laid his spear across his shoulders and glided by me with long graceful steps, his legs like stilts beneath his *shuka*, his speed forcing me to double-time. Only in a place where the land stretched out as though leading the way, did it seem possible to walk in silence with a man I'd just met and feel complete comfort.

His footprints were fragments of tire treads.

Hours later, the brown rectangles of two villages appeared in the distance. I walked shoulder to shoulder with the warrior, feeling like a king. The blue of the sky was intense and unreal, as in pictures of earth from space. Near the first *boma*, two boys in *shukas* walked toward us, making eye contact but keeping their heads down. I extended my hand expecting to shake, but the boys stopped a meter in front of us, bowed their shaven heads, and leaned in, one toward the man, the other toward me.

I watched the elder for a sign of what to do. When he laid his palm on the head of the boy in front of him, I did the same to the boy before me. The boys switched places and we repeated. It wasn't hair I touched, but warm skin, the skull, and I thought of the Shabbat Priestly Prayer at synagogue when my father had placed his hand on *my* head under his prayer shawl.

The bigger boy, by responsibility or honor, took my bag. A dry acacia fence lined the mud wall of the village. Goats everywhere shook their tails and baaed. Children with flies dotting their mouths and yellow crust around their eyes paraded forward in overwhelming numbers, all with their heads bowed. The men stood back, bright teeth shining in their smiles, not directing the children, only watching. I touched one head after another, as if I'd been asked to bless a nation. The village back in the Mara seemed now hardly a village at all. I shooed and shooed a fly from my lips until I noticed Maasai kids unbothered by bugs feeding on their snot. The *boma* was dirty, the ground moist with mashed piles of cow dung. The smell of the soil was soft and warm, a detail, I imagined, that in the life of a child did not change—so that even manure might be loved.

All the men shook my hand. Then old women shuffled over, slumped at the shoulders and leaning on walking sticks like keepers of a pact, their heads held high. Two old mamas took turns pulling my nose and playing with my hair, the world here like one people at home might have imagined existed only in myth, a distant civilization of tall thin figures more alien than kin. The large boy from outside the *boma* lifted my pack from the dung and led me with several men to a hut, where smoke, solid as a curtain, hit me in the doorway. My eyes burned as I groped over a mud wall fragile enough to break in my hands. Someone took my arm and helped me to sit on a cowskin bed. The hut was pitch-black but for the coals of a fire and a ray of light slicing through the smoke from a tiny window. A woman poked the coals, blew, set a silver pot over fresh flames. I unzipped my pack and handed chocolate bars to the man seated at the fire who seemed to be my host. But he set the chocolates aside.

As Maasai entered and sat around me, the woman sprinkled leaves into the pot. She removed the leather cap from a beaded gourd, raised the gourd to her eyes and dumped milk into the tea, then spun a stirring stick between her palms. She poured boiling tea into a cup with a broken handle, then to another and back, again and again, to cool it for drinking. My maternal grandma always did the same even though we urged her just to add cold water.

After two cups of tea, a man led me outside. I drew crisp, smokeless air into my lungs, then held my breath as we dove into another dark *manyatta*. I sat at the fire in silence, eyes stinging, barely able to breathe air of an atmosphere from a different time. *Ugali*, a sticky starch made from ground corn, was set in front of me with a bowl of goat meat stew—two common bowls. The man showed me how to claw into the *ugali* and he laughed when I used both hands to keep my *ugali* ball from disintegrating. As I scooped food into my mouth, I realized that on my hands were the germs of the entire village.

I moved from house to house through the afternoon, counting cups of tea until my stomach at fourteen was close to bursting. But at least I was no longer thirsty. And what a paltry welcoming my small family and I could have given a wandering Maasai. And how foolish I'd been for thinking I needed to give a gift to my host—the chocolates—when everyone had been waiting to honor me, a solitary traveler, by sharing.

And asking for nothing. Language was artifice. Warmth didn't necessitate words. What was small talk next to singing? As I lay that night in my sleeping bag on a lumpy bed of sticks and hide, I struggled to measure my obligation to the Israeli Army against the budding individualism I'd inherited from my mother. I thought, My life in Israel and even Israel itself were just specks on an endless horizon. Everything I believed about myself, my family, and other cultures, I'd inherited from my *own* culture. The lens of my upbringing had been pulled away, and I hadn't even known it existed. How could I have made a real choice about where I fit in the world when I'd been ignorant of what choices there were?

I woke late and alone in the *manyatta* and pawed for my glasses, then laced up my boots, laughing at myself for lacking the confidence to go barefoot when women strolled through the dirt as though walking on carpet. Children gathered outside as I blew balloons, children who were proud to carry water and wood and to tend to calves and who were listened to by their elders when they spoke.

An English-speaking Maasai was brought from another *boma*. We helped that afternoon in the herding of cattle and he instructed me on the handling of predators.

"The lion is coming?" the Maasai said. "Make the *shuka* big or to hold the bag like you big. Take the bag, put it down, make you so two people. If cheetah come to you, no move. If cheetah *run* to you, no move."

We met a man with scars across his chest, slashing scars from a lion's claws. In the past, the man said, three or four *moran*—warriors— left the village and wandered, carrying clubs, knives and spears, sleeping on the ground and hunting for meat, the only time besides periods of great wanting when Maasai culture permitted the hunting of animals. The journey of the *moran* was the ultimate test of the bush: to find and slay a male lion. Felling a lion with a thrown spear wasn't the most honorable kill. Nor was distracting a lion and flanking him. The *bravest* warrior, who if he lived would be known forever for his actions, would kneel in front of the charging lion, plant the dull end of his spear in the ground, the shaft gripped in his hands, blade pointed outward at his face. And he would wait for the lion's attack, wait for the lion to lunge and impale himself on the spear, as he learned whether he had the courage to hold himself still.

The Maasai stood before me, broad shouldered, chest gleaming in the light, his scars so long and thick he'd almost been sliced in half, and I realized then that what made him who he was was *not* what he knew but what he had done. And the importance of what he'd done was not that he'd survived his confrontation with the lion, but that he'd looked for the lion and faced the lion when every instinct in his body had screamed to run, to back away, to take shelter. There was nothing he could bring to that moment, no skill, no wisdom from some elder about *how to kill a lion*. He'd simply planted his spear in the ground and waited, so the lion would either kill him or cut him so deeply he would be forever changed.

I wasn't going to the academy to study biology or physics after the army. Not any more. No matter what might happen to me, I was headed straight for the teeth and the claws.

THE ARMY

My grandfather Moshe told stories of his life in Iraq, of a Tigris River teeming with fish, of markets overflowing with a hundred varieties of dates and of nomads bringing to Bagdad their buffalo-milk cream. Jews and Arabs had lived in peace on avenues lined with coffee shops and they'd all spoken Arabic. Moshe had worked as the accountant for a fabric merchant and, before commuting each morning to the market on foot, he'd turned toward Jerusalem and prayed in Hebrew. *On the rivers of Babylon we sat and cried and remembered Zion.* Moshe believed his lineage in Iraq stretched back to the time of Abraham. But when he prayed, he prayed as his forefathers had: for the creation of a Jewish state.

My mother was born in Iraq in '49 and three years later moved with Moshe, my pregnant grandmother, and my aunt to newly created Israel. Waiting for them was a bath of DDT at Ben Gurion Airport and a shack at Camp David in Haifa. But for Moshe these were barely nuisances, and little mattered more than that the impossible wish had been achieved. The load of tradition, dragged through the centuries on the backs of Jews, was set down within a new state, the ancient quest completed before my birth.

More traditional than religious, Grandpa Moshe believed that the country he'd helped to establish was mine to protect, a task to me that was not a warrior's but a watchman's. Facing boot camp, I had no choice but to do my part in protecting aunts and elders and everyone who'd done their share. Evading the draft was unthinkable, synonymous with cutting ties to Israel and family. But at eighteen when I arrived at the base in Tel Ha'Shomer, my quest had become not to create or protect borders, but to erase them.

My first uniform was baggy enough that my sister and a cousin could have taken shelter in the sleeves. The glasses dwarfing my nose kept me out of combat boot camp and the upper-level courses, and it was impossible to feel a sense of achievement when other rookies faced far greater daily challenges than I. My M-16 was with me always, stuck between the bedsprings and my green mattress when I slept, just beyond the stream of water when I washed in the open showers, the thin strap cutting into my neck as I walked, barrel banging against doorjambs. Commanders delighted in ordering us to refill sand buckets at the fire posts, to whitewash walls, to rake the unending cascade of leaves falling from eucalyptus trees, which seemed to have been planted solely for our torture.

In a professional course after boot camp, I learned radio communication and encrypted communication for combat. None of it interested me. Nor did it interest a short guy named Elad, who, within hordes of zealous rookies, kept his eyes on the floor as though waiting for world's end. While mopping the cafeteria one day, I said hello, and Elad glared at me. "The killer got up a bit before dawn," he said. "Then he put on his boots. He walked up a really long hall. After a while he got to a door. This guy said, 'Father? Yes, Son. I want to *kill* you.'"

Elad frowned when he realized I was still beside him. But then his desire to drive me off morphed into the hunch that I might be a kindred spirit. We started talking about music; Elad played the pickups of his guitar with a nail. "But I have time for nothing now," he said. "I hate the slave work, not because it's hard but because it's useless."

We pushed aside the tables in the dining hall instead of cleaning and squared off for water hockey, for jousting with squeegees and mops, an Olympics that ended with blood and the infirmary.

Ofer was another rookie, quiet and solitary. Ofer had lost a friend in a bombing of a *trempiada*, a station where soldiers hitchhiked to and from a remote camp. His commanders refused to let him attend the funeral. So disconsolate was Ofer that he joined the pact Elad and I made to reclaim our lives. We vowed either to be stationed where we could sleep at home with evenings free—*kalab*—or to be assigned as cooks or drivers who spent one week on the base and one week off—*weekweek*. We didn't care that soldiers with *weekweek* were those the army didn't want around more than half the time. We called our strategy The Art of War of *Weekweek*.

After the professional course, I was stationed in Tel Aviv where the buildings of the base loomed over us like threats. My unit, responsible for communications support for special operations, was unique in that we could not leave the base. Time passed with an impossible slowness. The yelling I endured was generic and impersonal, which only made it worse, and I thought constantly of the Maasai who knew far better why they carried their spears. I slept in bed wearing boots for nighttime shift duty—two hours at a guard post, two hours in bed, two hours at a post. In the helmet pouch of my combat vest I stashed a Swahili phrasebook and the *Lonely Planet Guide to Central Africa*. I traded for shifts at isolated posts so that I could read about Zaire.

"I don't want to be promoted," I told my commander. "I don't want you to value what I'm doing. I *want* to be a good soldier. I want to be a *great* soldier, but if I'm a great soldier, you'll promote me, and then I'll have even less free time. I'm stuck on the base and I can't even visit my home, which is five minutes away. Do you see a problem?"

Elad, "The Dwarf," had hung a noose over his bed when he was fifteen, and he had little trouble convincing his mental health officer he was on the verge of suicide. He was removed from Northern Command and reassigned as a driver, and he spent his evenings making industrial music, playing guitar with small electrified motors and shards of glass. For their ability to wave wands and restore lives, mental health officers were called "magicians."

Ofer's big ears had earned him the nickname "The Bat." He was also in Northern Command, stationed on Mount Harmon on the Lebanese border, living in tunnels beneath the snow. He spent hours in therapy, honing the ruse of depression and, for his finale in the Art of War of *Weekweek*, he left a suicide note. But the formulas of army legend had become cliché, and Ofer's note was one of *three* found that afternoon in the unit.

"Ofir, let's cut the bullshit. I want you to make a list," said my new direct commander, who had the muscular build of an athlete and the alien ears of a *swala twiga*. He relayed stories, not of sacrifice to country, but of personal challenge. "Divide a page in two. On one side write what would be good if you go to the psychologist and get *weekweek*, and on the other, say, the benefits of going to the field in Lebanon. The question is how far can you go?"

Elad, Ofer, and I were handpicked for daylong officers' course exams. Elad saw his selection as further proof the army was a farce and he used the opportunity to aim for full discharge, seeking both to fail and to be mentally examined for his answers. After a year of being reduced to an automaton, of feeling drugged by routine and the cumulative agony of pointless tasks, I was as happy as Ofer that the army was now asking us to think, and I cancelled my appointment with the magician.

The desert landscape of Mizpa Ramon in the Negev imparted a sense of freedom absent within the walls of a military base. In officers' training, Ofer and I learned to use explosives and fuses, how to treat mass casualties, burns, cut limbs, fractures, battle wounds. *A good paramedic is an improviser.* Our daily goals were no nobler but they were practical, and for the first time the military was adventurous. We crawled up hills blindfolded. We were woken in the night to run for hours, to trek with twenty-kilogram packs, to carry a member of our unit for thirty kilometers on a stretcher, drills I never ceased to imagine were on the savannah. We learned to pace our walking and to know our range and we studied command, the management of soldiers on the battlefield, philosophy, principles and the ethics of war and self-management for maintaining control in extreme situations. I led my unit of ten cadets in a simulated field exercise, my commander batting my helmet, knocking my head from side to side, as I tried to give orders before we stormed a hill, breathing dust, firing blank cartridges, and I committed errors, both tactical and mental, that led to the theoretical deaths of nearly all my men.

In my self-critique before the unit, I said, "I should have spread my soldiers wider and known the terrain better. Under stress, I got lost." But I was always getting lost; my inner compass insisted on spinning its own way. Adding to the critique, my bunkmate, Shahar, said, "You're also not such a glamorous commander." But we had "space" to make mistakes, and even costly ones were desirable as tools for learning.

The company was in the field, daytime, simulating battlefield movements, when my friend Assaf accidentally raised an antenna from an armored personnel carrier into a high voltage power line. He was evacuated to the hospital, and the company came together to wait. Anxious cadets walked in circles around improvised tents. Assaf's training officer was found crying in the grass. When the highest ranking officer of the base appeared, a man I'd seen only once, I knew it would be bad. He said, "It is with great regret that I inform you that at 16:30 Assaf Avni passed away." My friends grabbed each other and sobbed. The commander looked down, then said, "God gave us a great gift that we forget things. All pain eventually hurts less."

Everyone had stopped listening and I thought, Why am I the only one not crying?

"Continue as usual," was the word from the magicians. "You don't need to stop and process this. Continue in your routine. The routine protects you."

When I finally got a weekend off, I stayed in my room at home and listened to "Hotel California" for hours, which Assaf had played in the barracks on a guitar missing a string. When my tears finally came, the melancholy was like a drug. And the draw of it I couldn't explain.

Summer of 1996, after eight months of officer's training, I got my rank and was transferred to a colorless world of concrete and sand that made me long for the hated eucalyptus trees. My office I painted peach, outfitted with a bar and three stools and decorated with a print, *The Metamorphosis of Narcissus*. I played Jimi Hendrix tapes and turned the office into a night spot, Ofir's *Janana* Bar, where I served well-sugared instant coffee to my soldiers. The aquarium that I brought in with two leopard geckos finally earned me a commander's wrath: "You can't just do what you want! This is the army!"

My need to be in Africa had grown almost pathological. It hardly mattered that my connection to the continent was as tenuous as the encapsulated revelations of a three-week trip. In Africa, I believed, waited not just the experiences I needed to continue building myself, but my very purpose. Whatever contribution I might make in my life would not be in someone else's army.

As an officer, I had to give a fourth year to the Israel Defense Forces, and Ofer and I began holding "Africa meetings" at the Prozac Bar in Tel Aviv. Ofer had taken me to get contact lenses, and my glasses were gone and with it the nickname "The Blind." On the way to the bar I changed out of my uniform into a velvet shirt and purple bellbottoms. I carried my M-16 on my back and *Heart of Darkness* in my bag. Ofer, the primary architect of my makeover into coolness, wore black vinyl pants. Both of us wore three earrings. And no one in the Prozac Bar believed we were officers.

"The meeting has begun at 20:37," I said, following army protocol. "People present are Ofer and Ofir. Comments?" Ofer had just started to smoke, and his cigarette burned only along the bottom, back toward his throat. I asked if we should register "one badly smoked cigarette" under "any other business." And I stirred into my Nescafé as many packets of sugar as the water in the coffee mug would absorb—seven.

"*Sabbaba Ugalák,*" I said, invoking our language of odd words and cult music phrases. "Third point on the agenda: Cheetah attack procedures. If a cheetah attacks, we stand perfectly still. Do we agree?"

Ofer nearly spit up his beer. "Are you serious?"

"A cheetah makes false attacks, to intimidate. If we stand perfectly still, she'll run right by. Now a leopard—not so much, so we ought to move. Write it down."

Ofer laughed and wrote it down and told Galit, our waitress, that he planned to make her fall in love with him. Ofer had a vast circle of friends he'd brought me into and was always dreaming up excursions.

While stationed in Gaza, Ofer had been in charge of monitoring forty-one kilometers of border with field trackers and radar.

"Agenda item six," I said. "If we have a problem with the authorities, we should try to 'settle' the problem before reaching the police station. Thieves often pose as policemen. Do we agree?"

"Indeed, I smell you."

"Now, if we hire a plane in Kinshasa and parachute into the jungle, we try to land near a river. Do we agree?"

Ofer laughed. "We don't even know how to parachute. Why near a river?"

"If something goes wrong, like, breaking our legs, we can float downstream."

Ofer went quiet. But then a smile crept back across his face. He said, "Okay. Smell you. Being burned by cannibals preparations. What do we do?"

"No worries. If we're about to be burned alive, we throw teargas pills into the fire—I stole some from the base—and we disappear. Poof."

Ofer ordered another drink. He'd once said he would give his life for me. My girlfriend at the time, Gal, was jealous of Ofer. Shahar called us a married couple. Ofer and I had promised, even after taking brides, to live next door to each other. We vowed at seventy to skydive in wheelchairs. *Ofer and Ofir. Ofir and Ofer.* We danced with friends at clubs like Echoes and Kat Balu and dreamed that when peace came we would guide the first Israeli tourists into Syria.

Ofer and I were drafted on the same day and then discharged on the same day in October 1998. A few weeks on, we sat at a table in a mall near an eye doctor's office. We had appointments for Lasik surgery, as the jungle was no place for contact lenses. Ofer and I had worn our oldest, thickest glasses that day, and we looked like scuba divers. We had the same diopter, minus ten, which meant that without corrective lenses we bumped into walls. As our appointments neared, we nodded in ceremony and pulled our glasses away from our eyes. The mob around us swirled into a blur of colors. The volume of everything seemed to soften. We leaned our heads together and continued to talk. "My brother," Ofer said, "Kenya will be the dream and adventure of our lives."

1998—1999

. . . The Point That Must Be Reached.

KENYA

THE BUTT OF A GUN

Our first day in Nairobi, Ofer and I rose at dawn in a dirty room at Hotel Iqbal. Dead traffic lights leaned over buckled sidewalks. Abandoned cars sat in an alley heaped with bricks. A brown eagle glided overhead. The city was humming with so many people that in Israel it would have been a parade. Bus attendants called to passersby, "*Kssst kssst*," over laughter, radios and revving engines. Larger coaches were adorned in graffitied names: "Born Bad" and "Prince of Nairobi."

The taste of *matatu* exhaust filled me with joy.

Ofer and I strolled up the street as leisurely as we would have in Tel Aviv. He swaggered, holding a cigarette at his side with the chic of a man being filmed. When tourist hunters descended telling stories of safaris, Ofer said, "We can see elephants, you say? Here in Kenya? Did they break out of a zoo?" Skyscrapers rose beyond Kenyatta Avenue, though the ubiquitous decay made clear that the glorious era of their construction, when Kenya was the jewel of East Africa, had passed. Further on was the Hilton, a cinema, a man on the sidewalk gripping a billy club. Ofer was feasting on the unending wonder of details in the chaos, my enjoyment channeled through him. I felt cleansed being back in Africa, with Israel swept away and exchanged for Kenya by the impossible ease and completeness of air travel. Ofer pointed at a street boy trying to grab a dog by the tail. A child sold cigarettes and bubblegum, "One bob. One bob." Ofer gave the boy his half-smoked cigarette and said, "Mister, I'll come back later for a refund; this cigarette isn't working." And the boy laughed.

Out of the corner of my eye: the man in the blue uniform was waving his billy club.

"Your girlfriend's not going to be happy," Ofer said, looking in the other direction, "when she learns we're going to the bush for five years. We're going to drive this whole continent insane."

The man swung his club overhead, smashed it down into my shoulder, my back. I dropped to the cement. Wrapped my arms around my head as the blows rained down. From nowhere a soldier charged Ofer with an Uzi. Was it a *coup*? The man with the club struck me on the back, neck, arms, grunting with each blow like someone I'd betrayed. My cheek was flush to the concrete. The men left us.

I peeked out from under my hands at Ofer. We stumbled to our feet and ran. Pedestrians with shopping bags were surreally calm. People across the road walked as if it were any day. Ofer grimaced, rubbed his head, checked himself for blood. He said, "They beat us because we're white." I stopped and looked back at where we'd been attacked: a black truck parked on the sidewalk, with a windowless back-end, was an armored car; men were moving money into a bank and we'd walked straight into them.

I clutched my throbbing neck and laughed. "What an experience! Shit!"

Ofer glared at me as if he might beat me himself.

"Where the fuck was the experience in that?" he said. "The guy beat me with the butt of an Uzi. You like being beaten? We could be dead."

"We're alive, no?" I said, still laughing. "We're okay."

He didn't respond.

"Half a day in Nairobi," I said, "and we've already had our first adventure!"

Planet Safari sat atop an eleven-story building, an oasis for travelers hustled in by street touts paid a commission for bringing them, and for bringing us; Ofer had to see the Maasai Mara as I had. And he infuriated Planet's manager, Lucy, by bargaining for the cheapest safari she'd ever sold. Ofer said, "If the Mara's grass is not well watered, we're coming back for a refund."

"You're little bandits," Lucy said and then almost smiled.

Four green canvas tents were set up on the open-air patio for travelers, who were slicing papaya, sipping yogurt, reading *Rough Guides*. I felt an ecstasy akin to my first day in Hell's Gate when I'd bounded from ostrich to antelope—lucky, unconflicted, giddy and young. That evening, after Ofer and I cooked *shakshouka* for Planet's employees, I asked the sleepy-eyed night watchman, Paul Muangi, in Swahili where I could get a drink of water because the pipes and the plastic barrels were dry.

"*Mzungu*," he said with a smile, meaning white man, "you should speak in your *shalom shalom* language; you just asked me for *shit*. *Kunywa*, not *kunya*. We ran out of one, we have lots of the other." Paul chuckled and swiveled in the boss's leather chair under a portrait of President Moi. "Go to the roof and see where the water is: in the Hilton's blue swimming pool. *Here*? We barely have water for cooking *ugali*. Oppression of the poor, my friend, oppression of the poor."

Across Moi Avenue was the unlit River Road area, and I told Muangi that Ofer and I planned to walk there in the night.

"No no no," Muangi said. "You want to get robbed? There's a reason it's called *Nairobbery*."

Impatience was a product of the long wait to return. We needed to know what was really out in the dark, to know whether Nairobi's reputation was deserved and whether we were ready to face it. If Africa were to be my home, I couldn't choose to walk only where people promised I would be safe. An hour before midnight, Muangi unlocked Planet's gate, and Ofer and I rode the elevator down with the seriousness of men summoned for an operation in the field. Ofer stretched his stiff neck, rubbed the bruises he'd earned that morning from the Uzi. Buildings in central Nairobi were guarded by *askaris*, who carried clubs, nightsticks, and whips, and we woke a man sleeping face-down at a table who had a club in his lap. He yanked a great mass of keys from his pocket, fiddled like a jailer for the right one, and opened the door.

The sidewalk on our side of Moi Avenue had a giant curio shop and Nando's and the Chicken Inn, a strip of well-lit retail bordering the blackness. Street children moved on the dark side of Moi with bottles of sniffing glue at their mouths, as if they alone were comfortable there. The distant horns of fifty *matatus* calling for passengers clamored like instruments of the devil's orchestra.

We crossed. Islands of light broke the darkness: a light bulb between the bars of a window, one buzzing streetlamp, a flashlight. Shops were shuttered, barricaded by metal doors, locked with padlocks so stout they seemed exaggerations. I could hear Ofer breathing as we marched side by side, fists clenched, boots thudding on the pavement in a feeble warning to anyone near. I could feel that my hardening in the army would not be as much help as I wanted. Ahead in the darkness was an intersection we knew from daytime, to the right a construction zone blocked by a metal wall. I squinted, struggled to see, my night vision so poor after the surgery that my eyes felt wrapped in cellophane. I didn't want Ofer knowing I was nervous, didn't want us amplifying each other's fear—as I gripped the teargas in my pocket.

Beyond Tom Mboya Avenue, children sang in a saucer of light. I exhaled. Apartments, tangled in fire escapes, rose to the left. Ofer was thinking what I was and we crossed toward the children. From the right five meters off and rushing us was a flashlight pointed at my face, blinding me as to who held it. Adrenaline came, the rush of wind spilling into the chest. I stepped in front of Ofer, rotated the safety cap on the teargas and went straight at the man.

"Show me your passports!" he said, shoving the flashlight up to my eyes. "This is the police."

I leaned out of the light beam. I couldn't see his face, but he wore no uniform. I pivoted, seized his wrist with my left hand, jerked his flashlight aside and swung my body against him, aiming the teargas at his eyes.

"Show me you're a policeman or I'll spray," I said.

I felt no tension where I gripped his arm. He didn't struggle to pull away. But stood so calmly in the road he seemed bored. Then he called over his shoulder in a voice devoid of fear. Footsteps. Men dashed around the corner. One was in uniform.

From a hero to a fool in a single breath. I released the man's arm.

"This guy here," he said to the others, "just tried to attack me with teargas."

I could only imagine what Ofer was thinking: Please register "under any other insanity," Ofir's complete lack of a brain.

"Attacking a policeman," said one officer. "Do you know what this means?"

I'd given them an opportunity for a bribe for which they wouldn't have prayed.

"*Mzungu*," said the first officer, "people go to prison for this. Do you attack officers in *your* country?"

"I was just protecting myself. You have no uniform. I didn't know."

Every officer surrounding us in the dark shouted in unison.

"Just get them to the station," said the first man.

Ofer and I made eye contact under a streetlight as they escorted us toward a military truck. When an officer pushed him into the truck's cab, Ofer said, "Maybe we can settle this here."

The men roared. "We promise you a night in a Kenyan jail you'll never forget!"

I rode in the wagon, seated on a bench and guarded by half a dozen men. The truck rattled and bounced through potholes and seemed to be coming loose from its wheels. My attempt to mount a defense only got me yelled at. I thought of my mother, always ready with uncommon advice: *You'll find your way out and then be happy you were here.* I turned and looked through the back window into the cab of the truck. Ofer was chatting with the lone man in uniform.

The truck down-shifted. We U-turned.

I looked back at Ofer. He was pointing toward a halo in the darkness: a lit restaurant. The truck braked, throwing the men against me. The uniformed officer leaned out the front window and yelled, "We're dropping them here." He shook Ofer's hand and apologized, and we scurried into the restaurant, The Chicken Licken.

"Ofer, what the hell did you tell him?" I said.

Ofer lit a cigarette. "I said we're Israeli officers. And the man asked, 'Are you connected to the unit that came with the dogs? That helped in the rescue after the U.S. embassy was bombed?' And I told him, 'Of course! You think we're tourists? We are officers *in that unit.*'"

We laughed and I apologized.

Ofer exhaled smoke and stared at me. "Next time you decide to attack a policeman, *you* will be the one spending the night in jail."

The *matatu* engine was hot as a furnace. Dust stuck to my sweaty arms and dripped as mud. "*Simama hapa,*" I called out to the conductor by the door.

The driver didn't slow.

"Stop here!" I said. "Down. In the valley."

"There's nothing, *mzungu*. It's just trees. There's no station," the conductor said.

Ofer looked at me and raised his eyebrows.

The *matatu* crossed the bridge and zipped up the valley's far side.

"Stop!" I reached out the window and banged the metal shell of the van.

The driver braked, and the conductor slid open the door. The Kenyan passengers were shaking their heads, all certain I was confused about getting off a bus in the bush.

A woman said, "Where are you *going*?"

"No no, it's okay, mama," I said, crawling over two men to reach the door. "We need this river. We're following this river."

Men shouted at the driver in Swahili and pointed at us.

"Don't worry!" I said. "We're dropping here."

Ofer stepped out of the van and wiped sweat from his eyes. Yellow grass grew along the broken tarmac. We fetched our bags from the rear of the van and stood on the narrow road leading to Narok, deep in Maasai country. I stepped away from the van. Ofer walked beside me, uneasy, stroking his scruff and looking back at the Kenyans. The van puttered away with riders hanging out the windows and holding up their hands to see if we would change our minds. Then they disappeared over the hill.

The army was in the past. And we were just going to walk, finally, now that I stood on the far side of the barriers to things that were simple and good. Somewhere, days or weeks ahead, the river flowing through this valley would intersect another road, and we would hitchhike from there back to Nairobi. Or perhaps the river on my map was not this river at all. Perhaps this one snaked across the border into Tanzania. I didn't know and it didn't matter.

Thick vegetation on both sides of the bridge fenced off the river, which we could hear but not see. I tightened the straps of my food-filled backpack and stepped off the tarmac into the brush. Ofer groaned, flexed and crashed through the thicket. I ducked and slid sideways to find a path, snapped through a chandelier of dead limbs. The dry pine forest was as impenetrable as a crowd of people holding hands. The murmur of the river led us through an opening in the brush, down an embankment toward sandy exposed ground. We came over a rise into view of our river, and it was hardly a stream. Ofer disentangled a twig from his hair and smiled—to tell me I didn't know what I was doing.

I turned and continued the battle with the brush.

"It's great fun walking on your savannah," Ofer said, touching a scrape on his forehead and checking his fingers for blood.

"Let's move away from the river," I said. "Maybe the brush thins out."

"Don't you think we should open the map?"

"We don't need a map."

Ofer shook his head as Shahar and other cadets had done when I'd gotten us lost.

"Look, Ofer, we can't get lost because we're not aiming to go anywhere, at least not anywhere in particular."

I checked the compass to appease him, and we climbed out of the gulch. Quickly, as if we'd gained a thousand meters, the trees grew tall, the walking easy, and the canopy cast a shadow over moist, leaf-covered terrain. Another hundred steps and the vegetation knotted around us, and we crashed through branches trying not to get poked in the eyes. The sound of water came back to us and fell away as we navigated a maze of ravines. With each hour we trekked, I felt further from delivering the villages and the endless savannah I'd promised Ofer. Had I been alone, I wouldn't have cared that the landscape was ugly and disappointing. It wouldn't have been. It just would have been new.

Ofer and I hadn't looked at each other in at least an hour.

"Please register under violations of the Geneva Convention," Ofer said, smiling, "the torture methods Ofir and his African pals dreamed up for our trip."

"Listen!" I said, raising a finger.

Cowbells.

"Maasai! Say '*sopa*' when we see them, Ofer, and raise your hands to your chest."

We scurried up the gulch as the bells chimed somewhere in front of us.

Our search for the cattle, though, was as futile as our walking had been. Ditches, trees, ravines—the landscape was a puzzle. Then the joyful cry of cowbells grew clear. Through the leaves, we spotted patches of brown and black. Cows in motion. We ran downhill, flung by gravity toward the herd. I scanned for a red *shuka* among cattle that were not the small milk cows of Israel but massive, horned animals like those of the bible.

From the thicket behind us: a roar. A Maasai rushing.

I raised my hands. "*Sopa!*"

He shouted, charged. Ofer and I backpedaled. The old man closed the gap, bent down and raised up with a spear in one hand and a rock in the other. "*Sopa! Sopa!*" I said, slashing away through the trees, yelling greetings as we barreled on without stopping, and I lost myself in the whirling of my legs as panic and exhilaration merged.

Ofer stopped ahead of me in a dry creek bed. Huffing, hands on his knees, he said, "Nice people, your Maasai pals."

I shouted another greeting into the forest and turned to Ofer. "He's an old man. Imagine how he felt with us jumping out of nowhere onto his cows wearing these backpacks. He was just shocked, probably a bit afraid."

"Are you serious? Afraid? So fucking what? He chased us with a spear!"

"Ofer, he's old."

"A spear in my back would hurt less because he's a grandfather? I can't wait to tell Shahar about your crap."

I wanted to return, to face the old man, to find a way to persuade him we'd come as friends. But Ofer and I continued on at a pace just shy of running, over a terrain of ditches slicing in all directions like broken spokes of a wheel. Where the savannah flared out in front of us, Ofer threw down his pack. We unlaced our boots, shook out the debris, and I pitched my tent with the door pointing back toward the woods.

"You think we're too close?" Ofer said.

"I don't think he's chasing us. He's just an old man."

"Well, we shouldn't build a fire," Ofer said, pacing beside the tent. "If anyone *is* looking, the smoke and then the light will lead them here."

Long ago I'd stolen small pulleys from an army base supply room so I could rig a trip-line around my tent, but they were useless with the trees so far apart. Instead, I lined the perimeter with dry wood. Birdcalls and the soft colors of dusk eased the tension between us. I opened a pack of cookies and handed them to Ofer. Ofer unscrewed his canteen and passed it to me. Leaves rustled over the ground as in a poem. I was *energized*. I understood now that it was not epic landscapes I'd been after or the welcoming of a Maasai village; what I yearned for from Africa was the shock of the unexpected, even if it came from a club or the butt of a gun.

"What if he returned to the village," Ofer said, "and explained that two men tried to hurt him? Wouldn't they search for us?"

"That would be a huge misunderstanding."

"Well, he *might* have claimed to be the hero who chased us away."

We heard singing later, and I said, "It's far from here, and remember when we heard the cowbells, how hard it was to find them? And that was in daylight."

"Nope. This is their territory. Your pals find us if they want."

I unrolled my maroon sleeping bag and lay back in the tent. Ofer's worries gained traction in my thoughts as the night stretched out through the blackness. What would happen if I unzipped the tent door onto the tips of ten spears? In misunderstandings were shitty deaths. An animal rustled in the brush and I crawled out to scope the ground; the night was empty in the flashlight's beam. I climbed back into the tent and silently rehearsed my Swahili for a confrontation.

A scratching on the tent woke me. Chills climbed my back as I slid past Ofer and shined the light outside. Trees stood in the cold like guards, the reach of the flashlight marking the edge of how little was known, the wilds humbling in the messages they gave. The eerie call of a bushbaby traveled into the tent with me as I zipped the door closed.

Ofer pulled his sleeping bag over his head. The scratching came again, now inside the tent. We jumped, slung our bags aside—it was a mouse stuck under the nylon floor.

When I woke at dawn, Ofer was sitting on his sleeping bag with his back to me, the tent unzipped, his legs sticking into the sunlight.

"Ofer, you're okay?"

"We have to talk."

I sat up and brushed a fly from my face.

"This is not for me," he said. "I won't go on like this. Being beaten, being arrested, being stressed, being chased, afraid, unable to sleep." His voice was phlegmy, hoarse. "Maybe you didn't eat enough shit in the military, but I did. I want adventures, not punishment. I don't see how you can enjoy this."

I said nothing for several minutes, then, "Ofer, this *is* what I came for."

I pushed out of the sleeping bag and walked across the soil to a tree stump. Ofer and I had joked for years that we could read each other's minds. It was with him alone that I'd considered sharing my life in Africa. And what I saw as a horizon and a challenge was for my best friend an angry crazed man trying to do us harm. Ofer continued his criticism of me, calling the trip bullshit, calling me self-absorbed "like in Israel," blaming me for misleading him through the long buildup of our supposed common dream; his words hurt in a way only a best friend's could. I didn't try to convince Ofer he was wrong. But I refused to be forced to measure my dreams against his anger and disappointment. I refused to be made to doubt my path.

As we packed in silence, I glanced at his face to see if I could do so without crying. "Ofer, you lead," I said, forcing the words out and pointing. "The river's probably over there. Narok should be in that direction. We can get to the road by afternoon and find a *matatu*. You choose the way."

Back in Nairobi, I paced the streets alone to avoid thinking. The pavement and buildings were dirty, dusty, blackened. Lepers begged for coins. *Matatus* blew soot into my face. I made giant circles, walking the blocks near Planet Safari with my head bowed, and I couldn't help but think of Erez Shtark, another friend who'd died in the army—in a helicopter crash near the Lebanese border.

A young Kenyan girl approached me on the street and said, "Are you okay?"

Her face was so soft against the backdrop of the brutal, buzzing capital.

"Thank you. But you don't have to worry about me," I said and walked on.

"Ofer," I said the next day at Planet, "we're still Ofer and Ofir. Let's have a journey together, a fun journey, and we'll do the things you want. Three weeks. Then Elad will be here and you can travel with him. And I'll do what I need to do."

Ofer scratched his scruff and smiled for the first time in days. We headed up Moi Avenue to the Chicken Inn, which we'd nicknamed the "Azrieli Center," after the palatial shopping mall in Tel Aviv. And we ordered chicken and Cokes to cement our fragile truce.

We turned Kenya into a playground. We outran a brush fire that burned a third of Hell's Gate, hitchhiked in a Cessna, chased giraffes, skipped from mosque to mosque giving greetings from the Holy Land. But sadness remained, underlying the wonderment and joy of our weeks together. On Lamu island, as we listened to a tape Shahar had made for our trip, melancholy rose to the surface to consume us both. "*Last night I dreamt that somebody loved me*," Morrissey sang. "*No fault no harm, just another false alarm*." Our brotherhood assumed the dynamic of a failed romance, with Ofer hoping to rediscover our old magic and to continue traveling, while I was closed to it. Until then, I hadn't realized exactly what I'd chosen by returning to Africa: my journey could be nothing but alone.

KAKUYA

The landscape was severe, dissected by mountains and cliffs, a world so broken it seemed a god had taken a slab of stone and smashed it upon the earth. Cutting through the wasteland was a river, the best route I had for going anywhere. I was four days southeast of Narok, hungry, sick, wedged on a tongue of rocks between the river and a cliff so high I couldn't see the top. The scattered Maasai settlements I'd found could barely feed themselves. Rainwater had leaked one night through the manure roof of a *manyatta* and pooled on my cowskin bed, turning my sleeping bag brown. I'd woken with a cough and the reminder of the struggle of genes here to survive.

I tripped, regained balance, skinning my hand where I skidded on the shale, knocking rocks into the river. I'd fallen into the water that morning, twisted my leg in the very place I'd spotted a crocodile. My boots were still sodden, socks bunched at the toes, my travelers checks a damp mass in the hidden inner pocket my mother had sewn into my pants.

The land dropped away, and the canyon narrowed as the river tumbled into rapids, swallowing the belt of rocks on which I'd walked.

I sidled across a shelf in the canyon wall, back to the river, as in a stunt my sister and I might have tried as kids while Dad waited at the flat to inspect our wounds: "That might need a stitch." My pack was so heavy and wet it seemed to be tugging me backwards off the ledge, as if the land disapproved that I'd brought more than my body. The sun disappeared beyond the canyon's mouth, and fatigue came in errant footsteps, like a loosening of the muscles of the legs. I shook out my tent and pitched it on a pile of rocks beside a tree. A leopard across the gorge that morning had quelled any urge to sleep naked under the stars.

I gathered wood that had likely traveled the miles downstream that I had. The logs of my fire fell between the rocks as they burned. I knelt beside the muddy river, its surface level with the tent floor, and I drank from my hands. After a dinner of lukewarm onion soup, a hundred calories of powder and salt, I climbed into the tent, clothed against the dampness of my sleeping bag. A beautiful exhaustion descended as I watched firelight playing on the nylon wall. I lay curled in the rocks like an infant. Spooling in my mind were sentences of a letter Ofer had written: "I'm angry at the entire world, angry for a wasted period with you . . . angry with you because you gave me up."

A wave of thunder filled the silence.

Not rain. It can't be rain. After a scorching, cloudless day?

Thunder boomed through the canyon. I shoved away the sleeping bag, seized the rain fly, and scampered out, the wind suddenly whipping, the glowing, misshapen tent as fragile as paper on the rocks. I shook out the rain fly, which was pitiful in my hands, thinner than a tablecloth. The wind nearly yanked it from me as I clipped one of its corners to the tent. The belly of the blackness ripped open, and the storm plummeted into the canyon, pouring down my back, dousing the fire, filling the air with the stench of wet ash. The rain fly snapped in the wind, and I pawed for it in the dark, grabbing a loose corner and lunging through the unzipped door. Lightning flashed as I wrapped the fly around the tent and around my head like a shawl.

Rain pounded the nylon roof. But pattered on the riverbank with a ghostly quiet. Was the canyon flooding? I stuck my head into the storm and shined the flashlight on the river and looked up at the cliff knowing I might have to climb. Rocks cracked upriver. Rock struck rock. Muffled. Then one second of silence. Then the sound, *Brruuup*, of a boulder dunking into the river. High overhead, the crack of rocks. Silence. Then the *Brruuup* of a diving boulder hitting the river with such force it sucked its splash into the water behind it. *Brruuup Brruuup*. The cliff was coming apart. I folded my legs against my chest, pressed my back to the tree against which I'd pitched my tent. It was all I had, one thin tree any boulder would obliterate. The tent tipped on its side in a gust of wind and nearly toppled into the river. I fought the wet walls off my face. Rocks crashed up and down the canyon, just meters away, and I saw my end, smashed in the tent as I cowered, afraid even to move my hands. What am I doing here? You didn't come because you had something to prove? You didn't, right? Or—no. I breathed. I said to myself, You are where you should be. This is the land you had to be a part of, and the land led you here. The night I measured in the uncountable times I thought the danger had passed, from cracking rock to cracking rock, one hope to the next, the promise of safety contained within each second. The rain finally lightened. The cliff began to hold. And I shivered in the darkness, hearing nothing but the whisper of water.

I woke initiated. I felt it in breathing, in leaping along the river. *God will not look you over for medals, degrees, or diplomas, but for scars.* The beauty of the day declared to me that I'd earned the right to belong here.

The landscape was endless, devoid of signs of man.

Near noon, I came finally to the muddy banks of *Ewaso Nyiro*, Brown River. Coughing and foodless, I slipped off my pack, peeled away my clothes and dunked a rock into the river, as the Maasai do, to scare the crocodiles. I rushed into the current, fell back in the water and opened my mouth to drink.

When I climbed out, I pulled on underwear and scanned the gentle hills beyond the river, my cough sticky in my lungs. I toed into the water, balancing the backpack on my head, legs spread for balance, steps diagonal to the current. The water climbed as I inched across the muddy river bottom until I was on my tiptoes, the river at my chin and the backpack casting a shadow over my face. Farther out, when I brought my legs together to keep my mouth from going under, the current swept me off my feet. I swam—two seconds—and my strength failed under the weight of the pack. It splashed into the river, bobbed. I hooked an arm around it and side-stroked, struggled against the current that swept me downstream. I staggered up the far banks, heaving. Then threw myself across the sand.

Three hours into the hills, I found a path. I scanned the gravel for footprints, for the tire marks of sandals. My backpack was still dripping. I fantasized about hot *ugali* and passing the night near a fire with a family in some togetherness still alive in the time after Ofer. The trail vanished; it had likely been carved by animals who were as indifferent as I to particular points in the landscape. I didn't regret parting with Ofer, but the cost of solitude was clear.

Snared in a bush was a shred of a red *shuka*. I walked up and over the next hill, gaining views of the dark rings of three *bomas*. "Sopa!" I called out as I neared a cattle herd. I raised my hands and stopped until I saw that the two young Maasai were smiling. They approached, bowed and leaned forward, and I placed my hand on their skulls. I followed in silence to the thorn-bush fence where men were gathering to welcome me. An elder took my hands and pulled me into the village.

"*Sopa sopa sopa*," I said.

All eyes went to my waterlogged pack when I let it thud to the ground. A girl touched my hair and ran off laughing. Two old mamas seized my wrists and inspected my earrings. I sketched my route in the dirt with a stick and relayed the story in Swahili to the Maasai gathered in the cow dug, though I lacked the language to share how it'd felt surviving the storm. The direction I'd come surprised them: "the mountains."

A tall slim man in a striped *shuka* worked his way through the crowd.

"Are you one of the lost ones?" he said, stroking his moustache.

I laughed. "You speak English?"

"Yes, the only one. They called me from another *boma*."

A boy picked up my backpack.

"Let's go," the man said.

A skeleton of sticks showed in the cracked mud walls of his *manyatta*.

"My name is Isaac Ololkupai," he said, ducking through the door into the dark hut. "Sit. I think you could use a cup of tea."

His sideways glance made clear he knew I needed more than tea.

A fire burned within three rectangular stones forming a hearth that was almost a shrine. The smoke-stained poles holding up the roof were as dark and smooth as ebony. The scent of Isaac's home reminded me of childhood when my father had returned from the army reserves and I'd rushed into his arms to absorb the smell of sweat from his uniform and beard. I pulled off my boots, and Isaac served me a cup and then a second cup of tea, his chest visible where his *shuka* was pulled back. He dragged a metal box across the dirt floor and opened a disintegrating photo album and pointed to a picture of a school forty kilometers away, just a day's walk for a Maasai.

"I was the one in the family my father chose to send to school," said Isaac, who was in his thirties. He had a few grays curling in his hair. He pointed to a photograph of himself in trousers and a button-down shirt. "I got a job at Mara Sarova, the safari lodge." Among pictures of villages was a photograph of Isaac at a computer. "I was there three years. I was good at my job. I was advancing. But I decided I had to come back here. I wanted to be with my father and herd cattle. This is my home. *This*," Isaac said and motioned with his hands, "is worth far more than I had in the other world."

We walked that evening to the *manyatta* of his father. "My old man," Isaac called him. He sat on a stool outside his hut, wielding a cow-tail flyswatter. The wrinkles and lines on his forehead were a checkerboard of decades, and age had given his skin a sheen of silver. I knelt before him, held his hands and said, "*Sopa*."

His eyes were milky with cataracts, his voice weak.

"The old man says he dreamed of your arrival," Isaac said, translating. "He says your arrival is a blessing to the village."

To talk with such a man was an honor that put to doubt one's worthiness.

I asked Isaac how to say "Grandfather" in KiMaasai.

"*Kakuya*."

Still kneeling, gripping the elder's cold, fragile hands, I thanked him. *"Asante,* Kakuya. *Asante sana."*

In a field among trees, Isaac taught me how to shoot a bow and arrow. He taught me the names and uses of plants and how to track animals from downwind and he encouraged me to practice Swahili with other Maasai. I laughed at how amazing it would have been to have Isaac beside me in boyhood helping to catch snakes. "Feel welcome," Isaac seemed always to say. "Do what you want."

I'd seen Kakuya walking alone between *bomas,* slumped over but holding his head up, his shoulders thin as a shirt on a hanger. He had four wives.

"How old is Kakuya?"

"Nobody really knows," Isaac said. "From the memories he has, we think he should be about ninety-four."

Kakuya was the only survivor of his age group, the oldest Maasai in the area, and he sat outside his house eating an ear of dry roasted corn, corn I could not chew, the difference in the hardness of our teeth a simple proof of the softness of modern ways.

"Father, can I ask for your wisdom?" I said to Kakuya through Isaac.

Kakuya smiled, nodded. His right earring looked like a tiny brass bell.

"What's the difference between the life today and the life of the Maasai when you were a child?"

Kakuya spoke for several minutes. His soft, gravely voice seemed to have its source in a world barely heard. "In my time, the Maasai did not live in *bomas.* We were more nomads and had small houses made of sticks and leather. It was a time of great bravery for the Maasai. We did have good relations with other tribes. The Luhya gave us steel. They knew how to work the steel. The Akamba made pottery and traded with us."

All I knew of the Akamba was that they were the best *askaris* in Nairobi.

"When was the first time white men arrived?" I said.

"I remember it well. I was very young. It was British soldiers who came. One soldier gave me a piece of hard candy, a sweet. He showed me to put it in my mouth." Kukuya twisted up his face and reached into his mouth with two fingers. "The taste was horrible." He pretended to yank out the candy and throw it down. "It's the most horrible memory I had as a child."

Isaac laughed with the old man and said, "It's the first time I've heard that story."

Kakuya's enthusiasm to tell stories was as great as my desire to hear them, and we reached the point where I didn't have to ask him questions. As Isaac listened to Kakuya before translating, I thought of the times I'd shushed cousins and aunts in an attempt to give Grandpa Moshe the stage he deserved to read the Saturday blessing. My family "felt sorry" for my grandfather because of his age. But to try to take care of him was an insult when they should have been listening.

"The old man has given you a name," Isaac said. "You are Lamayan. It means 'The one who brings blessings.'"

I thought, How on earth could I ever deserve this?

Two weeks later, Isaac draped blankets over my shoulders and wrapped me in a *shuka*. "Lamayan, take this," he said, handing me a smooth stick and then laughing. "I think we're going to surprise a few people at the wedding." We strode for hours on the savannah, long past dusk when I wouldn't have walked alone. But Isaac, with his spear across his shoulders, was merely strolling in his neighborhood.

Singing and drumming, barely audible, reached out to us from the vast night as we crossed a space that seemed not to be real. We arrived to a *boma* filled with men drinking honey wine and dancing with spears, shooting themselves into the air without bending their knees. The warriors, *moran*, who'd likely traveled a day or more to be together, did not notice me in the dark. Isaac put his arms at his sides and shot into the air and nodded for me to do the same. One by one, as I leapt, the Maasai met my gaze. Then jumped back with their spears. They slapped their knees and laughed when they saw Isaac. Many came to shake my hand and chat in Swahili or to talk to me through Isaac in KiMaasai. I felt as drunk after a single taste of wine as the *moran* who were dancing and stumbling as though they'd been at it since lunch. What a rush to be accepted by warriors. I wished my sister could see me, my sister who'd encouraged me to play electric guitar instead of breeding lizards.

The celebration hardly paused for dawn. Men stayed in one *boma*, women in another. Outside the fence, elders sat on cow skins and prayed, oblivious to the commotion behind them. The groom was adorned in ochre, his hair, forehead and sideburns red. Half circles of ochre paint, like the scales on a reptile, decorated his bare legs above gray socks and dress shoes with the laces gone. The groom stood near his *manyatta*, waiting for the bride to arrive from her village.

His mouth hung open as if his stomach were unsettled, and I approached. His father spoke for him, bragged about how long it had taken to arrange the marriage. With so many eyes on me, I couldn't help but feel that my presence was a distraction and I backed away into the crowd.

Cattle lazed in the dirt like overfed pets.

The first of the bride's caravan sang its way into the *boma*. The entourage was a festival of color, spectacular and showy against the brown earth. The bride had to be proud, I thought, for the communities that had traveled from the far corners of the bush to celebrate the creation of her family. I was falling in love with the Maasai, with their hospitality and patience, their connection to nature, the respect of elders and of children, their courage, pride, resilience and joy.

The bride walked across the *boma*. Old women before her sprinkled liquid from calabashes onto the ground, a tradition incompatible with concrete. Discs of orange and blue ringed the bride's neck, and the long spires of a beaded crown rose like feathers from her forehead. Her massive earrings were of the most impractical shapes.

Song encircled the groom, and I thought again of my sister whose own time in the army, I hoped, was passing without pain and who would meet a good man someday for her own fine wedding. The mothers of the betrothed negotiated the dowry's final terms while the bride waited outside the groom's hut for the invitation to enter. A female relative carried a blue trunk on her back, held in place by a tump line, a trunk filled with gifts from the bride's family for her new life. People sang and danced. The bride stood motionless, focused on the ground. She was beautiful, the ceremony magnificent. I moved through the dancers for a better view of her face. Silver chains curled under her cheekbones. Two silver pendants lay on the bridge of her nose. She was frowning. Her eyes were melancholic. She was in despair. And no one was consoling or helping her.

Hours later, walking back to Isaac's *boma* and feeling almost betrayed, I tried to hide my disappointment that the marriage seemed wrong.

"Isaac," I said, finally, "do you think the bride was sad?"

"Yes."

His matter-of-fact answer clashed with the intensity of my emotions. "But why?"

"She'd never seen her husband," Isaac said as he loped through the grass beside me, spear in hand. "She hadn't chosen her mother-in-law. Many times the mother-in-law is harsh with a young bride; she has more authority over the bride than the husband and can ruin her life."

Isaac, himself, had fallen in love with his wife before asking her to marry him. They'd gone to school together.

"It was probably the first time the bride has ever left her village," Isaac said. "She was frightened, and she has reason to be."

I felt guilty for looking at my *shuka* and being less proud to wear it now; this life, I realized, was not one I could have ever embraced completely. But as a nomad, myself, as a guest moving from culture to culture, could I pick the values I found beautiful and take them with me and simply leave the others behind?

The Maasai burned a fire through the night near the entrance of Isaac's *boma*, to guard against leopards prowling for goats. A leopard was chased off one night, and I stayed late at the fire the rest of the week, hoping she would show herself on return.

Isaac had told me that the rainy season began each year when two stars came together, a pair of bright stars side by side in the night sky, part of the legacy I was determined to capture. I set up my camera to take a four-hour exposure and I imagined that the two stars would leave long, nearly parallel scratches on the film as they rose from the east. When I removed my hand from the lens, though, and let in the light, I understood how far I was from capturing the *emotion* of actually waiting for the two stars to meet and of what Kakuya might feel when walking in first rains that would bring new grass up from the stubble.

"There's a lion!" Isaac said one afternoon.

I grabbed my knife, trembling, and we ran, the village emptying onto the savannah. Isaac had told me that four *moran* his age had been killed by lions when he was younger. But this lion was already far away.

Light shone through tiny holes in the thin walls of Kakuya's hut. I sat with him, our feet bare on the dirt. Through Isaac, I said to Kakuya, "Tell me one thing that is good in life."

"Cattle," Kakuya said and he explained how the Maasai drank the blood and milk of their cattle, which I'd known even as a boy.

"Tell me one thing that's bad."

Kakuya spoke and Isaac listened. "The old man says 'Education.'"

"No, no, I meant a bad thing."

"I know," Isaac said with a smile. "He said 'Education.' Let me ask him why."

Isaac leaned in as his father spoke.

"My old man says that when the white man brought education he didn't bring it as a gift. He brought it only to some people. The white man didn't spread education equally. It wasn't shared. Education was used by one tribe against another, as power."

Isaac walked me out of their territory.

"Lamayan, will you be lost enough to be back here again?"

"You'll see me soon."

"You're a part of us. You always have a place in my *manyatta*."

AN EQUAL FOE

My camel looked smaller this morning. The light caught his eye-lashes, exaggerating the movement of his eyes. His ears wiggled and he scampered across the corral and swung his head back toward me, as if to determine whether I were responsible for his quarantine from the other camels. It was early morning, the shadows of the acacia trees long across the savannah—central Kenya, north of Nanyuki, land of the Samburu tribe.

My camel seemed far too odd and expressive to be made into a beast of burden, more like a companion in an animated film who might suddenly tell a joke. The few camels there were in central Kenya were raised for milk, meat, and hide. But I planned to use him for transport. I was headed to the remotest area on the map of East Africa, Turkana, a desert hundreds of kilometers north inhabited by tribesmen more isolated than the Maasai. Hominid fossils found in Turkana had earned it the name "cradle of humanity."

My camel's hump was half bald, patchy with pubescence. Thick veins wound around his stomach like ant tunnels on a tree. He reminded me of the giraffes I'd chased, with knotty legs and too many joints. I was bringing him along to carry my water, as Lake Turkana, a soda lake, was undrinkable. Though I didn't really need an excuse to travel with a camel. From the Samburu family who'd sold him to me I'd hidden my ignorance of all things related to camels. "Yes, this male looks strong. Enough. Fifteen thousand shillings is too much for a camel of his size. I'll give 13,000 ($185). If you supply the trainers."

Training was a disaster, with a Samburu named Tanai teaching me to yell, "*Tor! Tor!*" while a half-Turkana man named Jonah whacked the camel's ass with a cane. The camel repaid the violence by roaring, screaming, and spitting grassy green bile into my eyes. Our first short walks were duels of stubbornness and cruelty.

On day five of training, when the camel, Jonah, and I returned from a trip to the bore hole, I said, "Tanai, tomorrow, I'm taking the camel to the river. Alone."

"Jonah needs to go behind you," Tanai said in Swahili.

"No. I'm doing it alone. I'm going alone."

Tanai thought I didn't understand. He drew a diagram in the sand and pointed. "You. Camel. Jonah."

I shook my head. "Tomorrow. I go alone. I'm walking alone. One man. Me." I erased Jonah from the sand and slapped my chest. "*Mtu moja. Mimi.*"

"Lamayan, it's not possible," Tanai said, his eye twitching. I realized then that what I'd seen as a stage in the camel's training—towing him from the front and whipping him from the back as he fought like a bull—was to Tanai the proper method of travel. "The camel is a clever animal," he said. "If no one goes behind him he knows you can't control him. You *have* to take another man for the journey."

"How much time to train him to go with one man?" I said.

Tanai scratched his chin. "*Mwezi moja.*" One month.

Defeated, I retired to the house.

The Samburu family lived in an isolated wood cabin, its inner walls plastered with peeling newspaper and pages from old calendars. They had a pickup, a long-drop outhouse toilet, wheat fields, a garden, and cattle grazing in a pasture to the south. The father, who had four boys, wore a beaded bracelet, a link to his nomadic roots and a life more like Kakuya's. His wife had high cheekbones and wore shawls of purple, red, and blue—festive and royal but still of the bush. In their cut, low hanging earlobes they wore no earrings.

"I'm going *alone*," I said at dawn to the camel trainers.

"Camel, you and I are going to the river!"

I got the bridle on him, whacked his ass with a stick, yanked the rope, yelled, "*Brrrh, brrrh!*" The camels lips parted and he sprayed my face with half-digested grass from the pit of his stomach. Then he looked away, satisfied I'd gotten my punishment, and followed me out of the corral.

My purple Bacardi shirt was soon soaked with sweat as I fought my camel over every millimeter of scorching ground. Flies traveled back and forth between the camel and me, as if some horrid ecosystem were forming between us. I dashed to his rump to whack him with the cane, then ran to the front to pull him, and in the process I walked twice as far, while the stinking grassy green bile baked on my face.

"*Brrrh, brrrh*, you stupid monster! We go we go we go!"

In dozens of countries, men raced *on* camels. *My* camel wedged himself into the thorny branches of an acacia bush and wouldn't move. When I yanked the braided sisal rope, he swung his long neck toward me, releasing the rope's tension, sending me backwards into the thorns. He swung his jaw and bared ugly yellow teeth in silent mockery. Then roared.

Exhausted and cramping, I dragged the camel to the river, his stubbornness exceeded only by mine. I tied him up, stripped and threw myself into the water.

Dusk caught us before we got back to the farm. The camel had made a strategy of parking himself in acacia and then staring at me, his pupils shaped like antique keyholes. I thrust my neck out, said, "*Brrrh, brrrh!*" The camel screamed and skipped forward and rammed me into thorns. I smashed the cane over his back, and what I'd seen as violence just days before was now both ordinary and essential.

"You want to sleep here?" I yelled. "Is that what you want?"

Darkness at the equator came like a falling curtain, with the sun dropping straight over the horizon. Stars appeared like little warnings. I stumbled into bushes, dodged silhouetted trees.

Something charged! A hiss through the grass. Rushing feet. I lunged, clung to the camel's neck. A current shot through my spine. Animals sliced by on both sides. Screeching. Hyenas tearing though the trees, their laughter seething in the darkness.

The camel was frozen, everything silent. I lifted my chin and tuned my ears to the distance, my jaw tensed as if focusing my hearing. I rotated my head, hoping if the hyenas charged again, it would be to the broadside of the camel, with his flesh between us. Three hyenas cried off to the side, far off. And I exhaled. And courage became cowardice. I was trembling. My legs wanted me running but I was safer with the camel whose instincts were finally aligned with mine. We hurried together toward the house, I watching the camel to see if he were picking up sounds beyond my range.

A light. A flashlight. It was Tanai.

After leaving Isaac, I'd returned to Nairobi and scoured the bookshops on Moi Avenue for the names of photographers who'd worked in Kenya, because photography could help turn my journey into a life. After two weeks of searching, I found British photographer Duncan Willetts, a survivor of the Bang Bang Club, a group of photojournalists who'd made a name for themselves in war zones. His house was in Westlands, the yard lush, blooming with bougainvillea. Willetts greeted me outside and said, "Can you believe these bloody Maasai are grazing their cattle in my grass?"

Failed rains had brought herders to the gardens of Nairobi, a town that a century earlier had been a Maasai watering hole.

Willetts praised me for my first attempts to get difficult images. He appreciated the idea of traveling with a camel and then directed me toward Nyahururu where I could find one.

At dawn, I grabbed the wood saddle Tanai and I had carved with machetes. I slung it onto the camel's back and tied sisal ropes around his belly before he pitched it. I strapped my cooking pot and backpack to the saddle and wedged my machete in, the handle within easy reach. The family stuffed gifts into the saddle pouches: honey, tea, and *ugali* powder, demonstrating why the word for "stranger" in Swahili, *mgeni*, was the same as "guest." The Samburu mother poured me cup after cup of camel milk tea, as if she knew I was embarking on a period of great wanting. I gave her boys my Pink Floyd tapes and said good-bye.

The camel and I turned and began our journey. I'd named him Lapa, "moon" in KiSamburu. The coolness of the early morning burned away in the African sun, and green belts of savannah gave way to brown. Circular elephant tracks, lined as delicately as fingerprints, were pressed into the dirt two hours from the farm. I moved through a grove of trees and tied Lapa to a branch, got my camera, and crept toward a clearing through a cluster of twisted, broken tree trunks. Six elephants, I saw. Seven. The babies seemed as small and harmless as rabbits. For two idyllic seconds, I watched elephants moving together. One trumpeted. Charged. Ears flaring. I snapped a photograph and ducked between branches. The elephants stormed through the trees, flattening an acacia, another, the ground thundering with the weight of animals and crashing wood. One small elephant rammed a tree trunk that stopped him with a crack. I stumbled and tripped, just meters from being crushed, and I ran until the elephants were no longer behind me, and I continued to run.

I circled back downwind from the herd. Lapa was traumatized, jerking his head. "Shh, shh." He shuddered when I touched him. I took the rope, and he spun around as though he'd lost his bearings. Then he began pulling in the direction of the farm. I turned him north, toward Turkana, and ran between his head and ass, hitting and tugging. But he was deadweight. After an hour of frustration, we headed back to the house.

I set out the next morning with a neighboring Samburu teenager who walked behind Lapa with the cane. Then we came upon elephant tracks. The boy stopped and fidgeted with his *shuka*, clearly concerned by the prospect of marauding giants. He said, "This journey is too long for me. I forgot. I have work on the farm." He handed me the cane and hurried off. He'd agreed to a trip of five hundred kilometers and hadn't made five.

I stood in silence, downcast, wondering how I would ever get moving. My mind drifted to trips I'd made to see the parents of Erez Shtark after he died in the helicopter crash. Weekend after weekend I'd made the long drive from the army base, alone, to bring to Erez's parents small doses of the happiness and energy they'd lost and to show them that their son was not forgotten. Ofer called my trips an obsession. On the drives home from the Shtarks' house I played *Final Cut* on the stereo, again and again, every time I drove, to create a ceremony of melancholy out of a longing to feel something real.

From the trees in front of me, wearing a beaded headband and carrying a spear with a goatskin sheath, came a young Samburu warrior walking south. He was relaxed and confident. I opened a packet of biscuits, took one, and put the rest in his hand. He looked down at the biscuits, then up at me, confused, for the give and take of the West was not the way of the bush. I felt ashamed that the biscuits were almost a bribe.

I pointed north. In Swahili, I said, "I need to go *there*. I walked with a boy. He left, afraid. The camel needs two people. Me. You. Do we go?"

Not sure whether he'd understood, I handed him the cane and said, "*Tuende.*" Let's go. I clucked my tongue. Lapa began to walk. Within one minute of materializing from nowhere, the Samburu turned in behind the camel and followed.

We reached the river and swung north and slept that night in his grandmother's *boma*. In the morning, we drank tea with milk and sugar. I checked the compass, aimed us at a tree on a distant ridge. And we walked. I had one direction: north. Saying Lake Turkana was my destination was akin to saying I was walking to Syria. My map was so crude, it had an illustrated giraffe in the middle of it. I didn't care if I reached Turkana by way of Ethiopia or if I missed the lake entirely. Walking, for now, was to be my life. Destination was an excuse. And my compass was a tool for continuing to be lost, for staying away from roads, for ensuring I didn't end up in Nanyuki, Maralal, or some place actually on a map.

I shortened the rope and pulled Lapa with my arms. I lengthened it and towed the beast over my shoulder to spread the toil of dragging him through the muscles of my back. Flies clustered on my eyelashes. Lapa screamed at me, spit, pulled me backwards, rammed my chest, kicked at the Samburu. That evening, the soft light of dusk returned texture to the savannah, details the midday sun washed out. The grass glowed in the same way hair on my arms caught the light, as though overwhelmed by the sun. I pitched the tent and lit a fire and waited for moonrise to summon shapes of animals from the darkness. The night was cold, and the warrior and I slept in the tent under my sleeping bag. And I tried to imagine his thoughts. Perhaps when your home was the bush, any journey crossing yours became your own. I woke to add wood to the fire, to chase off an animal that yelped and skipped away. With moonlight bright on the savannah, I set up my camera to photograph a hint of the magic of being out in the dark beside leaping flames. For a moment, I let myself forget that the fire burned to keep predators away, burned to keep us alive. My shortness of breath made clear that the urge to be as wild as the savannah ran counter to instinct.

We woke with sunrise and continued. Without breakfast. In early morning, it was easy to navigate by the sun. We followed a ribbon of trees that was like a hand holding back the heat, then crossed an expanse of loose volcanic rock that made Lapa snort and flail. Below us in the distance was a herd of a hundred elephants—the energy of the world in motion—an image of such magnificence, I doubted for a moment what I saw.

Some mornings I rekindled the wood of the night's fire, filled the kettle, and boiled tea. When I made *ugali* and set the pot between us, the Samburu and I talked little and he ate far more than I. Often he offered to help with Lapa or with the food, but I told him I could manage. Next to Isaac, he was barely a warrior. But he was at home on the plains, capable of handling whatever we met. And I was here to push myself beyond the point where I could be saved from my mistakes.

I drove us at a pace of roughly thirty kilometers a day. We stopped in *bomas* of the Samburu who fed us *sukuma wiki*, plentiful, simple food meant to *stretch the week*. Villagers gave us groundnuts and replenished our stock of *ugali* powder and filled my jerricans with water and Samburu beer—sweet like champagne but not strong. There was little distinction in the villages between what was theirs and what was not. And how could anything repay them for giving up their beds to strangers or slaughtering a goat their children had raised? Money, save for occasional trips to markets to buy salt or cloth, was not used in daily life. Before setting out with Lapa, I'd considered heading back to a town to get more cash; I had just $50. But I'd thought, If villagers have no place to drink but from a river, then I will drink from a river. If they can live virtually without money, then so can I.

One day, a man told us about a bandit attack on a road two days east. Another Samburu said, "It's far to Turkana. Take care; they are bad people."

Lapa was falling into rhythm, fighting less each day, walking without stopping, though still under the shadow of the cane.

Slicing across the savannah with the promise of water was a band of green, a forest climbing up through a crack. We hurried downhill, scaring gazelles. I tied Lapa near a patch of grass, stripped bare and jumped in tandem with the warrior—into a river filled with Samburu who were swimming and scrubbing clothes. Women fled up the river-banks and covered their breasts at the sight of me. Small boys giggled, swam close, and I grabbed them under the arms and flung them into the air; and the river swallowed their laughter. I sank into the cool water to rest my swollen, blistered feet, to scrub my scrapes and insect bites, to wash the camel's sourness from my exhausted body. Light shone on the water with a brightness that sparkled *through* my eyelids. Deep in the river, feeling that I'd slipped inside the earth, I drank of the source that kept the village alive.

Two dozen laughing Samburu led us up a path, and I sensed that the warrior was ready to head home. While Lapa munched on the cactus fence surrounding the *boma*, we divided up the food given to us in our time together. I pulled out my Walkman, tapes, and enough batteries to last for months, and I put everything in his hands. "Thank you," I said. "You're a good friend." And he was gone before nightfall.

I left the village the next morning, joined by a curious and talkative warrior with the Christian name of Stanley. And I stopped counting the days. I tracked our progress by the angle at which Samburu pointed to distant villages. I felt tiny in the landscape, which stretched on as though Israel were a myth and there were nothing in the world but the plains. Samburu walked on distant hills, red dots, as small to me as I was to them, all of us moving through a land we could not fill. The sun was brutal, the ground dry and shade-less. The grasses of past rains were yellow, the earth waiting for its crust to be broken.

My body was changing, the fight with Lapa thickening my arms. Blisters formed and healed almost without my noticing. I quenched my thirst with the Samburu beer villagers poured into my jerricans like the inexhaustible blessing of the tribe. I couldn't imagine how I'd spent four years in the army living someone else's life. As I traveled further and further from what I knew, I wanted my old beliefs to slip away and the ropes connecting me to my past to snap for good. Borders were artificial; geographical or cultural, they were excuses. I thought of Isaac, who'd said of his village, "This is my home." His comment was to me as much a statement that he had chosen the culture that fit him as it was an indication that I had yet to find my own.

By week three, the camel was regressing.

Lapa's body twitched, unsettling a coat of flies. He opened his mouth and sprayed me with rotting grass. I yanked the rope. He screamed, his eyes bulging, jaw swinging. Violence rose within me like the emotions of someone I didn't know. I broke the cane across the camel's ass, cracked tree limbs on his knees, gritted my teeth and yelled until my chest hurt. *Adherence to mission* was a principle driven into me by the army.

"You shouldn't beat him," Stanley said. "It just makes him resist."

Stanley wasn't yet immune to the charm of Lapa's eyelashes.

"Maybe he's afraid of heights. *Wasiwasi*," Stanley said

"What good is a camel in the mountains if he's afraid of hills? Turkana is full of mountains!"

We climbed for hours as the plains lengthened behind us. A stream ran just off parallel from the route we'd made. The midday sun was as vicious as the flies dive-bombing my face. Lapa stopped and wouldn't move.

"You brown dragon, I'll feed you to hyenas!"

Lapa was grinning, staring at me. We weren't going to reach Turkana together. He seemed to see a scam in what I wanted to be. The battle was between my desire to continue in an arbitrary direction and his to go nowhere. My camel felt like the baggage of all I'd come from, a confused legacy abusive to the idea of finding a new way.

Just as quickly as he'd stopped, Lapa began to move. I towed the rope over my shoulder, plowed through the gravel, dragged him on as if I were towing a tank over a pass. The trail we followed cut across a hill toward the outpost of Amaya.

The camel slipped, screamed. The rope pulled free from my hand as he fell, flipped and tumbled downhill. A bush stopped him ten meters below. He was bawling, on his back, legs thrashing the air. He looked so small flailing on the side of the hill.

I felt instant relief that the climax had come. Then guilt.

Stanley and I scurried down to him. We yanked the saddle ropes and flipped him while trying not to get kicked in the teeth. I slapped Lapa once and he scampered back to the path, intact, save for patches of hair clawed out by thorns. I emptied the saddle pouches into my backpack. Stanley took the saddle on his shoulders. We tried to continue but Lapa wouldn't move.

I left the camel with Stanley and set out alone for Amaya, feeling again and again that I'd forgotten something, as after I'd handed in the rifle that rode for years on my back. Then, as though a new season had already been reached, a rainstorm swept in, which the elders in Amaya gave me credit for bringing. The English-speaking chief greeted me with the enthusiasm he might have shown for a returning son. We hiked back to Stanley with an entourage and a camel expert armed with a rope. I kept my distance from Lapa, not wanting to see his face and thinking of a line from a Sinead O'Connor song about divorce: *I'll meet you later in somebody's office.*

Stanley hesitated and then held out his hands when I gave him a few shillings and all of our food. He headed south. The chief and I walked east to Maralal. He paid for my hotel room without telling me and negotiated a deal to sell Lapa to a white Kenyan who raced camels. Selling the camel for slaughter would have brought more money, but I felt I didn't have the right.

EXODUS

In Maralal, I pushed my new monster by the horns, a bicycle I'd designed and had welded with baskets for holding jerricans. Shacks filled the unpaved town, temporary solutions to the absence of a roof—for Turkana and Samburu who'd left the bush behind, who'd been lured by modernization, pushed by poverty or both. The new paint on my bike frame was still wet, but I was too impatient to pass another minute in town where packs of orphaned street boys wandered in the dust; and I found that I loathed even the sight of light bulbs. I pedaled up a dirt road, weak from diarrhea that had struck just hours after I'd sold Lapa. The bike bore the weight of my backpack, thirty liters of water and two and a half kilograms of sugar. I put a postcard into the mail to my parents and pushed off at the edge of town, down a hill as steep as a ski jump. The bike rattled and jerked over the uneven road, instantly out of control as it shot downhill through the trees, the seat ramming my *inkulal*, the brakes useless and the back tire in the air, as I held on for dear life and planned how best to crash. The road finally flattened and began up a hill, and my momentum carried me not to the top but just three meters up, where the overloaded bike stalled and flipped over backwards.

I kicked it aside and climbed onto a boulder to eat bread drizzled with Samburu honey. Ragged children rushed at me from plastic-roofed roadside shacks, two boys wearing T-shirts that were hardly more than collars. "Give me sweets," they screamed. "Give me one bob!" A boy lunged for my backpack. I jumped down and chased him off. A small boy approached. He wore a yellow shirt and sat against a tree at the bottom of the hill. He waited. And I watched him, wishing he'd make his move so I could drive him away; in *bomas* no one had to beg. I wrapped my bread up and continued with the bike. When I looked back, the small boy in the yellow shirt was searching where I'd sat for crumbs. I took all my bread, smothered it with honey, and left it for him on a rock.

I dumped much of my water and pushed the bike for hours on foot up the road to Poror, and a French bird researcher stopped his jeep and asked if I needed help. When I told him I'd designed the bike to carry water through Turkana, he said, "No, no. You can drink water from the lake. Just add acid."

I could hear laughter rumbling out of the pit of Lapa's stomach.

I sold the bike in Poror, bought lemons I hoped could deliver this acid, and descended into the Suguta Valley, where I crawled through acacia fields that tore from my backpack the wet socks I'd tied to the outside to dry. I drank from puddles full of tadpoles and got caught in a storm and learned that the Great Rift Valley, here, was a refuge for gun runners, road bandits, cattle raiders, fugitives, and *watu simba*, lion men, as the villagers in Moridjo called them. I hitchhiked around Suguta, suppressing the thought that the spirit of my journey across Kenya had been lost.

Back on foot, I aimed for the black mountains said to "cork" the lake's southern end. The terrain was gentle grassland. Willow trees, with shadows shaped like the hairdos of Rastas, offered shelter from the sun. I'd learned from a Somali family in South Horr that a bore hole lay somewhere between the black mountains and the road. I headed for it, more or less, hoping the presence of villagers would make it possible to find this speck within a hundred square kilometers.

The ground became black, barren, contorted, as strange under my boots as a place I might have reached in a dream. I struggled to hold a direction, to judge distance. After an hour I came upon four Turkana women. Two were yelling at each other, shaking fists, their bracelets clattering on their arms—until they spotted me. All four Turkana wore oversized metal earrings and leather loincloths. The lip ring of one woman dangled below her chin like a golden beard. The two young women stood before me as unembarrassed as the grandmothers, all with their breasts exposed. I stammered and stared at the ground, and they spoke to me, as though trying keys, in full Turkana sentences.

"Mama," I said in Swahili to one grandmother, just glancing at her, "where is the water, the way to the water, the hole in the ground?" I pointed in three directions.

A woman smiled and walked, and I followed, hoping it would be easy for her to point me to the bore hole. She stopped, reached down behind a bush, then stood up holding a cup of water.

The terrain morphed almost as soon as I said good-bye, into a reddish bedrock of tiny columns, carved as if by acid. Columns three at a time cracked under my boots soles. I stumbled, cut my hands. How could people walk, much less live here? My right boot lodged in a rut and I broke off a chunk of rock prying myself free. I got stuck again, and it seemed I'd become either a giant for whom the world was too small or an insect who could travel but a meter in a day. The land was full of ridges that peaked at the level of my eyes, an endless series of obstacles. The rocks sliced into my boots, drew blood from my arms, as though the ground itself rejected the premise of being crossed. The ridges ran north to south, dipping and rising like the spines of a herd of extinct and petrified animals who'd died in some great migration.

One massive spine after another.

I couldn't see the horizon or guess how close I was to the lake. But I found a path when the sun was high. Then lost it a dozen steps on as though it were merely a landing strip for birds. A cluster of hot, wind-polished boulders gave views of a ribbon winding through the desolation where feet or hooves had trampled the rock to gravel. I lost and re-found the path through the afternoon, which led me away from the volcanoes at the lake's southern tip. The landscape morphed again, from black rock to yellow grass to eroded, column-filled bedrock, as if under the spell of a sorcerer.

I approached a village, slowly, my body feeling with chills what my brain was slow to tell me—the village was abandoned. Several domed huts, with full, shaggy coats of hay, might have been used just days before. Others, shedding their thatch, sat on the gravel like balding skulls. None were large enough to shelter adults.

I knelt by a ring of rocks encircling charred chunks of wood, then lifted my head. The silence was like a pressure in the ears. Neither an insect nor a rustling tree. Had the villagers been raided, forced to leave? Had they left while a fire was still burning? As I kicked through thatch blown to the ground, I understood why the Maasai burned the bomas they abandoned: so not to leave their legacy to the elements and shame.

I searched for tracks, for ribbons of crushed gravel. I cut back toward the black mountains, east to west across the rocky spines, fearing I was in a dead land. The ground was breathing, its heat in my throat. The backpack jockeyed up and down on my back, exaggerating and mimicking the movements of my body. Turkana would have killed Lapa had he not killed me first, and the reddish rock would have melted, shredded the tires off my bike. What plans I'd had!

When I reached the last barricade, I found that I stood on a ridge. Whatever might have betrayed the people of the abandoned village was not the lake. Calm as a mirror and waveless from above, Lake Turkana flared into the distance, a turquoise treasure worthy of the land's effort to guard it. The lake was too tranquil not to be older than everything. And I stood, humbled by the thought that the taste of its waters had been known by first men. I followed the lakeshore with my eyes—three days crossing to the black mountains, which plunged into the water, and three days more as the shoreline ran over ridges and boulders before disappearing in the sunlight.

I spotted calabashes below me: women marching up from the lake, five Turkana whose massive bodies said more strongly than the land that I had not been born here. The women wore leather loincloths. Red beads. Ochre. Hooped necklaces. They didn't chat or joke or look at each other as they moved. They held their shoulders back and scowled and stopped, it seemed, only because I stood in their path.

"*Ejyo'k*," I said, greeting them as I'd been taught in South Horr.

They didn't respond. Sweat dotted their scalps at the base of their mohawks. Water splashed in the blackened, silver pot atop one woman's head. Another women spoke to her. Then she spoke to the next, as though an order were passing down the line. They stood in formation, naked, as unwelcoming as the rock. I reached into my backpack for a bag of crumbling biscuits the size of a soccer ball. A woman balanced the calabash on her head with her right hand and extended her left. Two women reached out with both hands, calabashes steady. They swallowed the biscuits and motioned for more.

The women turned and walked single file on a path as narrow as a goat trail, headed for what I could only imagine was some austere place. As I followed, I thought, Why weren't their children with them? And where were all the men?

The last woman in line turned and poked me and opened her hand. I left them, veering off trail as fast as if I'd been told to go. I descended to the lake and was soon splashing my face with water. The lake bottom was a collage of glittering pebbles—tan, red, and black—bits of shell and quartz. I cupped my palms and dipped them between waves. The water was electrified with the taste of minerals—fresh, cold, and good—which yielded to an aftertaste of dead fish.

For half an hour I followed the shoreline, stepping between stones, until I saw, perched above the lake, an old man draped with a maroon and gray blanket. I quickened my step, excited by the sight of an elder, hopeful he might help me to understand what had happened here. He had frizzy white hair, a face lined with the passing of years, and he sat bare-assed on a rock. Scars ran down his calves nearly to his sandals, which were made of twine, fishbone, and tire. The man's massive flat feet seemed to belong to an animal far heavier than he, and his robe looked like the kind of covering that in the army we'd called a "scabies blanket."

Where were his daughters, his sons? Where was his village? And why was he here so far from a settlement?

With a chisel-shaped knife he gutted a wildcat, an animal that barely looked like food. Sight of him was as inconceivable as the thought of Kakuya lying alone on the savannah eating a rat, with his people lost to him. The old man jutted his arm at me, then bunched his fingers at his mouth and held them there. Then stuck out his hand again to beg as he sat utterly alone.

Lake Turkana was a vast and silent companion. I spent a sweaty night on the shore in my tent. *Ugali* crumbs, which I tossed into the water to test for fish, floated untouched and drifted back ashore at my feet. I walked toward the black mountains. An elder passed on the lakeshore and did not look up. Half an hour later, a woman appeared carrying nothing but a small wooden headrest. A naked man walked by with a spear. Then an old woman cradling an infant. They were all moving in the same direction opposite me, traveling alone toward Loyangalani, some three days away, migrating as if a battle had been lost and there were nothing left to do but leave for the nearest town.

Could I imagine Isaac on this path, were the story of his people to end? Would he rush to find refuge at a safari lodge? Or cling to the wreckage and try to rebuild?

The exodus of Turkana stretched through the afternoon, solitary figures who would not address me beyond begging for food. The hostility and coldness of the people tore away any pretense that I should have been headed into the land they'd fled.

The heat was heavy on my face. I raised my eyes to find a boy herding goats up in the rocks. Naked, around eight years old, the boy smiled when I spoke Swahili. He bounded up the cliff, rock to rock, showing me the path to a plateau. A girl in a leather skirt herded the goats into a corral. A fishing net lay over a hut. Two naked children covered in white dust stood on goatskins, and a young woman looked up when she heard the boy and me talking. She wore a white skirt and one necklace, and her bare chest was streaked with the same dust that coated the children, as if they'd been holding on to her.

Taking my hands and keeping her gaze on my eyes, she pulled me into the space between three small huts as impermanent as bales of hay. An old man lay on the ground, too weak to rise but thrilled to shake my hand. He spoke in Turkana as the children sat around the fire. The young woman translated his words into Swahili. "He says you're the first outsider to come in thirteen years."

The woman stared at me, grinning. She was eighteen years old. The two larger children were her siblings, though she didn't say whether the small ones were her own. The longer I watched her work the fire, boil water, and make tea, the more beautiful she became, her sweetness a salve for the hardness of so many others who were leaving these mountains.

I asked her to teach me "thank you" in KiTurkana when she handed me a teacup.

"*Ej'ok enoi.*"

She said her name was Elizabeth.

"Have you been to church?" I said, confused. "Or to school?"

She shook her head.

How in such a place could she have gotten a name like Elizabeth?

I stepped to the edge of the cliff. The lake was brilliant in the evening light, its shores rimmed in a halo of salt left by waves. Beyond the mountains on the far shore, the land seemed to end, as if the lake marked the world's true edge. I looked back at Elizabeth, at the children, and saw a spear propped against one of the huts. I imagined a *moran* waking on the day he was to leave his *boma* and begin his quest. And I wondered what it was like for one's culture to protect within it an elemental question of a man's worth. Pulling Lapa to the river seemed a year in the past. Leaving the road with Ofer felt like a memory a decade old. I struggled to imagine that people could pass a lifetime without knowing such a place existed.

The children curled up on goatskins, and Elizabeth showed me where to lie on a tarp. The tiny hay igloos, *akai*, that seemed built for children, I now saw were for the storage of pots and fish traps. The only roofs they had were above their tools and not their heads. I stripped to my trousers and lay back without blankets, exposed to the stars, the warm wind our cover. Elizabeth sat and began to sing in KiTurkana. Her voice, like a flute, drifted over her brothers and sisters as they fell asleep.

At sunrise, the girls separated a goat from the herd, slaughtered it with a spear, and cooked a feast to celebrate my visit.

"If I had money," Elizabeth said, "I would buy a pen and notebook like yours."

I'd been writing details in my diary. "You know how to write?" I said.

She looked at me as if offended. "Yes."

I ripped the middle pages from my notebook and gave her my pen. "It's for you."

She folded the paper and held it in her lap, then started to interview me as I had done her. "Where are you coming from?"

"Central Kenya," I said, playing along, though she knew the answer.

She wrote and glanced up. "Where are you going?"

"North to Ethiopia."

As Elizabeth asked me questions and wrote on the page, I walked around and looked over her shoulder. Her tight lines ran perpendicular to the lines of the page. The hundreds of characters she'd drawn were all U's turned sideways.

She put the paper in my hand and smiled proudly.

"Very nice!" I said.

She took the paper back and continued the interview.

"Elizabeth," I said, "where are all the men?"

"*Wamekufa*," she said, pointing north. They're being killed.

In the days I walked beside the lake, my skin darkened and my body strengthened. When I happened to hit my arm or leg on a rock I could feel I was becoming as hard as the ground. The barbs of a low hanging palm branch sliced into my stomach as I walked one evening, and sight of the blood made me happy.

The shoreline plunged into the lake as a cliff, forcing me to climb around, to climb for hours on treacherous slopes. Where the banks ran smooth, I strode near flamingoes, and water seeped through cracks in my boot soles. My trousers turned the color of dirt and shredded at the knees because I wetted them to stay cool during the day. Onshore were fins and bones, jagged ribs I couldn't fathom were from fish. I built small fires and cooked *ugali*, plain or with a salt cube. And lay back exhausted on my sleeping bag, no longer using the tent and thankful that a dearth of animals made night a time of total rest. I woke, though, from the old reflex of needing to add wood to the night's fire.

Without a tent to block the light, I rose the instant the sun began to mute the darkness. Fishermen's camps stood days apart on the lakeshore, settlements of two or three men. From afar the huts were indistinguishable from boulders, as nondescript as rounded and hardy shrubs. The naked men wore fishbone necklaces. They mended nets and worked their drying racks. And they greeted me with silence and stares. In one camp a bag of sugar solved the problem of getting me fed, and a bowl of mush was put into my hands. We slept side by side on burlap sacks. And the family-less, village-less, hermitic fishermen sent me on with smoked fish and *ugali* powder for the days I traveled where no one lived, for the days I saw no signs of men but for burned wood washed up onshore and a broken headrest in the rocks, for the days I opened my mouth only to eat a small meal and sip from the lake.

A man and boy walked above me on a ridge. Across the man's shoulders was a G3 assault rifle. One of his arms was draped over the stock, the other over the barrel. He looked like he'd been put into a yoke. Cattle raiding, banditry, and warfare, intensified by weapons pouring over the border from Sudan and Somalia, had drained Turkana of its men. The lawlessness and the militias stretched back a century to the British. And extended drought was hammering the people.

The boy noticed me, and his father turned with the gun.

"*Hakuna*," I called out. I have nothing. I walked quickly but without running, swinging my arms in a show of strength, not turning my head to look back. If he became aggressive, I wanted him unsure of the outcome, for even lions avoided prey that put them at risk. The weak were eaten first.

The taste of the lake became so sweet and fresh that I closed my eyes to drink. I took one step and then a thousand more. My legs moved on their own until I no longer noticed I was moving. The landscape passed through me as I passed through it. For as many days as I could walk, there was land. If I'd started my journey with the aim of getting away from the civilization I knew, here there was nothing to get away from. Whether I moved one kilometer in a day or fifty was irrelevant.

In the emptiness I began to hear my voice, as stars shone clearly over a town that had been stripped of its lights. My voice was not louder but unmuffled, uninterrupted—for days—and listening to myself was as reassuring as being sung to in a language I was beginning to understand.

I found I was looking back on my life, on all the choices I'd made. The mistakes and anger and lost chances were like knots unraveling. I understood the conflicts with my sister Mor, who because of the attention I got had been doomed to follow and had lacked the room she needed to grow. I understood the conflict with Ofer, whose love for me and mine for him were far more dear than any difference in direction; with girlfriends, who I'd needed to love me so I could love myself. With each step I released more angst and insecurity, and I forgave others as I forgave myself. Could I live beyond judgment, full of empathy? Could I live as wisely in foresight as in hindsight and cast off the pettiness and prejudice of the ego?

I found that I was singing aloud. "Ode to My Family" by the Cranberries and Pink Floyd's "Shine on You Crazy Diamond." Was this dangerous? To be singing, dancing, laughing as I walked? Could there be a tribe of one? Or was I delusional, narcissistic?

I reached Lolelia, a fishermen's camp, four days after a man said I would arrive in two hours. Beyond the camp, pebbles onshore were so beautiful that I stopped and stared as if looking at gold or some rare mineral no one was around to claim. I thought of the field near my flat in Tel Aviv where in childhood I regularly found creatures I'd never seen: a centipede, a mole, a butterfly with red wings. One afternoon in high school, bulldozers flattened the field, scraped it to the dirt. Men planted Japanese trees in uniform rows, saplings with purple flowers and painted, white trunks. A steamroller packed down the earth so hard around the trees that nothing else grew. I never passed that way again but took the long way around, by road.

I knelt onshore and reached for a glittering stone. Was it possible to travel beyond the wreckage of the world and bring back fragments that did remain? Could I search for and return with old seeds?

I fumbled over my shoulder into the top pouch of my backpack and removed my diary. I leaned against a rock, using the pack as a cushion. The cover of the fifty-two-shilling notebook was as soft and worn as old hide, its inner staples rusted. I flipped through stories I'd written from street children in Nairobi, notes on aperture settings for photographs of moonlight and lanterns, plans for an adventure in DRC, thoughts before the journey: ". . . Whatever happens, I'm writing it all." I flipped to a Samburu legend about a woman who cut the rope that connected earth to god, to names and stories of dozens of friends like Celine Jot Achai who'd said, "The best moment of my life was when I got a letter that said I was accepted to school." I reached the description of a naked Turkana boatman I'd thought might strike me with his paddle and of a warrior who hesitated to take a balloon I'd blown. When the wind lifted the balloon from his hand and the balloon hovered at his nose, he ran off and did not return.

I put the notebook away. Just as quickly I grabbed it again, drew a line and wrote a kind of letter to my family: "When I first arrived here my life began—a different way of life. Everything is more intense— sorrow, joy, fear, excitement. But this is the only way I can live. I accept the risk. If I'm no longer with you—I have lived a beautiful life and have been fortunate to have fulfilled a dream. The life of a man is not measured by time but by action. I have touched, seen and experienced enough for a full and satisfying life. Lots of love to everyone. Me.

"I want you to try . . . to do something with all the images I've captured and the experiences I've written down in this book. At my funeral I want played at full volume, 'Great Gig in the Sky' by Pink Floyd. I'm sure I'll enjoy it. I want to leave you only happiness and joy. Thanks, Ofir."

Where the cliffs ended, rocks on the lakeshore yielded to sand. I wandered into the first Turkana village that was not just a camp and I received no welcome. Huts sat on the ground like giant woven baskets. The place, nearly lifeless but filled with people, seemed like an accumulation of all the individuals I'd passed in the shattered settlements, the dourness clashing with my elation from the prior days. I reached a second village similar to the first where fights broke out, even among girls, who shouted, grappled, threw fists. And I left the next morning as soon as there was enough light to see, frightened by the force that had undone the tribe.

At a kiosk in Eliye Springs stood a man who wore a shirt bearing the face of President Moi, the sole sign there was any government at all for this forgotten place. Days later, when malaria pushed my temperature to forty degrees, I lay on the sand in underwear, and villagers poured buckets of lake water over my shivering body. We waited out the day's heat, and they took me back in the moonlight for medicine to Kalokol, a town I'd tried to avoid where a paved road reached nearly to the lake like a hand. I drank from the second water tap I'd seen in two months. And I met a fisherman named Frederick who said, "My big brother went to look for a job in the far town and it's fifteen years and we didn't hear from him." I continued north, crossing cracked riverbeds that broke under my toes with a dryness of decades, riverbeds the rains seemed no longer to have use for.

Two days from the Ethiopian border, I reached Nachukui, a village connected to the others by a sandy track. An escort of excited villagers welcomed me with a warmth I'd felt only once in Turkana, with Elizabeth. The caravan ushered me to the straw house of the chief, and people shouted with excitement when I spoke a few Turkana words. They said, "You must meet Father Albert later. You must meet him." Two young women rushed through the door of the chief's hut and with handmade brooms hurriedly cleaned the spotless dirt floor, as if dirt could be cleaned.

A woman entered in a colorful dress she might have worn for a stroll in Nairobi. "You are welcome in our village," she said in English.

"Thank you. Are you the wife of the chief?"

She smiled. "I *am* the chief."

Words tripped over my lips as I bumbled through an apology.

She smiled, took no offense. Her name was Esther Apedetamana and she wore her pride in her shoulders. She walked me back across the sand to my own round hut, which had a thatched head of shaggy hair. Esther had won the election over seven others, some of whom had resisted the authority of a female chief. "It was difficult," she said. "Those who disrespected me—the police came and took them away."

Through the afternoon, men and women of Nachukui came to Esther with problems and disputes. She sat back and listened and consulted the elders and offered advice full of compassion. A girl came carrying Esther's two-week-old son, and she breastfed between visitors. Esther told me, "Tradition keeps a lot of young girls from going to school. I'm explaining to girls now there's no point in a life of only getting water and taking care of goats. Now they know a woman can be a chief, a doctor, anything."

After all the broken communities, I wondered what here had held people together.

My third day in Nachukui, Esther said, "I'll name my son Writer Ofir."

I walked with Esther and her cradled newborn through the village on Sunday. The sound of drumming rumbled out a church that rose from the sand like a warehouse—concrete walls, a zinc roof. From the doorway, the scene inside was a frenzy of motion. Women in colorful dresses danced wildly in the aisles, their bracelets clanging. Shoeless Turkana grandmothers jumped by the altar, spread their arms and legs in midair, ululated and swung around as they jumped to land each time facing someone new, the energy infectious enough to make anyone a disciple for a day. Dancing in the middle of the mamas, obscured by flying arms, was a white man with curly blond hair. He jumped as crazily as the Turkana while laughing and spinning in a white gown.

A robed Turkana signaled to the drummers to stop. Father Albert walked to the pulpit, draped a purple velvet sash around his neck and began a sermon in effortless Turkana.

Then he noticed me.

Father Albert moved through the aisle as he spoke to the congregation of fifty or sixty people, and in his words I found the names Sarah, Abraham, and Israel. He paused his sermon to stick out his tongue at two boys who were chatting, and the congregation laughed. From the altar, without changing his tone, he said in English, "I see we have a guest here." All heads turned toward me, the people smiling as though they'd been waiting to be introduced. "You are welcome in our community," he said. "From how far away did you manage to find us?"

I stood so I could be seen and I described my trip and then spoke of the River Jordan and the Sea of Galilee, hoping the stories would color his sermon. As Father Albert translated my words into Turkana, I realized how special was our communal conversation, the way he and everyone got to know me all at once, blurring the distinction between public and private. When the service ended, I walked outside to find that my backpack had been brought from my hut and placed in the bed of Albert's pickup.

Father Albert leaned back on the rear legs of a chair and propped his feet on a table in his house. A guitar sat against the wall. Warm light shone through the window. He struck a match and lit a cigarette.

"Jesus was the biggest hippie of all," he said through a cloud of smoke while looking at the match. "My friends and I used to be a group of hippies. Long hair, girls, music, drugs. We left Spain and rambled in Europe. I wasn't even eighteen. We were influenced by the sixties, idealistic, searching for something new, writing songs to change the world. It was great fun but we had no direction, and the drugs and girls pushed the ideology aside. Then I met Father Paco."

Albert had blue eyes and the look of an aging rock star.

"Most of the guys didn't want to hear about Christianity or even see old people. They gave him a hard time. But Father Paco was persistent. He kept on talking about what we might do with our ideals and in the end he got our attention. The old guy managed to convince many of us to follow him, then placed us in different spots. And we're all still hippies, Catholic Fathers around the world."

Father Albert and I talked into the night and drove the next morning through the village. Everywhere, people waved and rushed to the pickup, chatted with him in Turkana. When we happened upon two arguing men, Father Albert stepped down from the truck and crushed out his cigarette on the door. He listened to each man argue his case and then spoke like a kind of roving judge. We drove on, delivered building materials to a site where fifteen men were wielding hoes and shovels. I grabbed a bag of concrete from the pickup and handed it to a Ugandan, a teenager like half a dozen others who'd come to Father Albert from missions all over Africa. Father Albert had an abundance of projects in Nachukui—a school and water wells—and he paid a day's labor sometimes with bags of wheat and *ugali* powder.

"I can't let them become dependent on me," he said. "We need to get them back to fishing. They need nets big enough so they can fish together."

In the evenings at his mission, Father Albert led discussions and showed films, like *Bird on a Wire*, and he didn't hide the sex. He seemed eager to expose the Turkana to more than Christianity, and he encouraged the teenagers to talk to me. He said, "Ofir is different from you. Ask him questions."

"Where do you pray?" said the Ugandan.

Hesitant to answer, I looked at Father Albert. "I don't. I don't pray."

Father Albert nodded, letting me know it was all right, then two girls asked why I didn't pray.

"I don't believe in God."

"So what do you believe in if you don't believe in God?" the Ugandan said.

"Well, many things. Values, I—values I find, that I believe in, maybe even some values that I have in common with you, but without—"

"So," the Ugandan said, interrupting me, "if you think you have found something else, something good, why are you selfish in hiding it from others?"

I asked to borrow Father Albert's guitar one night and I went down to the lake to think. That I'd met him at the end of my journey in Turkana made it feel like fate—when he had so much to teach and was helping a community to thrive. I envied him. In all the years since my first trip to Kenya, I'd focused on building *myself*, while Father Albert seemed to have done that by building the lives of others. He made me feel small.

Later, smoking a cigarette, Father Albert came to sit beside me because he knew I had things I needed to share. I said, "I wish I could stay here and do what you are doing. I want to stay but, you know, I don't believe in God."

He ran a hand through his long blond hair and blew cigarette smoke toward the heavens. "A river must have its source, Ofir. You can't have a piece of river."

The back of the pickup filled with children as we bumped and skidded over rock and sand. Father Albert cut the engine, pulled off his sunglasses and crushed his cigarette on his shoe sole. He climbed onto a boulder perched over a small pool in the rocks beside the lake, stripped, and dove headfirst. Children pulled off their clothes and followed him in.

"Before I met Father Paco," Albert told me, "I was digging in the earth, digging and digging in different places. But they were just barren holes. Father Paco came and showed me a new way. He said, 'Find a place where you can dig and a tree can grow.'"

1999
The Search Upset
KENYA, NIGERIA, UGANDA

Kenya

KISSES AND THE SPOILS OF ACTIVISM

"Azaria, it's our son!" Mom called out. "It's Ofiri! It's Ofiri! Azaria!"

"Mom, listen."

"It's Ofiri! Azaria! It's Ofiri! Wow! Wow!"

She was screaming so loud, I had to hold the phone away from my ear.

"Mom, I just got to Nairobi and came straight to call you."

"Are you safe?" Dad said. "Is everything okay? You're not sick?"

"Yes. Would you listen?"

My parents wrestled over the phone, and I described the long days beside the lake and how I'd found so much within me that was new, and as I tried to explain everything at once the stories crashed into each other and the Hebrew stuck in my mouth.

"What were you eating?" Mom said. "We didn't understand from the postcard."

"Did you hear *anything* I was saying, Mom? Who cares what I was eating!"

I leaned back against the inside of the flimsy booth. Through a hole in my pants I could see my entire lower leg. "I'll call later," I said. "I love you."

When I looked up I found a petite woman in a round hat watching me through the booth's window. She had dark eyes, thick eyebrows. When I climbed out into the call center, she stared at me with an intensity that was almost rude.

"Where are you from?" she said in perfect Hebrew and then smiled.

"How did you know I'm Israeli?" That I was felt almost irrelevant.

"Maybe, sweetheart, because you were just shouting at your mother *in Hebrew*?"

"So what are you doing? How long have you been in Kenya?"

She fiddled with the hat string tied below her chin. "Not long. Four days."

"You won't believe how beautiful Kenya is."

"I didn't really come to travel here," she said. "I'm going to Kinshasa, to DRC."

For a second I thought Ofer might be around the corner telling her what to say. A cute, dark-eyed girl in a funny hat wearing zip-away safari pants and heading for a warzone. Her name was Rachel. If she'd come to Africa for an adventure, she deserved one. "Come with me," I said.

A week earlier, I bid goodbye to Father Albert and spent the last of my money on a bus ticket to Lokichokio, an aid camp on the Kenyan-Sudanese border; Father Albert had energized me to take my journey in a new direction, and at the Lodwar bus station I joined a group of nomads from another war-torn world. The three dozen passengers who boarded with bags and suitcases were Sudanese refugees. After short furloughs to search for loved ones and apply for asylum, many having visited Nairobi, they were returning to the camp.

The bus stopped not long after leaving Lodwar. People craned their necks to look through the windshield and then began to murmur. Standing in front of the bus was a man wearing Kenyan army pants.

"Everyone out!" he said in English, waving an AK-47. "Bring your bags."

I climbed down to the road in my shredded clothes.

"Line there! Backs to the bus, bags in front!"

Policemen worked the line. An officer stopped in front of a middle-aged man with tribal markings on his forehead. "What did *you* have to look for in Kenya?" the officer said. "Show me your papers!" Two men and their commander approached a woman. "Are you trying to hide something? Get the clothes out of your bag! Open it. You think this is Sudan?" The commander stopped in front of me. "Are you playing with us?" he said. "Give me your passport." And then to the soldiers, "Search him." He flashed a smile and said, "Ahh, you're from Israel. Welcome." Then he added to his men in Swahili, "These are the people who killed Jesus. Search everything well."

My underwear, notebooks, and cooking pots flew from my bag in the hands of the soldiers with the exaggeration of theater. After they moved on, I shook the dirt out of my sleeping bag and gathered my things. As our bus pulled away, nearly everyone sighed.

"Ahh, they're evil!" said one man. "Kenyan police are hyenas."

"Are there more roadblocks?" I said.

"Six more," said the man in front of me.

At the next barricade there was shouting, the emptying of bags, clothes tossed in the air like water spraying from busted pipes. A policeman shoved a man against the bus. Another was taken aside. An officer leaned into my face. With his booze-soured breath on my cheek, he said, "*Mzungu*, why don't you buy me a beer?"

I gripped his arm. "I have nothing in my pockets; why don't you buy *me* a beer?"

Everyone watched until the man shook free and walked off.

"You should thank God for staying in one piece," said a tall, dark Sudanese man as we climbed back onto the bus. "That was a very stupid thing to do."

At the third roadblock, the commander fanned through my passport without looking at it. "Your documents are not in order. You're under arrest, *mzungu*. Get in the truck. You're sleeping in jail."

I threw my backpack into the police jeep and leaned against the door. Policemen on both ends of the line ripped clothes from the bags of the Sudanese, who looked not at their harassers but at me; the abuse made us quick kin. When the Sudanese were finally gathering each others' clothes from the dirt, the commander turned and approached me.

I told him, "I'm happy to sleep in jail but I won't pay a bribe."

"Go, go back to the bus with the others, go."

To my left were three men still arguing with officers, holding creased documents, pointing to words and stamps that gave them permission to be outside the refugee camp. But they had no luck. The Sudanese watched their brothers through the rear window as the bus drove on.

At the next roadblock, we lined up with our bags. A policeman stepped toward the man on my right and shoved in the chest. The man stumbled backwards. His wife gasped.

"Tell your wife to shut up!" the policeman said.

The Sudanese man was thin in the shoulders, short. He glanced at his wife, looked away.

"You want to be beaten?" the policeman yelled. "Go down."

The man crouched, wrapped his arms around his knees.

"Come here! Open your bag."

He crawled forward and unzipped a small duffel bag. The officer pulled out a brown dress, which fell open from its delicate fold and dangled at the end of his hand. He tossed the dress on the ground with two more dresses and pulled out a pineapple, kicking aside the empty bag. The policeman took a machete from another soldier, then hacked the pineapple in two. He seized half the fruit in each hand, glared at the Sudanese man and brought one half of the pineapple to his mouth and tore out a chunk of flesh with his teeth. He threw down both halves, smiled and dragged a sleeve across his mouth.

"I searched your pineapple," the soldier said, viciously. "And it's okay!"

The soldier moved on, laughing with the other officers. The Sudanese man rose from the ground and walked past his wife without looking at her. I followed him around the bus, wanting to tell him that I was sorry I hadn't fought for him, that what he'd suffered was wrong, that I wished his wife hadn't seen him humiliated. I reached out to touch his shoulder but stopped. Tears were streaming down his face.

We reached Lokichokio, home to more than sixty aid agencies that I figured were doing their best to build the dislocated Sudanese a home. I arrived expecting to find characters from films about aid in Africa, the tired *doctor without borders*, the idealistic nurse vaccinating a child while speaking softly to visitors, young people wielding trowels and shovels. My naïve vision and my hope for a warm welcoming were dashed by the sight of a high white wall topped with barbed wire, the buildings, vehicles, and satellite dishes beyond reach. The NGO city looked like some kind of Oz beside the open field where refugees lived in tents. It was unclear to me if they were ever let in.

I pitched my own tent outside the locked gate and then wrote a letter to the UN coordinator, which I sent into the compound with Kenyan guards. That night, as I was eating food brought to me by refugees, two Kenyan officers drove up in a private vehicle and interrogated me as if I were a threat to security.

I said, "I came here to help. Who am I a threat to? The NGOs?"

"I don't want you in Loki!" said the lead officer. "Go back to Nairobi."

I didn't leave.

On the fourth day a blond woman arrived at my tent.

In Hebrew, she said, "What are you doing here?"

"I want to enter Sudan and volunteer to help the refugees."

She shook her head. "That's what's wrong with Israelis. Everyone says Israelis have an *attitude problem*. And you know what? They're right."

Her name was Aya.

"Listen, I'm sorry if I've caused any problems or offended anyone. I just felt for the Sudanese. I want to try to make some small difference. I'm not sure how. Tell me how I can do it."

"I'm the spokesperson for the United Nations here," she said, impatient but disarmed by my tone. "You think there are volunteers here? You really think there are volunteers? Volunteerism is passé. People have jobs, careers. You won't find a single volunteer in this camp. You can't get in and help just because you want to."

If all the organizations, which were here *for* the Sudanese, couldn't keep them from being abused and humiliated just beyond the boundaries of the camp—and on the peaceful side of the border—then were they capable of doing anything? Was the world's effort to help the refugees nothing but rhetoric and a ploy to fund the careers of privileged white workers? Had I not been Israeli, I might have argued with

Aya, told her that a man like Father Albert would have laughed at her proclamation that volunteerism, that activism, was passé. Or maybe he would have been as distraught as I was that the system had left no room for the individual to help.

Oil glistened in the mud. Truck exhaust seemed to cling to my eyelashes. I wove through the *matatus* near River Road with Rachel.

"*Beba beba beba!*" said a boy ushering passengers into a van.

Rachel was glancing from side to side, pausing, moving again, absorbed in the commotion. I tried to point out the soot-covered mural behind the *matatus*, of street children in torn clothes transformed into radiant, uniformed students. I pulled Rachel onto *matatu* number twenty-three, and she glanced out the window at girls standing by a mound of refuse, my wish that she would see Nairobi for how it was alive.

Rachel had worked as a tour guide in the army, leading soldiers through the Golan Heights and Judaea with a Beretta 9mm at her hip. She'd tended bar at club Kat Balu in the years after Ofer and I had danced there on tables, and she'd worked at a tobacco shop, whose manager she'd moved in with, fallen for, and then left before coming to Kenya; she said she'd come to Africa to live in wilder places so she could find those places within herself.

We dropped near Aga Khan Hospital and followed a path away from the road, between trees that led past orange honeysuckle. I plucked a flower and sucked out the sugar as Mor and I had done as kids, and my shyness hit as I was about to pass the flower to Rachel; she was running her hands through her thick black hair. At the gates of the park sat a man on a tree stump selling cones of peanuts wrapped in newspaper.

"*Rafiki!*" he said. "*Habari yako? Habari za Israel?*"

I told Rachel what he'd said and that *rafiki* meant "friend" and then I felt too much like a teacher. I picked two cornets of peanuts wrapped in cartoons, paid and passed one to Rachel, and we stepped under the park's cool canopy. People in work clothes slept on their bellies in the shade, legs spread, books and magazines over their faces, as though sweet afternoon naps had stretched into neglect. Deeper in the park, thick trees curtained us off from Nairobi. I stopped and watched and waited. A gray monkey ran at Rachel, jumped on her arm, swiped the cornet and scurried up a tree.

"Oh my god! Did you see that?" she said, pulling the peanuts from my hand and scanning the canopy.

A baby monkey eased himself down a tree trunk and crossed the grass and she tried to lure him to take her hand. A larger monkey sprinted, scaled Rachel's back and swiped the second cornet, then perched on her shoulder to eat. Rachel laughed and stroked the monkey's tail and didn't notice that I'd backed away to watch her. Monkeys descended en masse from the trees as though a signal had come from the deep heart of their biology. They rushed her, tugged her pants, hung from her belt.

Five cones of peanuts later, at the far end of the Monkey Park, the sound of rain drummed on distant tin roofs and swept over us as if we'd been caught beyond the end of our scene. We held hands and ran, laughing, searching for refuge in the downpour, breathing in the smell of wet grass. The rain soaked us by the time we found a gazebo. Rachel wiped water from her face with both hands and stepped toward me. We were panting, shivering, her wet tank top tight against her skin as my shirt was against mine. We pressed our bodies together, the cold our excuse. Rachel put her hands on my waist. I wrapped my arms around her back. I had too much to tell her. The warmth of her mouth was soft on my ear, and rain on the roof absorbed all but the sound of her singing, "Ode to My Family."

SCARS

"If Africa had to have an enema," photographer Duncan Willetts told me after my return from Turkana, "you'd shove it up Lagos." Just as I'd needed to venture out from the safe places in Nairobi, so too did I need to venture out of East Africa. I'd realized that the chance of making an impact was greater in a place that was both broken and wild enough to scare away most anyone who could help.

So I landed in Nigeria.

An *okada* whirred up the street, its headlamp like a cyclops's eye. Blinded, raising my arm to block the light, I shuffled out of the road. The day's heat had baked the sewage, the rotting food, the pollution. Lagos was pungent as jungle—tropical industry. I turned right. A car and bus swerved, and I nearly tripped into the foul open trench at the edge of the road. Bus riders stared when headlights caught me on the dark sidewalk; the only other white faces I'd seen in Lagos were albinos'. The dangers here were of a different magnitude than in Nairobi.

My black camera bag was secured between my ribcage and arm in the same way I'd carried my rifle in the army. A lone streetlight lit power lines tangled in the air like veins. I'd been woken in the night by gunshots. I'd seen bodies in the street in pools of blood. On my first visit to city center a truck raced by with men firing rifles in the air merely to move money between banks.

Food vendors sat along the road beside kerosene lamps, the smell of burning oil mixing with lamp smoke. Women wore crazed hairdos of pointy centipedes and balls of hair that clung to their heads like moons. I moved through the sellers to the mama who'd been feeding me. She crouched with a giant spoon before a vat of boiling oil.

"You have one *akara* for me, mama?" I said.

"Na not six now only one, *oibo*?" She scooped a bean cake from the oil onto a piece of newspaper and took my naira.

"I'll get more when I come back from the market."

Oju Elegba bridge was a massive overpass, the daily locus of vast traffic jams. Packed under the decayed bridge, like the clotted blood of some sick heart, was an armada of dented dirty yellow minivans, most of them parked and empty now with night. I crossed beneath the bridge and swung left and walked five minutes to where the bridge arced down to the level of the road. I stepped onto the shoulder, reversed direction and moved from streetlamp to streetlamp beside four lanes of weaving traffic as the curve of the bridge slowly lifted me off the ground. I stopped and turned toward the market below.

In the blackness sweeping out beyond the overpass, lit faces marked the course of a hidden path. The faces belonged to sellers who sat with goods and paraffin lamps that carved their tiny red portraits from the dark, just their chins, cheekbones, dimples, and eyes revealed, everything else blacked out, as if the lanterns, themselves, knew what made the sellers human. I steadied my wrists against the sooty railing of the bridge, camera in hand. I'd come to capture the lyricism and magic of these lit gods perched along the curve of a black river through Lagos.

I zipped my camera into my bag, glanced in the direction I'd come, at the well-lit sidewalk along the road. Then I looked to where the overpass descended on the far side into plains of darkness broken neither by streetlights nor kerosene lamps—toward a place in daytime I'd seen a corpse face-down on the cement. I headed there.

At the far end of the bridge, I reversed direction at street level. The absence of people, of sound, of growling motors quickened my step. Sweltering Lagos dripped like a hot steaming bathroom after a shower. I headed for the lit junction directly under the center of the bridge. There was just enough light to see shapes ahead in the darkness. Men running. Crossing the road and turning toward me. They shouted, called to each other. It was noise, I had no doubt, made with the intent to scare.

Five area boys stopped twenty meters away and went quiet, like predators focusing before an attack. Breathing through my mouth, my pulse drumming in my throat, I walked straight toward them; they were close enough to run me down if I fled. And as I marched I tried to project an utter lack of fear that they stood in front of me, side by side, blocking my way. I fought my feet and stormed forward to shock them as they had shocked me. Two steps before I reached their line, a man jammed his arm against a concrete rib of the bridge, blocking my path at the neck. I raised my fist overhead, hammered it down into his arm, walked through the opening without stopping, without turning my head to look back. I fought the urge to run, fought the urge to glance over my shoulder, and I kept my ears cocked for the sound of footsteps, of pipes, chains, or a man running up to strangle me with a rope. I reached the light of the bus junction, shaking, still clutching my camera.

After a month in Nigeria, the country for me became Fela's land. Fela Kuti the late musician had danced in his underwear calling Nigeria's dictators liars and thieves. Singing in pidgin English to be understood by the common man, he railed against Christianity, tyranny, injustice. Fela was jailed and beaten again and again for screaming at those who'd ruled Nigeria by the butt of a gun and often the barrel. And he'd lost his seventy-eight-year-old mother when government soldiers stormed his house and threw her out a window. They set fire to Fela's compound and cracked his skull. In "Coffin for Head of State," he sang of the funeral procession and of setting his mother's coffin down in front of Dodan Barracks where the president lived, so Ọbasanjọ would have to bury her.

Fela's son Seun Kuti had continued the tradition of playing with the old band at Fela's nightclub in Surulere, Lagos. I went one night. The lights came up as the guitarist introduced the rhythm. A shaker joined. Then the bass and drums. A sax sang over the groove, and Seun Kuti strode out wearing white bellbottoms and a sequined shirt. In purple pants I danced with everyone toward the stage. Seun thrust his hips at the crowd and roamed, claiming territory, arms back, his bowed chest sliding sideways. He sang, "*Some dey follow follow dem close dem eye. Some dey follow follow dem close dem mouth . . . close dem ear . . . close themselves. I say, dem close sense.*" The dancers and the saxophonist replied. Swaying to the slick groove of the Afrobeat, Fela's son sang, "*If you dey follow follow, make you open eye, open mouth, open sense. At dat time, at dat time, you no go fall.*"

Fela had been the mouthpiece of a movement, his lyrics the substance, his sexuality and daring the fuel. He shouted down popes and imams and corrupt leaders and called on Nigerians to fight against the military dictatorship of Abacha, who surrounded himself with 3,000 loyal thugs and stole billions of dollars from public coffers.

More than a million people turned out for Fela's funeral in Lagos.

Sweat flew off Seun's body. The skirts of the dancers flared. Men carried onstage a section of tree trunk that thundered when they set it down. A band elder climbed onto the massive drum and slammed his hands into the drumhead and it boomed with a power that rattled the chest. Nigerians danced and raised their arms. I thought of Lokichokio and the refugee camp, and how helpless I'd felt after the run-in with Aya, how I'd felt I was staring up a beast too massive to be seen in full. I imagined the Sudanese dancing to Fela's music, throwing their own clothes in the air, crawling over the barbed wire into the NGO city to take the money and food meant for them. I imagined them shouting with us here, dancing to a drum that sounded like a cannon.

Hundreds of kilometers north of Lagos, a red road cut through a forest of thin trees. Clouds blocked the sun, dulling the day's color. The breezeless, humid air clung to me like a hundred hands. I felt tired and lost, out of shape, as I headed into an area beyond Jebba sheltering isolated tribes. Tipsy Nigerians had said "There you find savages." But why I was going, I couldn't quite say.

Fulani women, elegant as royalty and wrapped in electric blue, passed with bowls on their heads. Tattoos rimmed their cheekbones, fanned out from the corners of their mouths. Some Fulani were dark-skinned, others light with blood that had come through the centuries from the north. I felt no desire to talk, though the women smiled and stopped to greet me. I waved and trudged on, each step as difficult and heavy as those I'd imagine Rachel taking up Mount Kenya after I'd sent her away two months earlier. We'd lived for weeks in a tent on the roof at Planet Safari and trekked to see Isaac and Kakuya—by the short route—and Isaac's wife had given Rachel the Maasai name of Nashepai. But Rachel deserved her own Turkana, and the power of being with her had left me with no urge to travel at all. I'd fallen for her. But broken off the relationship.

"My Ofir," Rachel had written in an email, "Don't be angry with me but I keep on thinking of coming to you . . . that's the only thing I can think of, my Ugalák child. I'm lost and I want to see you and it hurts. I don't deal with reality very well . . . Yours, Nashepai."

Hours on through the trees, I came to a hut painted with geometric designs. "Sanu!" said a man rushing up the path, greeting me in Hausa. He gripped my hand and led me through a clearing where the ground was covered with a yellow gravel of drying corn. Children snapped and spun spiral snail shells in the sand. Holding a book in the doorway of a mud hut was a Nigerian pastor named Leo, who said in English, "Oh, you're welcome here. You're very welcome in our village, my good friend. Let's put your bag inside. Wow, you must be traveling a very long time to carry such a big bag."

Leo's eyes were so far apart they seemed confused about whether they were ears.

He sat me on a stool in the shade outside his hut and surrounded me with enough pots of food, brought by neighbors, to feed two families. "I've got a treat for you," Leo said after he told me of the tradition of always keeping food ready in case a guest appeared. "I know you're the kind of man who'll enjoy it." Then, like my father pulling a Tarzan comic book out of his briefcase, Leo opened his hand to reveal a roasted cricket. I added salt and bit off the bug's head, which tasted like butter and slime.

On the dirt floor of Leo's hut sat a mass of dusty boxes filled with papers and notebooks, which he welcomed me to look through. The documents, inherited by Leo when he'd moved into the area, represented the work of countless missionaries. I pulled a rotten box between my knees, held up a piece of paper to the light slicing through the window: "Dedication and the Burning Bush." It was a sermon. "Abraham and the Christian Faith." A report on a meeting of missionaries in Eastern Nigeria. "First quarter 1997: Inter-Church Council Meeting." Data on the number of missionaries in the field, the number of missions with a pastor, reports on training, notes from a meeting of The Evangelist Church of West Africa (ECWA). A report on a seminar in Benin. A document from Ghana. "Lessons learned from reaching the Dukawa." "Spreading Jesus to places he has not been heard of." Fela was roaring in my head: *It is a known fact that for many thousand years, we Africans we had our own traditions. These moneymaking organizations, them come put we Africans in total confusion. Through Jesus Christ, our Lord. By the grace of almighty Lord.*

I pulled out a document, three pages made moldy and yellow by the bush. The document listed tribes with the percentages of Christians and Muslims in each. It was a tool in the fight to make them *all* Christians, a blueprint for those who would be glad to see Kakuya leave behind his culture and enter the church. More than a hundred tribes were listed, all with the percentage of converts. Flipping through the pages, I spotted the lone gap in the data. Just one tribe had no numbers beside it. Instead were the words, "Hostile Animists." The tribe was the Achipawa.

I bounded out of the hut. "Where is Leo? Where is Leo?" I said in Hausa to a boy with tattooed feathers on each cheek. He turned and ran into the forest, up the path leading to Leo's field and the river. I circled the hut until impatience set me in motion after the boy. Chickens scattered as I sprinted barefoot up the trail, and I spotted Leo through the trees holding a dead monkey by the tail.

"I bought us something good for dinner, Ofir."

"Leo, look what I found."

He handed the monkey and his hoe to the boy and inspected the document.

"All these tribes," I said, turning to the second page, "all with the percentage of Christians and Muslims except one, the Achipawa. Look!"

"I hadn't seen this."

"Do you think it's true?"

"This list is smaller tribes."

"You think the Achipawa are still untouched? Is it possible they attacked missionaries? Where are they? Why doesn't it say where they are?"

"It's a credible report," Leo said. "You see here? Calvary is the largest evangelist organization in Nigeria. It was written—let's see—six years ago. It's strange about the one tribe, I agree."

"You think I can find them?"

"It's possible. Why not?" He traced his finger over the page. "I'd say you need to meet the man who wrote the report, Brother Niyi Gbade."

I left Leo carrying a live chicken and many gifts from the Fulani. I roamed through towns where women wore Western bras as adornment and wigs resembling Napoleon's hat. I traveled in minivans across the savannah where the grass was as tall as the flipped-over, burned-out buses on the roadside. I fell sick with malaria and rested and gave away my shirts and socks and half the goods I carried, and I started inviting Nigerians, who had no place to sleep, to share my hotel rooms and beds.

In Ilorin, at the Second Evangelist Church of West Africa, where Leo had been ordained, I found my way into an office complex guarded by an unpainted wall and I showed the list of tribes to a pastor.

"Why do you look for Niyi Gbade?" the man said with suspicion.

"So do you know him?"

He shrugged. "No."

"Any idea where I should look?"

"You have a better chance in Jos. The headquarters of Calvary is there."

It was two days by bus to Jos.

I arrived a long time later.

The north was full of palaces and sultanates, with partial autonomy from Lagos, that had been in place since the Muslim wars in the early nineteenth century. At the Calvary Mission in Jos, I met a bald white man named Steve who drove a Land Rover.

"Niyi Gbade was here," Steve said, "but he's not anymore." He handed the report back to me. "Where are you staying?"

"I just came from the bus station."

"You can stay with us. C'mon."

The house was isolated and outside Jos, up a private dirt drive. Steve led me across the wood porch to his white wife, Sonia, who stood at the mosquito-net door.

"This is great. This is really nice that we have a new guest, Steve," she said, showing all her teeth. The house had a library. Their servants slept in a shack.

I sat down to dinner across from two well-dressed and motionless boys.

"And now we will say a prayer," Sonia said. "We are blessing the meal."

I clasped my hands, worried she would realize I didn't know exactly what to do. Every syllable for Sonia was its own word, and after the long prayer the boys attacked their food.

"Micah," Sonia said, "you know what we said about chewing with your mouth open. You don't want to provoke God's displeasure as you did yesterday, do you?"

When the boys began to tell Steve about the garden, Sonia interrupted. "We worked today, Joel and Micah. We worked today in the garden. They were planting flowers and vegetables. And they were working hard and God saw it. And you know, Joel and Micah, all the work for us is done and now it's God's work to make it grow."

I focused on eating politely and trying not to get everything dirty.

"Our work is with the Summer Institute of Linguistics," Sonia said. "Our goal is to get the bible into every spoken language, every tribal language in the world."

I hid behind my napkin. Here was the woman who would bulldoze the fields and plant Japanese trees in uniform rows. I wanted to offer my strength to the Achipawa, wherever they lived and whoever they were, to help them in the fight against the culture that would destroy theirs. Glaring at this woman, I vowed to be a missionary of a wholly different order.

Three weeks after leaving Leo, still looking for Niyi Gbade, I sat in a minivan with my backpack between my legs. Outside the window, the green hills were dotted with volcanic rock. I was crammed into the last row with five men, our shoulders angled sideways for the dearth of room. I slid back the sheet of glass rattling in its metal runner. The breeze blew into my face as I reveled in the joy of being nowhere.

Headscarves of the female passengers had been cut from the same cloth as their dresses. The man who'd said the prayer before the journey—"and the road is washed with the blood of Jesus!"—rode with a bible in his lap. Stickers decorated the inside of the bus: "Beware of hawkers," "No smoking," and the blessing, "*Wabillahi Tawfiq.*"

I thought of my grandfather Moshe, what he'd said during my quick stop in Israel before Nigeria. "You're traveling *again*? You had your trip. What about university or a job? What are you, the Wandering Jew?" He shook his head and muttered to himself, "The Wandering Jew." Then he reached into his pocket and gave me his tiny green book of Psalms.

Passengers whispered on the bus.

A man stood, peered over the woman in front of us. Another man leaned forward.

"Hey!"

The driver honked.

"That man's crazy!"

I gripped a metal rib of the bus' bare ceiling and got a view through the windshield. A minibus was headed straight for us, overtaking another car. The driver honked. People shouted as the distance closed. I grabbed the seat in front of me, pushed my back against the cushion and pressed my feet to the floor. I turned my head. The land dropped off beyond the right window. People shouted. My heart seemed to cough. We veered. *Whoosh.* A flash of white, the passing van. Then a collective sigh. I pulled my hands off the seat. We slowed and I swallowed.

The sound of gravel crackling on the underside of the minibus grew louder. Why? The tires ground against the rocks. The bus shook and the driver fought the wheel. The road curved left. We didn't. Women yelled. We slipped off the hill. Disconnected from the road. And entered a dream.

The sense of flying was in the guts.

Crushing metal. Thunder. My body struck, smashed upwards. Black. A shoulder. People flung. Enclosed in the roaring metal. Man thrown. Arm. My body slammed down against my spine. Shattering glass. Black. A woman crossing the space above the seats. Heads snapped downward. Black. We were rolling. The bus smashed into the earth.

Silence.

My left arm was torn. Cut to the bone. Blood gushed, pulsed. Grass lay beyond the window frame. People were piled, silent, drugged. I squeezed out through the window into high grass. The wheels of the bus were in the air, spinning. No one was moving.

"Go go go!" I said. "Get out of the bus!"

The cut across my biceps looked like a failed amputation. My lower arm dangled. Thick blood. There was no pain. Be quick. My medical kit. My backpack was covered in broken glass. I reached back into the bus, dragged the bag through the window. Two men and a woman crawled out of the pile. They staggered around, in shock. The road was back uphill. Too far up.

The silence was surreal. A man was staring at the sun. "Sir!" I gripped his shoulder and shook him. "Take that purple bag, please, sir. Come with me, let's go!"

A man moaned inside the bus.

Adrenaline fought me up the hill. Move, I said to myself. Twenty meters. Move. It's steep. I have no time. I looked back. You have enough time. The shocked man with the bag was coming, but far back, holding the pack over his shoulder. One step. One step. One step. Okay.

Where are the cars? The cars. Where are the cars?

I stood in the road and searched for cuts. A slice in my shirt. I hadn't even looked under my chin. My chest was split open, torn! How had I missed *this*? I touched the flesh, stopped, afraid my hand would slide into my ribcage. Why is there no pain? I couldn't stop staring. My chest was mangled, spewing blood. Stop staring. Look for cars. You don't have time. I scanned for cars, looked down at my chest. In five minutes I'm dying.

I can't die.

The man arrived with my backpack, stood by the road.

I couldn't remember the last town. How much time before I lose consciousness? I have to find a doctor. It could be far. An hour. It could be more. You'll find a doctor. Stay sharp. There's no way. Stay sharp.

Two minutes. A minibus. I stepped into the road, spread my legs and blocked his route. The driver stared at me and his mouth dropped open. The back of the van was empty. "4,000 naira! Take me to the nearest hospital! Quick!" I slid the door open and climbed onto the bench before he answered, then skidded across the vinyl in my blood.

The driver argued with the man in the passenger seat. The shocked man arrived with my bag. A third man from the crash limped to the van door, pulled himself in.

We weren't moving. Why weren't we moving?

"Take me to a doctor! Now!"

Blood pooled on the seat. My leg. Through a tear in my pants I found my groin cut, cut around to the hamstring. Near an artery. You'll bleed to death. The driver U-turned. We were moving. You're bleeding to death. Live to the hospital. Stay awake. Live to the hospital.

"Sir," I said to the shocked man, "open the bag."

He struggled with the clips. I reached for them, flipped open the hood. My camera bag fell out. The backpack was locked. I pulled the key from my pocket, held it out. "Sir, take the key," I said. "Good. Now open the lock."

He did and I shoved my hand in. I said, "Here. Take the green bag. Right there. Open it. Good. Now get out the green rubber." I fumbled the tourniquet trying to wrap it around my chest. No chance. The blood. No chance of stopping it there. I rolled the tourniquet into an L, tied it with the man's help around my biceps. I grabbed, held my chest. It's too far. Boulders passed along the road. I pressed against the right side of my groin, aiming for the pressure point. I'm losing all my blood. Where is the fucking hospital?

"Sir," I said. "You see this camera? Take it. Take the bag of the camera. Good." The words were heavy. "Now take this strap off the camera bag. Good. Now give it to me." I lifted my butt off the seat, leaned forward to get the strap around my leg, pulled, tied the strap, moved from one cut to the next, squeezing and pressing and holding my flesh together. Stay awake. My chest broke open again. Blood flowed from my leg. The strap wasn't tight. Blood was pouring out of my chest. I can't stay awake much longer.

The driver looked at me over his shoulder.

"Drive fast!"

He turned back to the road.

The shocked man stared at my shoulder. His expression scared me. A tickle. I let go of my chest and touched the back of my neck. Puréed. No. No. No. It was ground meat. Shit! I can't feel it. There was no way to stop the blood. How many cuts? Stay alive. It's too far. I'm going to die. You can't die.

"Are we near?" I yelled at the driver.

He didn't answer.

"Get that towel," I said to the shocked man. "Good. Put it here."

I pressed down on my leg, tightened the strap. Don't faint. I held my chest, grabbed a t-shirt, put it on the back of my neck and pushed against the seat. My good arm was weak. I blinked. Don't faint. I can make it. How far to the hospital? I can make it.

We slowed. Houses. A town.

A rush of energy. Don't faint. Please don't faint. I can't faint.

The shocked man who'd brought my bag argued with the driver in Hausa.

There was no pain. Why was there no pain?

"The driver isn't going to the clinic," said the shocked man. "He wants to go to the police station; he's afraid of being blamed when you die."

I fought the van for air. "Get me to the hospital now!"

The minibus stopped at a clinic. The door slid back. Sand. The glare. It was too bright. People reached out. I stepped down. "Hold me, I'm going to fall."

I collapsed into their arms. Dizzy.

They were walking me in. "I'm going to faint. Put me on a bed."

A man and a woman in robes. A bed.

"Where is the doctor? Where is he?"

"He's coming," the woman said. She was biting her lip. "He's coming."

"You!" I said to her. "Bring scissors."

"You!" I tried to lift my arm to point to the man. "Bring pen and paper. Hurry!"

The woman returned.

"Cut my clothes! Cut my clothes! Tell the doctor I have money to pay."

She sliced through my bloody jeans.

"I will live!"

The man rushed over.

"Write this down," I said. "009-972-36476623. Ofir Drori. You have it?"

"Yes."

"It's my mother's number. In Israel. Call her if I don't make it."

The women cut through my shirt.

Flashes. I was seeing flashes. "I have one cut on my neck. You hear me? One cut on my chest here. One on the thigh in the back and this one."

She pulled off my boots.

The picture before me froze. I moved my eyes, my head. The scene didn't change. Another flash and the woman was frozen in a different place. I had no time.

"Where is the doctor? I cannot die."

Another flash. The scene froze.

People shouted.

"I cannot die!" I tried to shake my eyes to the next picture. It was white, blurry. I felt my body lifted, thrown to another bed. Giant waves washed over me. I struggled against them. Waited out a wave so I could shout, "Where is the doctor?"

"I'm here."

"Doctor, I'm O−."

The sounds were coming from within me.

"Doctor, I'm allergic to Paramin."

I tried to shake myself from the dream.

"I have money. I will live."

There was light in the waves. The room dimmed.

I floated up.

"Doctor, will I live?"

"With God's help."

It got dark.

I'm alive.

I lay in a small room.

A black doctor with glasses stood over me. His face was a blur.

"I didn't think you'd make it," he said.

"Doctor, do I have two arms or one?"

"Two arms." He laughed. "You have two arms."

Rachel, I thought. I need to be with Rachel.

The surgery lasted two hours, required seven bags of IV fluid and three liters of blood they scrambled to get donated. "You kept shouting, though you weren't making any sense," the doctor said. "The stitches are very deep. Most are double stitches, like the figure eight. It will be a long time before they heal. I pulled a shard of glass out of your back. It nearly punctured your kidney. It's a miracle, a real miracle, that you're alive. The cut on your neck was close to the main artery. If the glass had cut you one centimeter more, it would have killed you on the spot."

I felt so alive I needed to move. "Doctor, I can drink. I need water. I'm feeling strong. I'm okay."

"Not a good idea."

I insisted and he was too soft and after one sip I vomited and fell asleep.

I lay in bed, sweating, lonely, itching in places I couldn't reach, defenseless against mosquitoes and the pain that tore through the drugs. At night I shouted for nurses up the hall who didn't hear me because they were sleeping. Visitors came to my bedside, passengers from the bus, people who'd seen me carried into the hospital and people who'd just heard about the accident. All of them, to show sympathy, said, "Sorry sorry sorry."

As I convalesced in the clinic, I grew more amazed by the doctor who, without running water and often without electricity, stayed armed against all the ills of the bush that arrived to him. I didn't know much about the other passengers; the plight of strangers hadn't registered as the blood was flowing.

The limping man, the third one from the crash, greeted me before his discharge.

"Already you're out!" I said. "The gods took care of you. Look at all my cuts. It's a miracle you came out of this so easy."

The man exited and the doctor entered.

"So was I the most seriously injured from the accident?" I said.

"Who knows? I only treated two of you. For those who didn't make it here—we probably won't ever know. But with your injuries, it depends how you look at it." The doctor smiled. "That other man had only one cut from the glass. But it took one of his testicles."

A TRIBE OF TWO

Rachel turned her back as she slipped off her clothes. On the far side of the bed I turned away, too, not wanting to judge her body, not wanting to be judged. A lamp glowed on the bedside table. The floors were hardwood, the curtains drawn. Wiggling out of my pants burned and tore at my body. My shoulder drooped. My head, because of the neck wound, was tilted like a bewildered dog's. I was drowsy from antibiotics. Held together by thread. Ugly. Clumsy pulling back the blanket and trying not to grunt as I swung my leg up to the mattress. It was cold in the room. I couldn't pull the blanket over me with my left hand or swivel to use my right. I inched backwards, half-crippled, half my muscles unavailable to me as I flopped my head onto the pillow like a fish. Then I fought and groaned just to turn and look across the mattress. Rachel was watching me from her pillow, her black hair covering one eye.

I'd landed in the morning at Entebbe without a visa, handing the local hyenas an excuse to badger me for a bribe. "We're going to send you back on the plane to Nigeria!" By the time Rachel arrived, I was drained of the energy to fight them. Sight of her, stomping across the airport like a brawler, clashed with the image of the dark-eyed beauty

I'd imagined lying beside me all those weeks in bed in Nigeria. She was heavier, wearing an unflattering brown shirt that made her look less like a traveler than a maid. She dealt with the police and pulled me through the airport, neither seeking a kiss nor glancing at me, and I thought, Maybe she sees *me* differently? Hadn't our feelings for each other intensified while we'd been apart? I'd bought a nice white shirt to wear off the plane and scrubbed the iodine stain from my neck. But with my wounds oozing and the shirt red with blood I'd had to change into black.

Outside the airport, Rachel closed the door of our cab, sealing off Uganda's noise. She slid beside me. Our cheeks met. I shut my eyes, and she said, "You didn't think I was going to let the police or anyone steal you away from me again, did you?"

On the bed, I lay like a terrified boy with his arms straight at his sides. Rachel said, "Are you in pain? Don't move, Ofirik." She traced her finger around my ear and pulled back the sheet a bit at a time, kissing around each wound as though to accept what Nigeria had done. She smelled like dessert, like a drink. But I was useless as a lover. And worse; I was dangerous. And I collapsed, smashed into her chest trying to hold myself up with one arm.

"Shh. It's okay," she said. "Does this hurt?" What protection there was in the dimness of the room, in the blankets and the strength of Rachel's body. "I'll find a way," she said and pulled the sheet over us.

We moved into a cabin at the Red Chili Hideaway, a Kampala hostel where backpackers pitched tents in the grass. A white doctor had sliced through the scar tissue over my chest wound, because fluid from an infection had forced the flesh apart and then started leaking. The nasty cave was full of undissolved stitches curling like black worms. Rachel sat on the bed between my legs and waved away the flies. She rolled gauze into strips and pressed them to the hole, then worked them into my chest with a matchstick, looking up again and again at my face to gauge whether she was hurting me. She pulled the fluid-soaked gauze out of the hole in my body like a magician drawing pink scarves from her sleeve and turned what might have been ugly into romance.

I yanked Rachel to the curb when a car passed—a side-effect that had become habit since the crash. Near the Kampala bus station, we ate *matoke*, a dish made from plantains, and Rachel joked, "Who the hell can make *ugali* out of fucking bananas?" She sang as we paid and walked up the road toward the market. I reached out and took her hand. She looked around, embarrassed, and pulled her hand back, hid it in her pocket. My stomach dropped away from my ribs, and I thought, Maybe she doesn't feel what I do.

An engine revved. A horn. Glass broke and metal scraped along the road. People flocked from all sides of the street to the accident. Rachel raced ahead of me, burst through the ring of onlookers.

"Don't touch him. Don't touch him," she said.

A motorcyclist lay bleeding and unconscious, his bike beside him on the pavement. Rachel leaned down and listened for his breath, then looked at his groin and touched it.

"Woo!" said the shocked crowd, as though she'd broken a taboo.

"A hard-on can mean you have a spinal injury," she said. "Lift his legs, Ofir."

She pinched his trapezius. The man's eyes opened and he talked to her. People on the street knelt down to take care of him. And we left the scene.

I freed the wooden curtain rod in our room at the hostel and ran into the grass, scaring off a red-headed agama; Rachel had gone with a white girl in an adventure vest for pizza. The curtain rod was thicker than a broomstick and twice as long. I lifted it with my bad arm, leaned back to get it up to shoulder level, twirled it from side to side, slashing and swinging the stick, to fight to regain a few ounces of strength. Weeks from being ready to wear a backpack, I was bleeding again when I returned to the room.

In the name of trying to give to Rachel the energy that Africa had given to me, I asked her to list all she wanted to do before she died. On the first line she wrote, "To be a pilot." We took a bus and then a private taxi and walked a kilometer along a road. Crossing an overgrown field and sure we were lost, we came upon shirtless men bent over and slicing at the grass with machetes. When I asked about the small airport, they straightened their backs, wiped their foreheads and pointed.

"The Israelis have returned to Entebbe," said Jeremy, an old British flying instructor who had a gray broom of a moustache and who showed me in his log book that he'd crashed five times; this didn't exactly instill confidence about fulfilling dreams. After three days in the classroom, Rachel and I climbed into separate one-engine Cessnas, each with our own instructor. I clamped the headphones over my ears, hit the switch. The plane clunked and spit as the propeller began to hum. The sun's reflection hid Rachel inside her cockpit. I held the throttle, inched my Cessna forward and watched as Rachel zipped up the runway and lifted clear of the ground.

I was terrified as I taxied into position.

"Bravo Alpha Tango, 386, request permission for takeoff. Over," I said.

"Bravo Alpha Tango, 386, you are cleared for takeoff. Over."

We accelerated, rose. The propeller rolled the plane left. The heavy controls petrified in my hands. "Kick the right rudder. Kick it!" Jeremy said, hammering his hand down on my leg. "Kick it! Right. Okay. From here we have nothing to crash into."

Below us were boats small as toys, the lake's edge and a carpet of green.

"Do you see them on your side?" Jeremy said. "Do you see them?"

I didn't want to look out of fear the plane would tumble as I turned. Still, it was the kind of moment that brought images from all parts of the past. I'd been frustrated by Rachel's inability to communicate during our weeks in Uganda. Love for me was all-encompassing; to hold anything back was unnatural. She'd said, "Ofir, I'm trying to open up. What you give me I've never had, not in a relationship, not with my family. Can you understand that? I don't have parents like yours. Okay? This 'total love' idea—I cannot do it in one day." She revealed also that for all the time I'd known her, I'd never once brought her to climax. How could I be so insensitive not to have known?

"There she is," Jeremy said. "Do you see her? Look how relaxed she is!"

Beyond the wing, Rachel's plane was beside mine, passing through the clouds.

We traveled to Israel soon thereafter. The hostility of our people toward each other made the atmosphere feel like that of the broken communities of Turkana, though with an abundance of medicine and food. We vowed never to stop being angry at Israel and all places like it. I was stronger now against the blank stares I'd always received from family and friends when I told stories of Africa, stronger in large part because Rachel defended so much of what I held dear. I found that my new need to give back was satisfied for a time by teaching in a private program at schools in central Israel. But home for us had morphed from a place we didn't want to be into a place we couldn't be. So Rachel and I headed back to Africa, to Ethiopia, in hopes of merging love and adventure with a plan of setting off together into the bush. And to know whether love was an exception to the rule that my journey had to be alone. Within a week of landing in Addis Ababa, I had the answer. It was tests I needed and scars I craved; and those awaiting me I could not share. The day I told Rachel I had to go on alone, I knew how far I was from being the noble man I'd promised myself to be while walking the shores of Lake Turkana. On our last day together, Rachel bought me a journal and wrote on the first page, "In the journey to the heart, I failed not once, but I continued, for I know that's where hope lies. Love, Rachel."

HUNGER

My horse, Konjo, had a white mane and freckles around his eyes, and he stared at the hippo as any boy would have who'd never left home. The hippo splashed, snorted, raised out of the river, inflated his lungs, changing his massiveness by degree. The water rippled where he sank and disappeared. I pulled Konjo by the reins and waded into the current, toeing over loose stones in the bed of the Gibe River, Ethiopia. There was no option but to cross; the bushy, boulder-strewn banks on our side, routinely difficult to follow, had become impassable where a mountain wedged against the water. The hippo surfaced just meters from us away like an emissary coming to inquire as to what we were. A second hippo made his display, snorting from afar. They were as cowardly as warthogs and would vanish with a clap. I sidestroked in the current, holding the reins, the horse swimming behind me. We were headed down the Gibe to the Omo River, which snaked and curled for untold months of trekking.

I'd bought Konjo in Addis Ababa and ridden him out of the capital on the highway, his metal shoes clanking on the tarmac, head jerking with panic at the sight of cars and carts. Though I could barely handle a horse, a village man named D'Jote Aberra saw me on Konjo and said, "You watched too many Westerns." After six days, two hundred kilometers of road, and an army of ants that gnawed Konjo's ankle to the bone, we arrived to the village of Abelti. Then rested, healed, and descended into the river valley, in part because no one could tell me what was there. Father Albert had been placed by Father Paco in Nachukui; the church or someone had determined the need. Hoping to find my own Turkana, I aimed for the edges of life where in risking myself I might learn to see. After four days in the valley, having found little more than monkeys and baboons, I was down to a day's worth of food.

The hippos snorted as we climbed out, dripping, onto the far side of the river. The banks were soon as impassable as those we'd left behind, and Konjo and I began up the side of the gorge. The sun was strong enough to boil away everything but the rocks, the wind carrying the scent of charred trees. We scrambled through brush, earning views of ridges blackened by fire. The horizon was hazed over, flames somewhere still sending up smoke. The Gibe stretched out below us in the heat. Konjo jumped to a ledge, and the saddle and backpack slipped down his legs to his ankles, and he jumped free. The saddle and pack tumbled down the slope through gravel and dust and disappeared. Crashed some hundred meters down into riverside trees. I tied Konjo to a limb and descended, first for the bag, then the saddle. An hour or so on, the horse jumped and the saddle fell again, down around his ankles before vanishing into the gorge. "Fuck!" My voice echoed with the boom of crashing gear. An hour and a half later, Konjo and I climbed on, minus the water bottle that had broken loose from the pack. The black soil was steep, staked with dead trees. I tugged the reins, and Konjo leapt, his shoes chinking against a boulder. His hind legs slipped, and he caught himself. The slope everywhere was as broken and loose as ground uprooted by pigs, unsafe for the horse to climb, unsafe to descend. I gave Konjo time to choose his steps. The river seemed to be falling away from us, our crack through Ethiopia deepening. I loosened the reins and clucked, and Konjo sprung by, brushing my shoulder. He looked back at me, with eyes so much kinder than Lapa's that he seemed naïve. "Konjo, let's go. Come on, boy." The soil slid away beneath his hooves. He caught himself, jumped. His head struck my back, lashing me against a boulder. I was a fool for bringing a horse to such a place, dumb again in so many ways. Konjo jumped, skidded on the rocks. The dirt gave out. His hooves clattered as he fell, his legs churning, and I was about to watch him slip away into the gorge when he thudded against a tree six meters down and stopped. Konjo was balanced on an outcropping, a large rock that a single rain might loosen from the mountainside. I took two steps toward him, slipped and fell on my back, slid downhill reaching out, grabbing for rocks as I sped toward the empty air, trying to dig into the mountain—the vision of my body flipping high over the gorge—when a dead tree rushed at me and I locked my hands around it. My body swung out into the air, butt and legs dangling over the edge. I lifted my leg, struggled for a foothold. The brittle tree, barely a stump, gripped the soil with weak roots. I shouted, slung my leg up. Pulled myself to safety and sat on a rock, panting, clasping my trembling thighs and trying to convince myself the ground wasn't still moving.

I spit dust from my mouth, picked gravel out of my bloody elbow and inched down to the horse. Konjo stood on a ledge that was like the last step of a staircase that had crumbled away. If I tried to force him to scramble back up the mountain, I feared he would resist, yank the reins, slip, and the steep slope of dirt and grass was as certain as a slide to send him plummeting into the canyon; my prodding or pulling was as much a risk to him as the ground. It was Konjo who had to choose his route, alone. Or was I just a coward for not wanting to watch him die? I unsheathed the dagger I'd bought at a market in Addis and steadied myself against the tree that had broken his fall. I climbed down to him and cut the ropes securing the backpack to the saddle. I lifted it off. I wedged the blade between his skin and the leather, sliced through the straps and put the saddle aside. "Konjo, I'm sorry," I said, rubbing his neck. "I hope the lions don't find you and I hope you find your way. Sorry, old friend." I descended the cliff and in the rapids of the Gibe sat naked while holding on to a rock. Then stood in the sun to be dried.

I walked until dusk and captured small frogs and fed them onto my fishhook. But I was too poor a fisherman to prove there were any fish alive at all. Dinner was boiled noodles, my food stock down to a can of beans. I drank straight from the river just to fill my stomach, and that night beside the tent I was scared without Konjo—loss of a fate tied to mine. *The trouble of many is the comfort of fools.* And he was a horse! The moon rose late in the gorge, peeling back the darkness so I could see I was not being hunted. Morning, baboons watched me from the far banks of the river. Colobus monkeys hung in the trees with tails long and white as pontiffs' robes. Tsetse flies burrowed into my hair, my pants, bit me behind the knees, bit my butt, face and arms. Maybe sleeping sickness was why no one lived here. As my stomach gurgled, I fished in deep water with caterpillars, hunted birds with rocks, kicked through the river around small cliffs. In the brush was a netted python, nonpoisonous, coiled. I photographed him, then stripped off my shirt and wrapped it around my hand in case he struck. He was thick and full of meat, and I could almost smell him roasting. I thought, He'll struggle but I can catch him by the neck, crush his head. I lunged. He uncoiled, knocking me to the ground as he shot to the river, a foe as un-wrestleable as a crocodile. Three meters long, the snake glided across the Gibe in curves. By late afternoon, my body was turning inward with hunger. I set my pot on the banks where the river was deep, dunked a rock to scare the crocodiles, then swam out with the dagger. I felt for clams with my toes and dove down the rock face. I wedged the knife between an upper and lower shell, cracked it open, cutting my hands as I scooped out the mollusk. I swam the teaspoon of snot to the cooking pot and worked along the rock face, prying open clams in the cold water with my hands at my waist and my mouth in the air. The current stole half the take, the energy I spent foraging likely greater than what was contained in the pot of slime waiting when I climbed out wet onto the slate-colored rock. Fire, salt and water, I hoped, would transform it into food. The soup boiled down to roasted brown medallions streaked green: algae-tasting and rubbery, two hours of effort swallowed within a minute. I killed insects and threw them on the water in hopes of scooping up fish with my backpack pouch. The beans I couldn't help but open. I warmed them and ate tiny spoonfuls, trying to erase the aftertaste of the excrement of clams. Morning, second full day without Konjo, sixth day on the river, I failed with rocks to bludgeon the monitor lizards sunning by the water. I spotted figures I thought from a distance were baboons. A mother and daughter! *"Akkam!"* I rushed to greet them. The girl wore a lime-green dress. Nothing they said could I understand. Two old men lounged in a hot spring in the rocks. With an Orominya phrasebook, I managed to explain what had happened, and a woman came with dry fibrous barley bread. One of the men, seeing me devour the food, opened a handkerchief full of roasted grains. The two men moved off to fish with ropes and hooks large enough for hanging meat, then returned a short time later with nothing, as if fishing were a whim. I tried to ask about their village, whether more people were near. The woman fixed me a glass of coffee, which I brought to my lips, longing for sugar. But it was sugar*less* and thick with salt, paralyzing, yet I drank all five cups she put in front of me—to avoid insulting her. There was a village somewhere, but how far away or whether there were others beyond it, I couldn't understand. That night I put my sleeping bag beside them on the straw, and *they* kept the fire burning to scare away hyenas. I looked up at the stars and worried that the ease with which I'd left Konjo was like the way I left places and people behind. Morning, they gave me half their bread. The women wore nice dresses. The men had rope, fish hooks. This prosperity I took as proof others were near. I continued alone, finished the bread by noon, and the day passed and I found no one. The cliffs and boulders disappeared from the river and there weren't even clams. I searched my backpack and found half a tube of concentrated milk paste. I squeezed the tube and swallowed it all. Time in Israel had shown me I wasn't as strong as I thought. Animals circled in the dark. A limb cracked outside. A yip. I unzipped the tent door, stuck my head into the night—the terrifying edge of a blackness filled with mouths. I battled the gorge from dawn to dusk of the eighth day and found no one, and sleep that night did not come. Fear lay with me in the tent as I tried to will myself onto my feet at first light. The gorge, the absence of vistas, compressed my thoughts until insights seemed to fall from the cliffs above. I had one water bottle, 1.5 liters, not enough for the fight through the heat to the top of the gorge. It was two days back to the hot spring. Or three? But what if they'd gone? It was nine days back to Abelti with nothing to eat but clams. I packed the tent and struggled against the cliffs, followed by clouds of tsetse flies that feasted on my blood, leaving welts on my face. I walked nearly all the hours of daylight and found no signs of anyone. Dinner was toothpaste.

I climbed an outcropping to watch light drain from the sky. A white bird alighted from shore and a crocodile snapped her jaws, missing. You've always found people. Why should it be different now? I woke in the dark and squeezed toothpaste into my mouth and in the morning I fell, jarred my leg trying to climb. I was lethargic from all the blood lost to tsetse flies. Two men held spears on the far banks! "*Akkam! Akkam!*" I waved and bounded downhill into the river and swam, the current sweeping me downstream like some crippled old zebra. I ran to them, sloshing, explained myself in broken Amharic, mimed the ordeal. They nodded. Their village was within a day of the river. They signaled for us to go. "*Mefeleg keretteet,*" I said in Amharic and raised my open hand. Five minutes. Please. I pointed to the bag and swam back across, kicking so hard I drove water into my nose. I wrapped my camera in plastic. When I lifted my head and looked to the far banks, there was no one. I jumped, shouted. "Whoa! Whoa! *Akkam! Akkam.*" I ran for a different view, whistled. *Damn.* They ran away. I crossed the river near hippos and stumbled up a tiny path, shouting and sucking into my throat the water that dripped from my hair. The path climbed, split three ways. I limped up the mountainside on the middle one. Found nobody. I struggled back and followed another path. I wasn't going to catch them. Darkness fell in a way it never had, ending my chance to hunt for food. Dinner was a bullion cube I rescued from the bowels of my pack. I set it on my tongue and sucked and thought, Had you tossed aside your fucking principles and offered them money you might not be eating a spice cube instead of a meal. Sleep did not come; even that was being stripped away. I lay on the rocks with a fear that seemed to emanate from my bones. Day eleven, I climbed out of the tent, heavy, limping, lacking the power to shoo the tsetse flies. This cannot break me. I straightened my back, sensed I might faint, braced myself against a rock. Then smiled when I heard Ofer's voice roaring through the gorge with his confidence from the army days: *River, is this all you have? This barely tickles!* Just wait for someone. I was dizzy, fearing I'd stumble, hit my head. I scraped algae and river weed from the rocks. Dried, covered with salt, the weed tasted of spinach but didn't feel like food; it lacked what made food fuel. Fat. Protein. Oil. Sugar. Veins were rising from my limbs. A crack showed beneath my biceps. Someone else will come on the trail.

Wait. Why hadn't I turned back? It took an eternity to calculate the day. February 28th, 2000? The day of Sharon's wedding, my cousin's wedding. As I lay in the dark, hearing only insects and the river, I imagined my family together, laughing, my sister, aunts, my mom. They would be telling stories at the reception beside a table filled with *food*. Mounds of chicken, steaks, salad, cream cakes. Operation meat pot. I squeezed toothpaste onto my tongue and in my journal wrote all I would want sent by speed post, "White chocolate. Chocolate filled with cherry cream. Rollada cake. Chocolate wafers, cakes filled with hazelnut cream, Bamba, nuts, orange peel coated in chocolate." I would spend every dollar I had in restaurants. The rituals of pleasure built around food were superfluous. No sleep. Toothpaste burned the length of my esophagus. Could I ever travel far enough that it would be okay just to live with Rachel? At dawn I turned back because no one was going to come. Trekking for months was no longer a thought; what more was there to face than the barrenness that had littered the earth with skeletons for eons? Day fourteen, I came upon a tree with pods I'd seen villagers eating in Abelti. Sour. Like lemon. Maybe it wasn't the same tree. I waited to see if the pods would bring some new hell down on my body, then filled my pack, struggling against the exhaustion of lifting my shriveling arms. I should have just traveled into an actual war zone. I smashed clamshells with rocks, sacrificing food for speed, the muffled underwater blows in slow motion. I was ill. I wasn't going to make it to the hot spring. A commotion of vultures. I climbed. The smell of decomposing flesh. I picked up a rock and summoned a roar. The dozen vultures, nearly as large as men, were feeding on the carcass of a baby hippo. I lunged, stomped my boots and they flew off to watch me from above. Meat had been cut away from the hippo's hide, the skin sliced straight. Leftovers of hunters, several days old. My teeth were useless for cutting the black hide, for chewing the fatty white flesh of the underside. With dry grass and sticks I lit a fire and roasted the hippo. It was as pointless as trying to cook a leather shoe. But oil beaded over the flame and rolled down the hide. I licked the droplets. I put the hide over the fire, licked, abandoned the reeking carcass. Farther on: children's voices up a ridge. A little strength. It lasted ten steps. Uphill. Blood splattered where I smashed a tsetse fly on my arm. Four boys. "*Akkam! Akkam!*" Taking no chances, I gave them a gift of my dagger. "*Mender. Inheed*," I said. Village. Go. We started up a narrow path curling through the rocks. I pushed down on my knees to help my thighs to lift me. The heat. Dead hippo on the tongue. The digestion of the very muscles powering my steps. I was too dehydrated to spit dust from my mouth. The distance between each boy and the next grew until the first one disappeared. The second. I shouted to the two boys still in view, "*Mettebeq. Mettebeq.* 100 birr." They didn't look back. "Wait. Wait." Please. How could they be so cruel? The sun fell beyond the gorge. I opened my tent on the rocky path and drank all but a last splash of water. Wake at dawn, before the heat. The rocks mashed my skeleton—hip joints, knees, vertebrae. Not one minute of sleep. At first light, I was about to leave behind my pack when I saw a man. Was it? He took the money out of my palm. He grabbed my bag, which was covered in Konjo's hair. Flies sucked blood from my face. I lacked the sharpness to talk. If I faint now at least he's here. My legs cramped. He gripped my hand and helped me with the long steps between boulders. We reached his hut on the ridge and he put a basket of wild figs in my lap. Smoked meat hung from the rafters above his wife's head. The sugar in the figs quenched me. I understood why a deer could approach a man for his salt. What relief to add something to the body. The couple watched me inhale the figs. Nausea. More food. Meat. Milk. Fat. Oil. The elements. But the taste of everything I'd left back in the gorge.

I smiled. I vomited.

Though I'd never felt weaker, I realized I was already stronger than I'd ever been.

And ready.

TOP: *Ofir participates in his first "bush" wedding with the Maasai in Kenya. The groom and the bride stand to Ofir's left.* BOTTOM LEFT: *The bride who, seen up close, reveals different feelings about her marriage than the celebrants around her.* BOTTOM RIGHT: *Maasai shoot a dull arrow at the neck of a cow and then collect the blood for drinking in a calabash.*

Isaac Olukupai in his manyatta. Isaac worked for three years in a safari lodge and then chose to return to his village to be with his father.

TOP: *Kakuya, Isaac's father of ninety-four years, the oldest Maasai in the area, who remembers the first arrival of white men.* BOTTOM: *Maasai children play a game at night moving charcoal from hand to hand.*

TOP: *Elephants drinking in Kenya.*
BOTTOM: *A baby elephant protected by adults.*

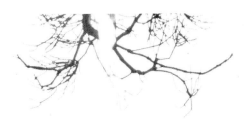

Ewaso Nyiro, Brown River in KiMaasai, which Ofir follows into the bush.

TOP: *A male lion stirs.* BOTTOM: *Cheetahs after a kill.*

TOP: *Giraffes.* BOTTOM: *The elephants in northern Kenya that charge Ofir when he sneaks close with a camera.*

Lapa, the stubborn, spitting camel resisting Ofir's efforts to move.

TOP: *Lake Turkana, the "cradle of humanity." An abandoned straw hut stands on its shore.* BOTTOM: *Elizabeth's sister with the goat they slaughtered to celebrate Ofir's arrival. Ofir is the first outsider to come in thirteen years.*

Elizabeth, a Turkana woman of great kindness, living in a harsh landscape drained of its men by banditry, cattle raiding, and drought.

A Turkana boatman guts a fish. Walking naked is common in the arid north of Kenya.

TOP: *Hippos on the Gibe River, Ethiopia, that Ofir happens upon while walking with his horse.* BOTTOM: *Cliffs along the river force Konjo and Ofir to cross the Gibe as a hippo snorts from a distance to scare them.*

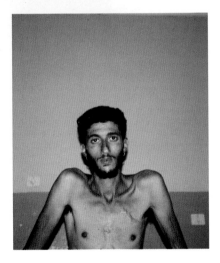

Ofir's trial of hunger on the Gibe: before (top), during (bottom left), and after (bottom right).

TOP: *Mukhtar Majairu, chairman of the amputees's camp in Freetown, Sierra Leone. After peace arrived to the country, Mukhtar came face to face again with the guerilla soldiers who'd maimed him.* BOTTOM: *Sina and Damba, Leonean victims of the country's brutal war.*

TOP: *A rally for peace in Freetown that ended with thirteen people dead.*
BOTTOM: *A corner of the front page of the newspaper Ofir opened the morning he fled Sierra Leone.*

TOP: *A lack of running water and functioning sewage systems mean that many Liberians have to bathe as this girl is.* BOTTOM: *"The War is Over" becomes the lead photo in Ofir's second published article. The civil war may have ended, but Liberians still live in totalitarian fear.*

Archie, a former child soldier who was forced to eat human flesh.

TOP: *A Nigerian boy in a market.* BOTTOM: *A tattooed mother in the Nigerian bush.*

TOP: *Fulani girls carrying* nono. BOTTOM: *The Nigerian near Leo's village who knew that when the god of the Achipawa spoke, he spoke with thunder.*

Achipawa huts near the top of Karishen.

TOP: *An Achipawa warrior stands with women and girls of his tribe.* BOTTOM: *A fisherman casting a net on the Niger River.*

TOP: *Ofir paddles a canoe down the Niger for six weeks in the summer of 2002 before traveling to Cameroon.* BOTTOM: *An adolescent gorilla.*

TOP: *David and Jack in the hotel room in Abong-Mbang, Cameroon, waiting for transport to the capital. Jack will have to ride in the trunk of a* clandeau. BOTTOM: *A mandrill: An endangered primate.*

TOP: *Inside the Nkoabang checkpoint on the edge of Yaoundé. Takam, the official, confiscates the bushmeat, takes the dealer into custody, and then sells the meat back to her, letting her go. Takam's coworker is sleeping at his desk.* BOTTOM: *A close-up of smoked bushmeat. The fingerprints of primates often survive the charring of their bodies.*

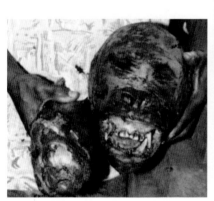

TOP and BOTTOM LEFT: *The tragedy of trafficked animal products, from bushmeat, to body parts, to skins, and the corpses of animals once meant to be sold as exotic pets.* BOTTOM RIGHT: *An elephant foot stool for sale in a shop, with a pair of tiny polished tusks. The wildlife trade is driving animals toward extinction.*

TOP: *Future roped to a tree branch in the hunter's rancid kitchen.* BOTTOM: *Ofir with another chimp saved from the pet-trade or from the cooking fire.*

TOP LEFT: *Future tied up and abused by the hunter.* TOP RIGHT: *Future with Kalebass, motorcycle taximan, musician, headmaster, and instructor of music teachers.* BOTTOM: *Ofir at work while Future sleeps on his back. Scars from Ofir's near-fatal bush crash in Nigeria are visible.*

TOP: *An arrest of an ape trafficker that led to the rescue of a baby chimp.* BOTTOM: *Ofir examines seized ivory for clues in an investigation. Julius stands in the background.*

TOP LEFT: *The logo of The Last Great Ape Organization adorned with Future's face.* TOP RIGHT: *Ofir shakes hands with the Minister of Wildlife and Forestry upon signing an agreement with the Cameroonian government in 2005.* MIDDLE: *Officer Julius after an arrest, discussing with Ofir the rescue of an endangered mandrill.* BOTTOM: *Vincent, LAGA's publishing machine, interviewing the* Fon *or king of Bali, Cameroon.*

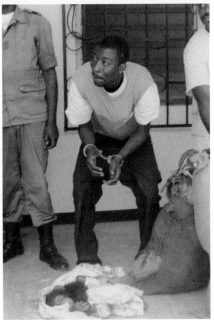

OPPOSITE TOP: *Ofir interviewed after a major ivory bust with tusks from more than a hundred killed elephants.* OPPOSITE MIDDLE: *Traffickers come from every country, and the reach of criminal activity is international. Here, an American wildlife dealer is put under arrest.* OPPOSITE BOTTOM: *In action, Temgoua, in his bright green uniform, and officer Julius.*

TOP: *A one-ton Ivory seizure. The sheer volume of seized "white gold" attests to the unending slaughter of elephants.* BOTTOM: *Apes and drugs: A trafficker arrested with a baby chimp and large quantities of cocaine and marijuana. The wildlife trade is closely linked with other forms of criminality. The baby chimp at his feet survived.*

The silverback wandered out of the jungle and into the town of Abong-Mbang. He was shot near the hospital by the retired gendarme. The photograph is as it was when the gendarme set it down in front of Ofir.

2000
War Zones
SIERRA LEONE & LIBERIA

CAN ACTIVISTS WRITE?

Freetown lay on a hill, a mosaic of trees and rusted roofs that at first glance looked more like a remote river outpost than a capital city on the Atlantic. Everywhere stood men in fatigues. There were buildings scarred by rockets, buildings reduced to blackened shells. Legless boys rented wheelchairs so they could beg. I sat on the balcony of my hotel room one night. The stars were nearly brighter than the lights of the city, and the evening breeze off the Atlantic was merciful in sweeping away the heat.

Sierra Leone was a country no one *chose* to visit, so visas were not issued to people without "reasons" for entering. My first application at the embassy in Ethiopia was denied; I couldn't very well write on the form: *Can't stop thinking about Sudanese refugee crying.* So I'd flown closer, to Ivory Coast, and found a man to write his aunt in the ministry in Freetown on my behalf. I declared that I was a writer researching children's games, the most innocuous "reason" for visiting I could conjure. And the visa came. I'd nearly died in Ethiopia for no cause but my own. And in a sense I wanted to enter Sierra Leone to relieve the lingering shame of the instances I'd failed to act for others, especially in Lokichokio. The tests I'd faced on the Gibe River had strengthened me, along with my urge and ability to give. It was April 2000, nine months after a peace accord had brought stability following a decade of war. Fast approaching was the country's Independence Day, a test of the fragile peace and of the process of the disarmament of the rebels that had not actually occurred.

From the moment I arrived in Freetown I was shadowed by secret service agents, who wrote in their notebooks about everything I did, forcing me actually to pretend to research children's games. When the agent got bored watching my impromptu "work" at Christ Church PR School and walked away, I asked the boy in front of me, Momoh, a slightly different kind of question: "What is your wish?"

"I want to be president," Momoh said.

"Why?"

"Because I want to rule the country. Because I want to do good things. Because I will give money to the people and I will bring the children to school."

"Now, not all of them are in school?"

"No."

"So what are they doing?"

"They cook or they fight."

I made notes in Hebrew, careful not to mix in English words; misrepresentation in a dictatorship was synonymous with threat.

A guard opened the gate, and I entered the Amputees' Camp, a community fenced off from the capital where banana trees grew in red soil. A one-armed child lost control of the UN food bag atop his head, and it fell onto the checkerboard on which two men played. Camp shelters had been assembled from bricks, scrap, and tree branches. Living in the camp were the families of nearly four hundred people slashed to pieces in the war.

Community chairman Mukhtar Majairu was play-wrestling with a woman in a house made of plastic "UNHCR" tarps. He jumped up and offered his right stem to shake. When I hesitated to grab it, the woman chided me for being flustered. The dull stump of Mukhtar's forearm looked like something born without a face.

"Laughing and playing around," he said as an apology, "it's the only way of dealing with the trauma."

As we strolled through the camp, Mukhtar told me his story. "It happened about two years ago. Rebels took our town, and we ran and hid in the forest. After some months, we were hearing West African forces were in control again. We tried to get back. On the way to town we came into an ambush. One after the other, rebels ordered civilians to put their heads on a tree stump and they cut their heads off. They murdered six. Then their commander said, 'Bring me the livers and hearts.'" Mukhtar breathed deeply, and his voice grew strong. "They were telling me to lie down. I did. They tied me and took me to the tree stump. They told me to put my right hand on that tree. I did. And they tried to chop it. But the machete wasn't sharp, and it took them two more blows to cut my hand off.

"And you know the next thing these people did? When I lay half-fainted on the dirt, they cut my right ear off. Then they put a letter addressed to President Kabbah in my pocket. It said, 'We've got the power.'

"I got up and I ran. Rebels were coming after me. I hid and then I heard them turn back because they thought I would die from these injuries. I managed to find West African troops and get medical care. I joined the community here and they elected me chairman."

Several months after the signing of the new peace accord, Mukhtar spotted two men in central Freetown. "I went to them and asked if they knew me. One of them said, 'No.' I showed my stump and I said, '*You* held me,' and I pointed to the other, 'and *you* cut my hand off.' They were shaking. They were shocked. One of them took money from his pocket and held it out. I told him, 'I don't want your money. I begged you not to do this, but you went on. You thought you killed me, and here I am. But I let you go in the name of peace. I forgive you.'"

Independence Day, April 27th, seemed to pass without incident. I found a pamphlet filled with the kinds of photos that were seldom published—mutilated bodies, a vulture perched by a corpse outside the Freetown morgue—scenes of the carnage from the prior January when Foday Sankoh and the Revolutionary United Front (RUF) fought their way into Freetown and terrorized the population for six days, leaving behind a decimated city and five thousand massacred. The UN-backed peace agreement that followed was called by some "a deal with the devil," for giving amnesty to rebels and leaving them in control of diamond mines. Now, sixteen months after the Freetown slaughter, rebels remained active in remote jungle, smuggling diamonds into Liberia. Foday Sankoh, from his fortress in Freetown, was said to be commanding them and trading diamonds to Liberian president Charles Taylor for arms.

Freetown's commercial center, P2, had three shops, one of them a diner whose owner looked Lebanese. I sat at a table just as he said, "Where are you from?"

Hesitant his friendliness might change, I said, "I'm from Israel."

"Ah, Israel! I'm from Lebanon, my brother. Lebanon, Israel—here, everything is different. Here, we are together. We are all friends."

I ate chicken, a great luxury in Sierra Leone, and the taste of the grease and the meat and the roasted skin reinforced for the hundredth time how lucky I felt to have experienced hunger in Ethiopia.

Wissam, the restaurateur, brought two coffees and joined me at my table.

"Ah, thanks!" I said and sipped. "The perfect amount of sugar." Almost.

Wissam cleaned his teeth with a piece of wood. He said, "I settled here eight years ago because of the problems in Lebanon. Me and my brother do a good business. *Alhamdulillah.* These people are blessed with quick forgetting. If you punch one and apologize, tomorrow nobody remembers. Look at the street. It looks almost like there has never been war. Everything is calm. This is their fortune."

In Freetown I'd heard story after story of nearly inconceivable tolerance and forgiveness. Save for a brutal few, Leoneans ought to have been held up as an example to everyone, especially to those of the region of my birth, because men like Mukhtar were no doubt carrying old seeds.

"But you know how it is in Africa," Wissam said, patting his bald head. "Everything can change in a day."

The morning after Independence Day, I headed toward the library of the British Council to learn more about the war. The streets were eerily empty, the shops at P2 shuttered, most Leoneans out of sight. An armored car passed. Near the charred, abandoned courthouse was a woman who appeared to be in a fight. I was anxious out on empty streets but I moved closer. The woman chased a car and threw a rock at the road. Her brown clothes were rags, her hair fuzzy and gray with ash-colored dust. She was young, maybe eighteen, and she threw another rock as if hurling a spear at the sea. But the rock dropped at her feet. She cried out to the characters fighting around her in the air.

More than eighty percent of Leonean women had been raped during the war. How many people knew this? I thought she might strike me, but I stepped in front of her. She dropped her arms to her sides. Her mouth was open, one shoulder slumped. Her wide eyes bore the distress of all she carried. And what they said was that the war had not ended and would never end.

I wanted to hug her, to take her someplace safe. "Are you okay?"

"Yes."

"God will help you," I said, stalling, reluctant to disconnect from her eyes.

She was like an atom spun loose from the world.

I walked on. Near the cotton tree roundabout, not far from P2, was a soldier at a post holding an RPG. "You! Come here." The sandbags he stood behind were leaking. He searched my small backpack and sent me to another post, which seemed to mark the entrance of a military base. Men beyond the gate were sorting ammunition.

"Who are you? What are you doing here?"

"Trying to get to the library."

"Everything's closed now," said another man. He had a Mickey Mouse sticker on the magazine of his rifle. "Do you even know what's happening?

"No."

"You don't know?" said the first one. "Go with this man."

I was rushed to another post. The base sat on a hill. Government soldiers sprinted across the soil and lined up for inspection.

"What's going on?" I said.

"It's all under control. You'd better stay here for now."

A soldier checked my passport at another post. "Where do you stay?" he said.

"The Leone."

"You need to get back there now."

"Is it safe?" said another soldier. "Maybe he should stay here."

"No. Go."

I moved with four civilians. We zigzagged through neighborhoods to avoid the main roads. Armored cars zipped by carrying UN soldiers. Leoneans peeked out from doorways. I gathered from rumors that the Nigerian-led West African peacekeeping force was pulling out of the country and UN soldiers were coming in. But conflict had flared during the West African retreat, when they'd tried to take a jeep that belonged to the old Leonean army. A man had been killed, and Sankoh's rebels, the radio announced, were preparing to attack.

After a few hours indoors, I returned to the street to search for food. I sat on a corner drinking a Coke and eating bread.

A civilian appeared. "Show me your ID."

I chewed and looked up. "I'll gladly show any document to a police officer. But why should I stop eating to show documents to civilians?"

People gathered. An argument brewed. "No one is in the streets but people with the rebels," a man yelled, and, as the pressure against me intensified, I stood and went with two angry men to the police station. I was passed from officer to officer, from one station to the next, as the men searched and re-searched my bag and read through my documents and every page of my notebook. Then a policeman found within the Hebrew, at the top of one page, the name Foday Sankoh.

"Do you have contact with the rebels?" the policeman said, newly hostile. "Why do you write his name? Have you met him?"

"There are Israelis *supporting* the rebels," an officer said. "With weapons!" *

---

* I didn't know that Yair Klein, a notorious Israeli arms dealer, was then serving a sixteen months sentence in the Freetown jail.

The men surrounded me.

"Do you have military training?"

"Yeah. Like all Israelis. But my job on the base was in maintenance, changing light bulbs, cleaning toilets, you know." I instantly regretted speaking. In a folder back at the hotel was my résumé, which stated that as a first lieutenant I'd commanded forty soldiers for two years. It was a detail that now felt ominous. After four hours of questioning, to my horror, the policemen drove me to the hotel, walked me up the stairs and continued the interrogation in my room. The folder sat on a high shelf in the closet, and I focused the officers on my face and on documents spread out on the table in front of them.

"I'm just researching children's games in Africa. How many times can I tell it to you? Look at this," I said, and held up a diagram of a kite made from bamboo and a plastic bag. "The boy who made this told me he wanted to be a preacher. Just a boy named Sa. I'm spending my time here with children." I showed them a sketch of a bottle cap game I'd learned of at a school. Then I read a page from the story I'd been writing about Lapa, my old camel.

A man pointed to the folder on the shelf and said, "Take that down."

I fished out a few papers and kept the folder closed and put it on the floor beside my foot. A policeman walked over, picked it up and pulled out a handful of documents, including my résumé.

I turned my back to him.

"Tell us again what you did as a soldier."

"Okay. I was the one going around changing bulbs, fixing doors, water taps, taking care of maintenance on the base."

"Are you sure?"

"Just handling things in the buildings. Scrubbing toilets, painting—"

"Take off your clothes. The trousers, too, take it off."

"How did you get these scars? Are you a mercenary?"

One of them patted my thighs around my Jockey shorts.

"Are you sure you didn't get this from fighting?"

"It was an accident in Nigeria."

"*Opoto*, I think a machete made this scar."

One officer continued to examine documents from the folder. I tried to distract him without looking in his direction, by arguing about the page in front of me, to make *it* seem suspicious. I got the résumé out of his hands, finally, and we returned to the police station, where the interrogation continued into the night.

May 8th, thousands of Leoneans marched for peace. They walked from city center past UN-manned machinegun posts toward the home of rebel leader Foday Sankoh. The new UN peacekeepers were a poorly armed, poorly trained hodgepodge of men who answered to command in their home countries. They had a mandate to defend themselves but not to attack. Sankoh and his rebels, testing the UN troops, had taken three hundred of them hostage.

Marchers sang in the road and waved banners: "RUF be human beings for once and let UNAMSIL do its job." People watched from roadside houses. Men held radios to their ears. The atmosphere was tense as we waited for an update on rebel movements.

People chanted, "We want peace!"

"Sankoh, we want no war!"

"Release UN soldiers!"

Three cars zipped through the crowd. A pickup. Men with guns. Another pickup appeared, a white Toyota with "Africare" on its door. Shouting, angry men rode in the back. Machinegunners on nearby hilltops seemed to be guarding Sankoh's house. An ex-militia fighter wore a brown cloak and a pointed hat that looked like the uniform for an army from a medieval forest. He'd once fought rebels on behalf of the people. Wiping sweat from his nose and waving his disarmament certificate, the man said, "We will fight again and the bullets will pass through our bodies and we will not be killed."

A boom thundered in the distance. An explosion. Boom. Boom.

The forward momentum of the marchers reversed into a chaos of running, the banners abandoned, the street suddenly too narrow. People tripped, fell into each other, screamed. Car horns blared. A fat woman held up her hands, yelled, and ran past me. Women tried to climb over a wall into a compound as if a river were about to sweep them away. A man looked backwards as he sprinted and said, "They shoot! They shoot!" I pumped my arms, ran fast enough not to be trampled, clutching two silver rings I'd bought for Rachel in Addis so they didn't fall from my pockets. I looked back. People will be killed before me; I won't be the first.

Through the massive crowd I saw a man named Anuk who lived near my hotel. He was covered in dust and holding one shoe.

"This is the end of peace," he said more to himself than to me.

Not knowing if people were being killed, I dashed to my hotel, wanting to get indoors. There was a knock within minutes. It was Sa, the eleven-year-old I'd befriended when I'd seen him flying his homemade kite.

"The rebels, they are bad," Sa said. "They will now kill many people because the war is coming back. You should go home to your country, okay? They will not kill you there. So are you leaving?"

"Sa, are *you* leaving?"

"No. The border to Guinea is closed."

"Do you want to leave, Sa?"

He looked at me as if I'd said something idiotic. "Everyone wants to leave."

In the entrance of Hotel Leone, I listened to the radio with Peter, who ran the hotel. The announcer said, "Violence erupted during the peace rally. Thirteen people were killed, many more wounded. There are rumors that protestors incited the shootings by throwing rocks."

The following day, May 9th, hundreds of people waited at the gates of the Guinean embassy. A guard spotted my white face in the sea of Africans and waved me through the crowd. I wasn't ready to leave, but I wanted options, and the visa came within minutes. I stepped back through the gate, which the guard shut behind me, and I could only respond to the gazes of the people who'd witnessed this favoritism by saying to myself, Tell their story. Tell their story. Fela was singing in my ear.

News came in pieces. Sankoh had vanished. Rebels were battling UN troops in the east, seizing towns. They'd taken some five hundred UN soldiers hostage. Embassies were evacuating, the international community leaving again. Peter and I sat in the entrance of the hotel that night, shirtless, slapping at mosquitoes, listening to the radio.

RUF rebels were closing in. One hundred kilometers from Freetown. Then seventy.

"They're going to capture Freetown again," Peter said. "You should leave. Don't stay here."

I told him that leaving now would feel like betrayal.

"No!" Peter said. "You're more at risk as a foreigner."

Sankoh came on the radio and spoke in a chilling voice that was high-pitched and almost too soft to hear. "The UN will not stop us," he said to the country. "We'll see what happens when we arrive to Freetown." He cackled and the radio went silent.

Morning, the RUF was just fifty kilometers from Freetown, engaged in heavy fighting, battling the UN with their own weapons and moving in armored cars and supply vehicles they'd seized along with the hostages. Rumors spread that a unit of the British army had arrived to guard Freetown. The radio announcer said, "All foreigners still in the country are urged to arrive to the evacuation center." Barefoot boys of the civilian militia strutted through town with bare chests, holding weapons given back to them by the government and carrying bottles of oil in their pockets to protect them from bullets.

Wissam's diner was locked with an overhead metal door.

"They all went to Guinea," said a man on the street.

My father called the hotel. "Listen, Ofirik, you have to leave now. I know what's happening. Mom already saw it on television: child soldiers and men with RPGs."

I packed and left for the evacuation center, an airstrip, where British soldiers stood in body armor, holding M-16's. My passport got me through the gate, and I approached a commander pointing white civilians to a military plane.

"I'm an Israeli," I told him.

"No. You have to get off the airstrip. Sir, I cannot evacuate you." He glanced at his clipboard. "Look, I have orders. I don't know why Israelis are not on the list. Believe me, if I could, I would take you with us."

I watched the British unit, who'd supposedly come to protect the city, merely coordinate the evacuation of foreigners. I was baffled. Was the world turning its back again on this tolerant people, a country of millions terrorized by small bands of crazed, drugged rebels?

I found that I didn't want to leave.

I was the last guest at Hotel Leone, and Peter and I stood in the entrance, watching the street for movement. We listened to the radio as if it alone knew whether the city would soon be in flames. By eight o'clock, the rebels were thirty kilometers from Freetown, a distance they could cover that night. I tried to conceal my fear from Peter as I searched for places to hide and planned my escape if a massacre began.

A boom on the street. People ran. Chairs fell. Doors slammed. Peter dashed inside. I followed, panicked, confused. I tripped. We ducked and turned down a staircase. I watched Peter, tried to remember the places I'd thought to hide. If they come. If they come in. What had I planned? I couldn't remember. I can jump. I can jump off the balcony in my room. Even if I break a leg I can disappear into the alleys.

Peter watched the entrance from a higher step and I watched him.

People shouted outside.

"It's okay. It's okay," Peter said. "It's only the neighbors."

I waited as he went to the door.

"Ofir, everyone is so tense. Two guys had a fight and one fell on a zinc roof."

It was a sleepless night of listening to the radio. How nice it would have been just to keep a fire burning to hold back hyenas.

The next morning, bag in hand, I went the amputee camp to say goodbye to Mukhtar, perhaps because I needed to hear that it was okay for me to go. At the port there were new armed UN posts and hordes of people jamming the dock, a new wave of refugees. When a man told me he'd been waiting three days for a ferry, I figured there was little chance of getting passage on a boat. I walked up the street to a post where two Nigerians in blue UN hats manned a mounted machinegun. I said to them, "You're looking at an *Oibo* with Nigerian blood in his veins! I was saved by your people. And why in *this* country can we not find a single good *akara* to eat?"

They laughed. Then one said, "You should go to a travel agency, my friend. Go."

The agency was open but all flights were fully booked or had been canceled. The woman at the desk told me to hurry to the airport, because if another plane did fly in, any empty seats would soon be gone. When I arrived at the airport, I said, "I'll take a flight to any-where." Never had I been so relieved to give away nearly every dollar I had—to get a seat on a plane to Guinea. But when we flew off I was torn, thinking of those who had no choice but to stay: Mukhtar, Sa, Peter, and the troubled young woman hurling rocks at the sea.

I opened a Leonean newspaper, *The Vision*, dated May 10, 2000, which I'd bought that morning. In the bottom right corner of the front page, I found an article with headline, "Israeli Arrested." It said, "Ofir Drori, an Israeli national was arrested by a journalist, Abubakar Sesay and handed over to the police for interrogation. His appearance was very suspicious. Ofir Drori was spotted standing by the Immigration department along Rawdon Street, doing nothing. When he was inter-rogated by the police he claimed to be a teacher. The police was not satisfied with his explanation so his documents were demanded. His passport shows that he is an Israeli national but he had in his posses-sion documents relating to the RUF . . ."

The rebels got no closer than thirty kilometers to Freetown. UN troops pushed them back and eight hundred British paratroopers arrived. They took control of the airport and strongholds around the capital. Foday Sankoh was captured.

I couldn't get on stage and sing in my underwear like Fela, but I could write the story—of how a fragile peace had nearly descended into anarchy, in a country of people who showed such forgiveness that they ought to have been revered the world over. Whether anyone else could expose the story, I didn't know. I wrote an article and sent it by speed post to my father with the rolls of film I'd shot. He went to Udi Ran, editor of *Teva Hadvarim*, The Nature of Things, and the eighteen-page article was published immediately in Israel. Finally my journey had led to meaningful action.

"COFFIN FOR HEAD OF STATE"

Archie was shirtless and he wore a pink plastic toy on a string around his neck.

"Hello," he whispered.

I sat beside him on the bench but facing the opposite direction.

"How old are you?" I said.

"Fourteen." Archie stared at a puddle by his feet.

"Is this your house?"

"Yes, I lived here two years," he said quickly. He was suspicious of me.

I'd found Archie through the Red Cross and a counselor working for the NGO Don Bosco.

"Do you see your counselor much?"

Archie shrugged and looked at the hut. "Not when it rains."

I swung around to his side of the bench and told him I'd been held by the authorities for three days after crossing into Liberia. "I told the police and the intelligence officers and the rest of those people that I worked in the army in maintenance, changing light bulbs, cleaning toilets. But I was really an officer with many men."

Archie let out a laugh and then stifled it.

"I told you this secret because I trust you," I said. "You can't tell it to anyone or I'll get in serious trouble. You promise?"

"I promise."

Archie had been a child soldier.

During my struggle to reach Monrovia from the Guinean border, I'd been accused of being a spy, accused of being a pink plump BBC journalist whose picture adorned an article I'd once printed off the Internet. Immigration, intelligence, police, and customs officials had fought over me, shot guns in the air, tried to sneak me away, tried to frame me with drugs. After three nights of harassment, I finally arrived in the capital followed by a secret service agent. A hotel manager, roused from sleep, handed me a key and a lantern and showed me to a dark room with a straw mattress. He said, "The generator doesn't work. There is no electricity in Monrovia. There is no electricity in this country. And we have no water. Welcome to Liberia."

A member of the Liberian community in Abidjan had arranged to get me a letter of invitation from a senator, and my visa was stuck into my passport in a parking lot in the open trunk of a car. I woke early my first morning in Monrovia to find the city far dirtier than I'd imagined in the dark. Vines grew up derelict power lines. The streets were covered with oil-stained sand. On the front steps of the congressional building, where I'd come by compulsion to meet the senator, a soldier aimed his mounted machinegun at my chest. "Wo! Come come come." After fourteen broken peace accords and a seven-year civil war, Liberia's rebel factions had been absorbed into the national army. "Don't move," the soldier said. "You have no business here." I gave him the senator's letter, which he held in both hands. He stared at the page for several minutes. Then I saw he had the letter upside down.

Archie had the body of a man—broad shoulders and muscular arms. The whites of his eyes were slightly yellowed, which was rare for a child. I'd won his trust and he began to talk.

"When they came, I was making a hole through the door to look at them," Archie said. He'd been nine years old at the time. "They burned the house. They killed my grandma and took my pa away. I knew they were taking him to the bridge to kill him. Boom! Into the water like all the rest.

"I was alone. Everybody was shooting but it only made me brave. I ran to the bridge. When I reached there an LPC man was pointing the gun at me. I told him, 'I don't care for the bullets. I came to see if the NPFL man killed my pa.' The man knew my pa. We saw his body there; I knew because the clothes. There was no head. I cried."

Archie walked with the Liberia Peace Council (LPC) rebel to his camp. "They gave me food and a place to sleep. Then they gave me an AK. They took it apart and I had to put it back together. Then they taught me how to shoot."

They gave him a war name, Bad Child.

"When they caught people they made me shoot them. I was small and whenever I shoot somebody I was falling back on the ground so I started leaning against trees not to fall. The first time I killed someone was not with a gun. They tied the man and made me stab him in the chest. I took the knife—choo!" Eyes narrowed, Archie thrust his hand out, twisted it. "I was stabbing him real hard. He died and I was crying. They shouted at me, 'Stupid! When you kill you can't cry. Next time we kill you too.'

"They gave me black shoes. My feet were too small so I put lots of paper inside. I got army trousers and name plates from dead bodies.

"They were too bad doing nasty nasty things. They were making 'surgeries.' One time they chose me to do it. If I say no they shoot me. They tied the pregnant woman. I cut her and pulled out the baby. I was holding his legs and waved him in the air, voom, voom, bang, I knocked it on the wall!" He mimicked the motion with his arm. "The whole brain scattered. Everybody laughed. I didn't laugh. I was wiping the blood from my face and tried hard not to cry. Everybody was laughing a bad bad laugh, 'Ha! Ha! Ha! Ha! Ha!' One day we captured a truck full of whites coming to fight us. So we took them and fucked them in the butt. All of them. Then we cut them to small small pieces. We threw them back to the car where they came from."

The war had ended in 1996 with more than 150,000 dead and half a million refugees. At war's end, most of Liberia's resources were in the hands of Charles Taylor, warlord, rebel leader of The National Patriotic

Front of Liberia (NPFL) and a man as brutal as Sankoh. Ahead of post-war presidential elections, the scepter of the African "Big Man" had hung over Liberia. People knew if Taylor didn't win, war would return. Fear spawned a saying that reached into the voting booth, "You killed my ma. You killed my pa. I vote for you." Taylor won, of course, and international observers declared the election "free and fair."

Archie escaped from the LPC but was captured by other rebels.

"The group was called Super Duper," Archie said. "The soldiers caught me and I knew if I didn't join them, they will kill me. I lied and told them I was a lieutenant. They were afraid and got me to their leader, Super Duper King. He liked me. He gave me an AK and a new knife. I was his bodyguard. Being the bodyguard of the King you have to be wicked. He would always choose me to kill people with the knife, vish-vish-vish, till the man is bleeding, then we had to lick the blood. If you don't lick they will beat you.

"We were eating human bodies, even raw ones. I took it and said I need to go pee-pee. That's how I threw it away most times. One time the King made me sit, and I was eating the human being.

"They made me use more drugs so I'll be brave. They put drugs in the food. They mixed gunpowder and sugarcane juice. It makes you do bad bad things.

"One time, when we caught a village and everybody had to go and make bad things, I heard a baby crying. I didn't want him to cry so I tried to feed him with cassava. He didn't want to eat, so I said, 'If you don't want to eat you want to die and I chucked him to the fire.' They gave you cocaine, so you start doing bad bad things."

Charles Taylor had been president of Liberia for three years by the time I arrived. When he was discovered to be an engineer of the war in Sierra Leone, and a major player in the trade of war diamonds, the EU cut off funds for the reconstruction of Liberia. The four-story Eurobank building, of the country's largest bank, was a burned husk with a papaya tree growing out of its second floor. Afternoon thunderstorms that deluged Monrovia seemed they might wash the decrepit city into its lagoons.

Taylor had suffocated the country's newspapers and shut down all radio stations save for two, one owned by his government, the other by him. International media, which Taylor couldn't control, he attacked with messages on billboards throughout the capital. They were straight out of Orwell: "Unbalanced news is also a human rights abuse." "Words can do more harm than bullets," was a message adorned with a cartoonish scene of bullets flying out of the mouth of a radio broadcaster to kill politicians—the oppressors made into victims. Taylor's face adorned billboards. He seemed to watch from everywhere. Liberians told me the world was against them. "Taylor will not be pulled by the nose," said a seller in a market. "He is his own man. He will not be manipulated." They said Leoneans were evil: "Those people deserve the war they got; they are war-liking people." Liberians were skittish in conversation, scared of being reported to the government, the country full of people turned into agents. War had erased families and villages, roads and buildings. Could it also erase the memory of what it meant to have rights?

Archie earned the rank of second lieutenant and commanded soldiers much older than he was. His troops were near the coast one day, and a ship of the Nigerian-led West African forces was visible offshore. Archie snuck away alone in hopes of reaching it.

"This time I took a small .45," he said. "You can't stay without a gun; everybody will harass you. When I came to shore I met a fisherman with a boat. I told him to get me to the ship and he said, 'I can't do it; you're a child.' I put the .45 to his ear and told him, 'You can't do it? I'll kill you.' He took me to the ship and I climbed and hid in a tire."

When the West African peacekeepers found Archie, they thought he'd gotten his fatigues from his parents and they took care of him without suspecting he had a weapon. Archie reached Monrovia and surrendered his pistol and found his mother. But fighting broke out again in Monrovia, and Archie's mother left him. She fled to Guinea.

"It was too dangerous so I ran to the barracks," Archie said. "I didn't want a gun but they told me I should fight. I fought hard. Everybody knew me. I killed lots of people. I got shot in the back. I was in the hospital and then went back to the fighting."

When the war finally ended, Archie was adopted by a neighbor. "People were afraid of me. They called me Rebel. Some of them tried to chase me. Even now when I cross the street, some people still call me Bad Child.

"The people I killed, they come to me in my dreams. They run after me and say, 'What did you have to kill me for?' Sometimes in the day I fight them. I'm the only one who sees them. People see me fighting the air. Sometimes, I can just sit and I see them hanging in the air, dead.

"When I went to school they gave me a pencil to write. I just drew; I didn't know how to write. One time I don't know what happened. I was tearing the notebook then I started beating the teacher real hard." Archie was swinging his hands. "You see, I have two hearts; one is good and one is bad and makes me do bad things. The good heart is saying, 'Stop! Stop!' The bad heart is saying, 'You can't stop! You can't stop!'"

Archie's story hit me like an illness. I had no choice but to write it. I had the ability to share such a story, thus writing became a responsibility. I was motivated by love for him but also by hatred. I wanted to take his words, a testimony of everyone's failure to help, and hit people with them. There were hundreds of thousands of boys like Archie still fighting across the world. The high of publishing the first article on Sierra Leone, of being heard and sharing a message, had morphed quickly into obligation. At night in Monrovia, I lay awake on the straw-filled mattress, unable to sleep and trying to cling to thoughts of things that were pure, Archie as a baby—adopted by Rachel and me.

Archie's story was published immediately in *Teva Hadvarim*.

Rachel wrote from Israel, "I thought you were not going to answer my emails and then I received this one and then the others and I thought, I'm going to die because of the excitement. My god, you always knew how to do this to me . . . I thought you forgot me . . . Ofir, I miss saying your name. They tell me I should step out of this mode, but I can't . . . It's not good for the soul but it's good for the poems . . ." A week later she wrote: "Can you take a picture of lightning? A reminder of rainy days. Do you know my favorite color is electric blue? Once I thought I could light the world with my anger. Now I am not sure if I can throw fire to the sky. Have beautiful dreams and be happy—this is the path you chose."

I returned to Archie with a soccer ball. He shouted and smiled and held his head against my chest, then looked down as we released from the hug. A kid with dreadlocks, Archie's friend, sat on the bench with us. Archie's foster father stepped out of the house and said to the friend, "Do you have it?" The boy gave the elder a handful of marijuana joints and took his money.

I wrote a postcard to Archie before I left Liberia: "Some people will say that you're a child. But you are not. You are grownup and strong—I don't mean in the muscles and in the shootings but in your heart. I know you're going to win. I know you'll find a way to be left in the end with only one heart—your good heart. Your brother, Ofir."

A DETOUR TO HEAR THE VOICE OF GOD

Niyi Gbade, the missionary who'd written "hostile animists" on the report in Pastor Leo's hut, crisscrossed Nigeria to outposts hundreds of kilometers apart. But I found him under my nose in Lagos, across the rail line from Fela's old neighborhood. A year after starting my search for the man, I entered a dark office in one of Africa's largest cities. I told Niyi I wanted to find the Achipawa and learn from them, that I believed the wisdom and beauty in old ways needed protection.

"No. I understand you," Niyi said, "but my heart tells me not to give you the information you are looking for. I am afraid your encounter with them will strengthen their local beliefs. I think our interests conflict."

I thanked him for being honest and direct.

"You know, the funny thing," I said, standing and pointing to my scarred neck, "is that I almost got killed just trying to meet you. Good luck in your mission."

I closed the door and walked down the dirty corridor.

I heard Niyi running.

"Listen," he said, catching his breath as he reached me, "all I will tell you is that you can find them between the Niger and Kebbi states."

The forest on the road to Leo's village was bright green, all the more vibrant after my time in half-ruined cities. The soil surrounding the huts was sandy, freshened and washed by rain. Fulani women wore elegant blue gowns as spotless as the cone-shaped flowers of yams.

Pastor Leo came out of his hut holding a machete and he hugged me.

"Ofir, you're just in time to help with the groundnuts."

Men gathered, their skin tones, noses, and the shapes of their heads as varied as migrants from a dozen different ages. Fulani girls in fine dresses encircled a chicken who escaped onto Leo's roof. A woman came with *nono* porridge, which they offered to Leo, who bought some for me. After one taste of the sour *nono*, I handed it back to Leo. Two Fulani girls were staring at me. The shorter one spoke and pointed at my face and Leo translated her words: "Even if he is very poor, I would still marry him."

I'd stopped to see Leo because he lived on the way to the Niger and Kebbi states and because he knew Nigeria well. I said, "Leo, do you think I should search in the bush in those areas? Or go first to the towns? Should I try to find other missionaries?"

Leo was surprised by the information I'd gotten. "There are people *here* who have been in those states or close to them. We're bound to find herders who've taken their cattle there. Maybe. We can try."

The next morning we followed a sandy path into woodlands. At the first village, people led us into the hut of an elder.

"*Sanu*," Leo said, greeting him.

"*Lafia*," said the old man.

They began a quick-draw of greetings, which I joined until I lost the rhythm. "*Lafia-sanu, sanu-lafia lo, lafia-lafia lo, sanu-sanu, sanu da aiki, lafia.*"

We sat in the shade. The man handed a kola nut to Leo. He broke it in two and gave half to me. Eating a kola nut was like chewing on an eraser, and I dipped mine into a spice-filled gourd. In Hausa, Leo explained our purpose in coming. The man shrugged, shook his head. "But we have food," he said to us. "Stay."

Leo looked over at women coming with the sour *nono*. He glanced at me and smiled. "Thanks. Maybe we'll stop on the way back."

The elder handed me one hundred naira as we left his mud hut; honors in the bush were endless.

In another village that afternoon, Leo and I exchanged long greetings in Hausa with the elders and accepted kola nuts and asked about the Niger and Kebbi states. We were pointed from one man to the next until there was no one left to talk to, and we were then invited to stay for a ceremony. Two men played stringed gourds and another sang like a storyteller, to a crowd of people sitting on mats. I was brought into a hut to take photographs, of a priest with a scalpel shaving all but a patch of hair on the head of an eight-day-old girl. The father, smiling and proud, sat outside in a ring of men. The mother held the shrieking bloody infant as the priest made cuts on her tiny belly and chest, protection from spirits, cuts that were barely scratches compared to the *brit milah*, the circumcision, of my eighth day in the world.

Leo and I continued. Farms on the edge of the village yielded to forest, which an hour later yielded back to farms and then to a cluster of huts. After twenty minutes of greetings and kola nut chewing, we learned in one sentence that the village elder knew nothing of the north and no one who did. The man asked us to stay for food just as a woman arrived with *masa*, rice donuts with sugar that Leo knew I loved.

"Of course we can stay," Leo said.

Villagers gave me money after I took their photograph. I said, "I don't think I can get the photos to you. There's no post office anywhere near here."

"We know. We're just happy you took our picture."

The following day, after trekking through many villages, we passed a boy selling lead shot in a pouch and then arrived at a hut. It was damp inside, the hard clay cold. A man with a rectangular gray beard and a face as thin as mine sat on a woven mat. Leo spoke in Dukawa, the language in which he preached. As soon as the words "Achipa" and "Achipawa" left Leo's mouth, the man swung his head toward me. He asked a question of Leo, his body language wholly different from the men who'd shrugged and offered us food. He leaned backwards as Leo spoke. Then shouted, waved his arms, and pointed at me. Leo pulled me up and we rushed out and sat on stools outside the door.

"He knows," Leo said.

A man did not often shout in his own house, especially in cultures in the bush, and we waited for him. He was stroking his beard when he finally walked outside. He thanked us for coming and told us to go in peace.

"He knows of the Achipawa but won't tell," Leo said as we strode into the forest.

"What? Why?"

"He doesn't want you to be killed, and *he* doesn't want to be killed."

"What does it mean he can be killed? Who will kill him?"

"It's not *someone* that will do it. He meant he will be killed traditionally."

I didn't press Leo to explain. In Nigeria, even politicians and priests had witchdoctors, and it pained Leo to acknowledge witchcraft.

"Don't worry," he said, knowing of my urge to return to the man. "We'll find someone. You'll see."

I was in the forest with three teenage boys when we saw what looked like a birthday cake on a rock: a coiled *bitis* viper. The morning was still cool and the sun hadn't reached the snake and he didn't move, except to inflate and hiss. I asked one of the boys for his machete and I severed the snake's head, which tumbled into the grass. The boys then insisted I cut off the tail. When Leo spotted me walking toward him with the snake dangling from my hand, he said, "Now *you* are the one bringing dinner." And he chuckled. "Ofir, the people here believe the tail is where the venom is."

Leo and I crossed the river, and I told him about the firefight and coup I'd been caught in in Ivory Coast after leaving Liberia. By late afternoon, we reached a village where people were angry over a Fulani whose cows had eaten a man's crops. They explained the conflict to Leo in hopes that his knowing might affect the reparation.

Leo turned to me and said, "The man I've been looking for is here."

He hadn't told me we were searching for anyone in particular.

"The man was born in Kebbi state," Leo said. "People say he has seen many things."

The old man was napping when we arrived at his hut. He jumped off his bed when he saw us, excited to have visitors. Green tattoos stretched from his face to his chest. Even his eyebrows were tattoos. Women began smashing wood under their feet, building fires. A boy ran off to get eggs. In the corner of the man's hut was a homemade gun that might have dated to wars two centuries in the past.

Leo spoke to the man in Hausa, then listened and translated for me.

"If you reach the mountain of the Achipawa," the elder told us, "you will meet a man who when he speaks you will hear thunder."

"Thunder?" I said to Leo. "Are you sure it's the right word? As in lightning and thunder?"

"Yes. He says you'll see what he means when you get there."

Then he gave us the names of two towns near Achipawa territory.

Donkeys and goats stood in the garbage-filled road of the northern town my bus wobbled into. Taxi mopeds, *kabu-kabus*, puttered by. I happened on an ECWA church and waited for someone to invite me inside or to invite me into his house. A man approached, greeted me, and within three sentences I exhausted my Hausa. Then he went off in search of the pastor, an English speaker. The pastor led me into his living room, where on the wall was a large colorfully drawn poster of Jesus knocking out Satan in a boxing match.

"The Achipawa let nobody in," the pastor told me. "Brother Bulus Demena is the one nearest to their territory and he's been there for years but cannot enter. No one can."

When I arrived in Bulus's town, I grabbed my bag and walked up to the minivan driver to pay my fare.

"It's okay," the driver said. "You don't have to pay. Someone paid for you."

"Who?"

"He already left. It's to welcome you here."

Outside the church, I sat on my backpack and watched giggling boys inch closer and closer to me. One boy held a faded Christian pamphlet bearing the face of a blond child. The boy pointed to the blond kid in the picture and said in Hausa, "You!" Then burst into laughter and ran away.

Bulus Demena was called from his farm and arrived with an English teacher named Elia Omaro. They led me to Bulus's house in the corner of the church compound. Tall, thin Pastor Bulus was an older man with the everlasting smile of a boy. A poster of the year 2000 doomsday adorned his living room wall. The poster depicted drawings of a dozen city scenes and selected Nigerians sucked up into to heaven as angels in white. Those playing soccer, kissing, doing karate, or drinking in bars were not going up.

Bulus didn't understand English, and Elia pronounced his words in a way that made him sound as though he were choking. As Bulus listened to me talk, his moustache spread like a pair of wings over his gummy smile. Elia laughed when I said I wanted to meet the Achipawa. He translated for Bulus and they both laughed.

"You don't understand. You cannot go. They are gah-DING their secrets," Elia said as though swallowing the word. "They are guarding their chief called god. No one enters. He is their god. He must not go down from the mountain, Karishen. They will not let you in. Don't go there."

Bulus offered me a chair and brought a Pepsi and half a dozen pots, eggs and *masa*, meat stew, chicken, enough food for a family of five though all for me, the kind of feast I'd fantasized about on the Gibe River in Ethiopia.

That night, I was about to go to sleep in Bulus's room, which he'd vacated for me, when he appeared at the door. Through Elia, Bulus said, "Timothy Karishen is the first Achipawa Christian. Probably the only speaking English. Tomorrow you can get closer to him. The vee-Huck-el can take you."

I didn't understand until he mimed *vehicle* with a steering wheel.

The next morning, Bulus's mouth dropped open when he saw me coming back from the market with a black billy goat; if I were going to meet god, I needed an offering. The animal and I squeezed into the back of a blue pickup and drove for hours, the road just tracks through the grass. The baby in the lap of the mother beside me had black eyes in which I could see the sky reflected.

At the end of the road were four houses with tin roofs. The goat and I leapt out, and I stretched my jaw, which was tight after the long jarring ride. People were as stunned as Bulus had been to see a white man with a goat. They fired question after question at me, though my Hausa was no use at all.

"Timothy Karishen," I said as I got my bag.

People kept speaking to me in Hausa.

"Timothy Karishen," I said, louder.

The third time I mentioned the name, a man nodded and took my bag and pushed his bicycle as he led me across a pasture. We waded through a stream, through rice fields, the pink sunset shining on the water. A boatman steadied his canoe at the banks of a river as I climbed in, the goat behind me, then the bicycle, then the man, which brought to mind brainteasers my father loved, of how to get a wolf, sheep, elephant and turtle across a river without any of them killing each other. On the far banks, we followed a narrow path in the darkness to a village with an outer wall made of woven mats.

"Welcome! Welcome!" It was Timothy. Word of guests traveled fast in the bush, and he'd known I was coming. He said, "I hear a lot of enjoyment from your visit."

A child took my bag and another took my goat, and food in calabashes and gourds was set down in front of me. Then I explained why I'd come.

"I can lead you to the elders," Timothy said. "And we see what they say. Eat, eat, there is more."

An older boy played a two-string gourd guitar.

The village was called *Angwan* Hassan, and Hassan, himself, sat by a fire.

"*Popo*," I said, greeting him in Achipawa.

"*Popo*," he answered. Then through Timothy he said, "You are protected by the god of the Achipawa, the Womo. He knows you are here as he knows everything."

Timothy, like Hassan, was relegated to the periphery of Achipawa territory. Timothy's father had taken him to live in a town as a boy and he lived now almost as an outcast because he'd seen the outside. His last name, Karishen, was the name of the Achipawa's mountain; whether he'd been stripped of his father's name I didn't want to ask.

"They allow me to be here," Timothy said. "When I came four years ago, no one is knowing to read or write. They did not know Christianity. Now, I build churches and we always have *many* worshipers."

The next morning at Timothy's church, which had a leaning mud pulpit and a mud cross, five people sang in a high, piercing octave, the sound like that of an ungifted cousin of mine warming up her saxophone. Timothy kept his parishioners for just two hymns, which would have been a warm-up for Bulus Demena, who'd been driven out of the territory after trying to build a large brick church.

Timothy, the goat, and I set out one morning. We met a man ascending the mountain who wore animal skins. One of his two trussed chickens I took and carried upside-down for him, and the man led us across a swamp, through fields of corn towering over our heads, land so fertile it seemed seeds could just be sprinkled on the ground. We crossed a stream, trekked through grassland. Three hours from Timothy's hut, we found Achipawa lining stones along the path. Tall and muscular young men, all wearing animal skins, stopped us, and Timothy had to explained my presence, explain that I'd come only as a friend. Other Achipawa were ascending the mountain slope, pulling goats and sheep, sacrifices for their god. Timothy motioned toward the highest point on the horizon, what seemed like a shrine of stacked boulders, like a totem of a giant bird. He said, "This is the Womo's automobile."

The massive rocks looked as immovable as anything could be. "Automobile?"

"It is our belief with this rock our Womo can go any place in the world in one second."

"But he can't just walk?"

"A Womo cannot leave his house his entire life."

We reached a tree where Timothy said we had to leave our shoes. As I unlaced my boots, I thought of what was told to Moses: *Shuck your shoes from your feet for the place you stand is holy ground.* We climbed for an hour on bedrock spotted with long leafy plants. Suddenly, at the top of a hill among trees, the first thatched roofs appeared. Bare-breasted women wore bouquets of green leaves between their legs. Men wore tight leather shorts secured with sticks. Strutting through the village were warriors who in wrestling matches would have pinned me in seconds.

"These are their holiday clothes," Timothy said. "For the Womo's holiday."

A man came forward and Timothy hurried to explain that I was no threat. In the doorway of a hut, a woman was weaving bark or leaves. Another woman used rocks to grind grains, spices, or dyes. A goat was led toward a man with a spear. The children didn't greet us. A young man waved us over, and we walked between huts to where four angry elders stood. Thin black lines around a man's eyes gave him a piercing stare. He shoved a water-filled gourd into my hands, another into Timothy's. I drank deeply. Mosquito larvae wiggled in the water. The elders eyed me with scorn.

Through Timothy I said, "The powers of the Achipawa god are known from a great distance. I came to bring respect from a faraway land and to give the Achipawa god the gift of this goat. The Womo is all-powerful."

"Where do you come from?" an elder asked through Timothy.

"Israeila," I said, as it was referred to in nearby towns by Hausa speakers.

"We don't know why you want to see the Womo."

The elders spoke to Timothy and then to each other. Though two of the men had not softened to my presence, Timothy said, "They allow us to continue to climb."

The bedrock, as we headed up the mountain, seemed to echo under our feet; Timothy said that Karishen was hollow, which I guessed was due to an aquifer or to air pockets sealed somehow by lava. We came upon shirtless ten-year-old boys working in a field, boys who had to labor for their future fathers-in-law for seven years.

We climbed to another layer of huts where people gathered beneath trees. A man rushed forward and Timothy seemed to say we'd been permitted to come.

"This is the blood ceremony," Timothy said, hurrying me to the side. "This is a secret you cannot see."

head between my legs, so not to be thought to be trying to look god in the eyes.

My pulse thumped in my ears.

Timothy knelt and greeted the Womo while looking at the floor. When Timothy looked at me, I knelt as he had and said, hesitantly, "*Popo*," not knowing whether it was a word meant merely for men.

The Womo did not respond.

One of the three helpers spoke to the Womo. Timothy looked at me, and there was silence, so I spoke. "I heard about the great powers of the Womo from very far. I come to pay my respects and to give the respect of my people. And I brought this goat as a gift." Timothy translated to the assistants and one of them spoke to the Womo and the Womo did not respond.

"Did you bring money?" one of the assistant priests said through Timothy.

"I did not bring money," I said. "Money can bring with it evil if it's used badly. My gift can bring only good."

Timothy smiled and relayed the answer to the priests and they did not relay my answer to the Womo.

The Womo spoke. His voice was hoarse, weak. Light shining through the window carved his faint silhouette. Out of the corner of my eye, I could see only that his arms were folded in his lap. When the Womo went silent, the assistants spoke to Timothy, repeating the Womo's words, and Timothy spoke to me. "The Womo accepts your gift and he thanks you for your gift. And he hears a lot of enjoyment when he sees you," Timothy said in his strange way.

I waited in silence.

The Womo spoke, a question, repeated to Timothy and then to me.

"The Womo asks you to tell him something about the place you come from."

"I come from a far place called Israeila. We have three gods that may actually be one god. But this god is in the sky and people cannot meet him. That is why I feel a great honor of meeting god here on earth."

Timothy nodded as he translated.

"The Achipawa are the first people to arrive to Nigeria," the Womo said. "In all the wars, people arrived to the mountain of Karishen to look for shelter because they knew that here with the powers of the Womo they were protected. The mountain of Karishen is the center of Nigeria."

I asked him, "Are you the one who brings the rains?"

"Yes."

The assistant priests added, "He controls the lightning and the thunder and the rising and setting of the sun. He decides who is born and who dies in all of Nigeria."

I could see now that the Womo wore clothes that were blue.

"How does the Womo know what happens outside," I said, "if he has to stay in his hut all his life?"

Timothy had told me that he read the fire.

"They are my ears," the Womo said of his assistant priests.

"The body of the Womo stays in the house," one priest said, "but the Womo can be in many different places at the same time. You talk to him here inside the house but he can be now in any other place in the world or even in three different places. In one day the Womo can go to any place in the world and come back."

The Womo asked me to tell him more about Israeila.

"There we do not let our cows go free to eat grass," I said. "We close them in small houses and it is the people who bring food to the cows."

"Cows in the house?" Timothy said to me. When the assistants heard Timothy's translation, they talked to each other for a minute before relaying my words to the Womo. And the Womo did not respond.

"Great Womo," I said, "I want to know more about the Achipawa. I ask for the permission of the Great Womo to stay in your land for a short time to learn your traditions."

The Womo gave his permission and invited me to return in a week to be with the Achipawa on his holiday. But he said, "Some ceremonies are closed. You cannot hear all the secrets of the Achipawa."

I was directed back into the tunnel as thunder rumbled outside. Timothy climbed out behind me into the daylight, the priests following. Thunder echoed again through the clouds, from one side of the sky to the other. Timothy pointed upward and said, "God."

"The Achipawa are not circumcised," Timothy told me a week later when we climbed back to the caldera's rim. "Me and you that are circumcised, we cannot go down to the dancing. We can watch from up."

Timothy and I had swum in rivers during our long walks, and he'd seen me without clothes.

"Would they check you?" I said.

"If you lie it will be dangerous. My brother lied and said he was not circumcised just to participate in the mountain ceremony. When he came back home, the place he was keeping his corn was burned."

Below us was a spectacle of topless women dancing in leaf skirts, their hair worked into giant Afros. Men wore plumes of feathers on their heads and danced holding bamboo poles. People moved in two circles that rotated in opposite directions, the singers dancing inward toward the soloist who held a bamboo shaft perhaps three stories high. Thunder roared as the dancers rushed the center soloist and withdrew, answering his words with song. Thunder came from the south. I set up my camera to photograph the lightning, the purple light, the Womo's rock automobile. But I felt it was not my right to photograph the ceremony, and part of me thought I shouldn't have come at all. As thunderclouds neared from the west, priests came to greet me on the rim. God sat shadowed in the doorway of his tunnel.

Lightning crashed. The sky darkened. And the arms of the storms merged. As lightning flashed again and again, I let go of rationalizing—that storms were inevitable over a high peak on the plains, that the existence of the Womo for the Achipawa was a survival mechanism. A few raindrops fell and then a billion. I wrapped my camera in my shirt, rescued a lens that fell to the ground. Timothy and I sprinted downhill as lightning ripped across the sky in sequence, a series of explosions. Bolts flashed one after the other, illuminating the view in front of us as we dashed toward a hut, the power of the storm echoing the power of their surviving. At that moment I couldn't say that the Womo *hadn't* brought the storm. And the singing of the Achipawa back in the caldera grew louder, loud enough, I understood, to hold back the great foe, modernity.

Timothy left his field, his family, and his church to lead me for two and a half weeks through the land of the Achipawa. Except for friendship, there was little I could give him in return. Of course he asked for nothing. In the man was a goodness as rare as anything I'd ever experienced. On the day I came to say good-bye, Timothy said, "If I have done something wrong to you and I know it, please, I'm sorry. If I have done something wrong to you, not knowing, please, I'm sorry."

THE COMPROMISE

Half of winter blew through the door as I stepped into the one-room flat in Tel Aviv that I shared with Rachel. It was hardly warmer inside than out, with cold air seeping in around the windows. I blew my nose and got another taste of the gourds my students had cut apart in class. Just one man in Israel, it seemed, grew gourds like those I knew from Africa. I'd piled them into Dad's car, dried them, and my students sawed them in half, releasing powdery spirits from the hollow fruits until we were sneezing and coated in dust. The students cleaned the gourds, added back the seeds and sealed the halves with hot glue. Then shook their rattles to Fela's song, "Yellow Fever," and learned it was a protest against Nigerian women bleaching their skin to look like white people.

I was teaching about tolerance. With the peace process collapsed, Israel needed the tolerance of men like Mukhtar more than ever. Instead of relying on dry classroom discussion, I aimed to nurture tolerance in my students by building their curiosity, hoping through direct experience they would learn to love and embrace what was different. We played *bao* and the Ethiopian game *tim-tim* and cooked *ugali* and looked at photographs of the Maasai bride to examine the choice of values. We made beaded Maasai necklaces. A people could be loved infinitely more by cooking their food and hearing the sound of their words from your lips.

West Africa had aged me. I'd returned to Israel in early 2001, longing for something protected, something safe. Parked in my father's car outside the dorms of The Hebrew University, I told Rachel I was ready to build a life with her. In Israel.

"I swore I'd never get back together with you," she said.

"Rach, just being with you anywhere, at the drycleaners, in the car—feels like home. It's taken me a long time to understand you're the most important part of my life."

"But what happens when you need to go back to Africa?"

"No. I just need to visit for a month or two a year, but my home will be here with you."

She looked at me with her dark watery eyes. In the awkward silence, Rachel and I couldn't resist each other. We reached over the gearshift and sealed the compromise with a kiss.

In our dilapidated one-room flat, I showered to wash the rancid gourd dust from my face. Rachel was late getting home; she worked for an Israeli security company. I walked naked until I began to shiver, then dressed, added a coat, Rachel's fleece, a blanket. I loathed winter. I paced back and forth between small windows on either end of the flat, windows, like gutters and poles I could climb down, now linked to Foday Sankoh and the half-traumatized need for escape routes.

I chose the schools at which I taught and set out to create an army of young activists. I had students write letters to the embassy of Ivory Coast to protest cacao farms that enslaved children. We discussed Jane Goodall's prediction that gorillas and chimpanzees would soon disappear from the wild, an impending tragedy that echoed the slow death of natural lands, the extinction of cultures, and the tenuousness that allowed the Achipawa to exist at all. I taught at Teva, where I'd gone as a boy, and lectured at Tel Aviv University. I spoke about child soldiers for Amnesty International, telling Archie's story. Teaching three days a week left long stretches of time for Rachel. We camped out and tubed down the River Jordan and ate breakfast once a week with my parents at their flat nearby. We spent evenings sometimes with Ofer, who worked for a cell phone company. Rachel and I shared many tender and beautiful days mixed with days of frustration.

I knelt in the apartment before the refrigerator. Time in the bush had made refrigerators forever like boxes of jewels. I gulped a cold Coke. Paced the room. Looked out the window at a view blocked by the roof of another apartment. I aimlessly opened the refrigerator again. I thought, Where in this life, in the well-constructed days, was the risk of being broken open? A memory uncurled, of a viper Mor and I had caught as kids and kept in an aquarium. We'd put our noses to the glass, causing the viper to fill her lungs and strike. Mor and I had held the viper's head down and petted her back day after day until she became docile. She stopped striking. And one morning we put a rat into the aquarium for her to eat, and the rat started gnawing on *her* back, feeding on the snake. The viper didn't move. So Mor and I let her go in the field.

Back at Planet Safari, not long after leaving the Achipawa, I was playing guitar in the closed office in which Paul Muangi slept. A beautiful young German woman walked in, shut the door, and watched me play. A few minutes later a man entered, looked at the woman, then at me and figured I was trying to serenade his girl—when I just wanted to be left alone. With my path out of the room blocked, I asked the guy why he'd come to Africa.

"To write a book."

"Nonfiction?"

"Fiction."

"I don't know why you'd write fiction. I'd just write my adventures the way they happened."

He cocked his head, thinking I was either a fool or full of myself. "*Adventures*?"

His name was David McDannald. Within five minutes, it was clear he was long past ready to ship the girl back to Germany and didn't care at all whether I'd been wooing her. David had left a job in New York with Goldman Sachs to live in a trailer on a West Texas ranch. He was a veteran traveler and had come to Africa on a one-way ticket. Our first conversation spanned six hours, and by the end of it we were friends.

David and I understood each other's quests and frustrations so well that I could tell him things I could not tell Ofer and Elad. After I moved in with Rachel, I wrote to him and revealed feelings I was barely able to admit to myself. December 20, 2001, I wrote, "Hey, Daudi, I really really miss you, man. I haven't opened my email for ages. I was stressed because of problems with Rach, growing bored of teaching and lecturing and feeling that I don't have the same vision for the book on children's games [and children's interviews that I'd actually begun to work on in earnest], like I don't have the same belief in its success. I'm stressed simply because I'm not in Africa." There *was* magic in what Rachel and I did together, in what we did for each other. I wrote later to David, "As for Rachel, I don't want to talk about it right now but I don't think it will work. Soon Africa will do its job of dividing me from the people I love and everything will be fine."

"You call yourself a writer?" David wrote back. "You write the same story again and again and pretend when you start you don't know the ending! Something important has kept you in Israel. Hide from it and it will plague you when you're back in the bush. As for me, I'm pretty well plagued. Half a year in New York and I'm already thinking of breaking my lease and flying to Ghana."

The prospect that I might leave again for Africa hung over Rachel and me like a sword. Or I hung it over Rachel like a sword. A quick trip I'd made to East and Southern Africa to compile more children's games had not slaked my need to be there. Some days, I thought of taking Rachel back with me. She labored to make me happy, asked again and again about my writing, encouraged me to take my camera everywhere, to photograph the ocean at night. *My* problems, my frustration over leaving my own path—the death of the urge—became *our* problems. Rachel and I fought, but she was incapable of becoming angry with me and instead grew to believe that she'd failed, that she couldn't make me happy, that she couldn't rescue me from our old vow always to be angry at places like Tel Aviv. She finally said my problems were "unsolvable" and she closed herself off. I loved her so deeply, though, that the thought of leaving, of actually going, seemed as impossible and painful as tearing off an arm. Talk of marriage had been so common that I never flinched when Rachel joked about getting pregnant.

The door opened. The air that blew into the apartment with Rachel cut through the blanket and coats I wore.

"Hi, honey," she said.

She was radiant, her teeth glowing like pearls, her black hair covering half her face. She said, "There was a horrible traffic jam because of the rain." She kissed me. "I'm exhausted."

Rachel wore the silver rings I'd bought for her in Addis Ababa. Her San Tropez pants were tight on her hips, and her breasts tugged against the safety pin that had replaced the top button of her thin brown shirt. She wiggled, slid her pants past her knees, pushed them away with a toe and climbed under the sheets, shedding her shirt and bra when we were sealed under the covers and warmed by our breathing. She scratched her nose on my neck in her cute way. Her skin grew cold as I kissed her down the arm to her hand then down the thigh to her ankle. We made love and she flung herself across the mattress like a warrioress who'd fought until she couldn't move.

"I love you, Ofirusch."

I was haunted by thoughts of opening my tent at dawn, by Lagos and the savannah and places where the world could be built each day from scratch.

I heard the words leaving my mouth: "Rach, I have to go back to Africa."

Her body tensed, as if something new had entered the room. I waited for her to cry, to scream, to hit me, to grab and smash something against the wall. She pulled her arms and legs in toward her core and rolled up and off the mattress. Rachel said nothing as she wrapped herself in a robe. She marched to the wall where my books were stacked, scooped them in her arms, opened the apartment door and tossed them outside. She slammed the door. A pile of my clothes she yanked off the tile and dumped outside atop the books. Slammed the door. Rachel grabbed my CDs, a towel, my sleeping bag, guitar and camera and heaved it all outside, making a dozen short trips in succession, each time opening and slamming the door, as if it were a moment for which she'd prepared, for which the strength had been gathered from across the years. I was sitting on the bed, a towel around my waist. When there was nothing more of mine to purge, she came for me, grabbed my arms and pulled me up, put two hands against my chest and drove me backwards across the room. Her face showed no anger or sadness. She pushed me outside. Slammed the door.

I stood for a long time in the cold, listening for movement within, trying to get a view of her through the curtain covering the window. I looked down at the pile of my things, pulled out my jeans and a leather coat and realized the only things she'd forgotten were my shoes. I left it all. None of it mattered. And headed for my parents' flat, the pavement wet and cold against my feet. I passed the drycleaners and the camera shop and I was as emotionless as Rachel had been. I wanted melancholy, some feeling commensurate with the act of pushing her away again. But I could only think of my horrid timing and my damn shoes.

Four days later, the weather changed in Tel Aviv, and the sun came out when for once I wanted winter. My mind swam with thoughts of marriage, pregnancy, family. Shahar, my bunkmate from the army, called her a "good soul," called me foolish for leaving her. Elad said, "Stay with Rach. She's a sweetheart." Memory and desire tore at my judgment of what I'd done. Had I learned nothing about how it felt to be on the other side of breaking things off with her? If I played guitar outside the door for a day. If I played for two days, a week, a year, if I toiled for seven years like Jacob and the Achipawa boys, would she open the door? Would she marry me?

I climbed the stairs to the flat, high on remorse, ready to lay myself at her feet. There was no answer when I knocked. My dad had come by a few days earlier and gotten all my things. I stepped left of the door and looked through the window. The curtain was gone. The door was open, the flat empty. I pushed in and found nothing but a picture of me, torn, and the silver Ethiopian rings.

Now came the melancholy I'd craved.

I headed for the sea.

The sun was strong, hot on my face, and I sat on the beach, squinting, clawing into the sand. Many times I'd paddled a surfboard out beyond the waves to float and think, where rays of light bounced from everywhere as if the stars had dropped into the ocean. The moment suddenly revealed itself to me, the false edge of the horizon where the sea and sky only appeared to touch, the halves of my life doomed never to merge. As I inhaled the salty air, I realized what people I loved may have already known: there was no choice. There never had been. I would never feel for anyone the love I felt for Rachel. I knew it as surely as my heart was thumping against my ribs. But I had already gone too far. Were I to stay and marry Rachel, I would blame her for untold unfinished journeys and dreams. Self-importance, yes. But mine. The man who could enjoy a parallel life with Rachel in Israel would be someone else. Without Africa I was not Ofir.

2002—PRESENT

LAGA

"I'M A GAMBLER"

Exhaust blew through Haut Nyong Voyage. An attendant in a blue smock corralled passengers on oil-soaked ground. Young men in slippers loaded sacks of onions onto a bus roof along with truck tires, a one-speed bicycle, and a dozen pieces of plaid Chinese-made luggage that were like zippered plastic bags. My bus, empty but for two men, was parked diagonally in the bus stand and looked as if it hadn't been driven in years.

I was headed for Abong-Mbang and the jungles of eastern Cameroon.

An older man cooked an omelet on a kerosene burner, a man as dignified and calm as the bus stop was shabby and chaotic. His beige button-down shirt made him look more like the manager of a fine restaurant than a guy perched over a homemade table.

A woman was shouting at the boys loading luggage.

"Mama, don't do this," the older man said in English as he scooped Nescafé into a glass. "We're trying to make the business run. Do you see? These boys load bags every day. Your suitcase will arrive as healthy as you."

His name was Julius. He was an Anglophone from the region in Cameroon near Nigeria, a village man who'd come to the capital to earn a living. My own trip to Yaoundé had come sooner than I'd expected. From Tel Aviv I'd flown to Nigeria and paddled six weeks down the Niger River, subsisting on cold *gari* and river water and the fruit villagers piled into my canoe. Unable to fight winds on the dammed Kainji Reservoir, I sold the canoe and moved north to write about Nigeria's growing religious tension and how Sharia Law was changing post-9/11. In Yelwa, a town festooned with murals, photos, and heart-studded stickers of Osama bin Laden, locals were angry to learn there was an Israeli among them. "What are you doing to the Palestinians?" one man shouted. "All Israelis should be killed," said another. When people contacted my host to coordinate my killing, I figured it was time to move.

I headed south to Cameroon; Jane Goodall's prediction that great apes would soon be extinct had grown from a concept into a mission. I would spend a month writing about apes and the bushmeat trade, then return to the human-rights battles on the Nigerian side.

Old Julius looked up after the first bus departed. "Your bus isn't going anywhere until afternoon," he said to me. "Come, let me buy you a drink at the bar just there."

I followed Julius through the bus station to a booth guarded by a short wall of blue fence plants. He brushed sand off the bench and motioned for me to sit, then ordered a large Coke and two glasses. Julius had full rounded cheeks and an infectious smile.

"You're traveling?" he said. "Where is your family? Do you have children?"

"My fiancée—she was basically that—well, she heard one too many times I was going back to Africa."

I told Old Julius about my reasons for coming to Cameroon, and he nodded when I mentioned extinction. He said, "In my village, northwest province, we had many, many animals. When I was young, elephants were coming through like just another herd of goats. Now? We don't have animals. In the East, they still have. But three or four vans come from there each day to this bus station, *loaded* with bushmeat. They are even smoking the meat just behind the station. Just here. In drums. The meat drops early morning. Some goes to a market near. Some goes direct to houses of rich people. But this is just one station. Just a station for Abong-Mbang. There are many stations. Across the road you have two more stations *just for Abong-Mbang*. I'm sure it's the same there."

I asked Old Julius about MINEF, the Ministry of Environment and Forestry, the government agency charged with protecting wildlife.

"The ministry?" Julius said. "Are you joking? MINEF? MINEF! These people *buy* bushmeat from *this* station! Some of them are part of the trade. Laws don't count in this country, my friend. People in MINEF are making money out of this. More than anyone."

I'd seen it. I'd spent twenty-four hours at the Nkoabang checkpoint on the eastern edge of Yaoundé, the primary gateway for bushmeat arriving by road from the rainforests of the East. Takam, a MINEF official at the checkpoint, was flattered by my interest in his problems and made a show of swaggering out to the road to flag down a minivan. But his confidence vanished, along with proof he'd ever inspected a vehicle (his job), when he hesitated, mumbled inaudibly to the driver, and climbed onto the roof rather than confronting passengers by searching *inside* the van. Takam wore a lime-green hat and an unbuttoned shirt with a jersey under it, and he rummaged through the luggage while people in the seats barked, yelled, and banged the windows. The driver inched forward and braked, jerking Takam on the roof, behavior that would have unholstered the gun of a policeman. Takam seemed to have little more authority than a luggage boy.

He did find a woven white sack and he took it to the roadside MINEF cabin, along with the woman who claimed it. Takam's co-worker slept, arms folded on his desk, head down. Empty beer bottles lined the wall. Takam opened the sack and dumped the bushmeat onto the floor. The cabin filled with the potent, oily smell of burned, rotten meat, a smell that was sticky in the throat. The meat had come from the national park near Lomié, the Dja. In the pile were hunks of blackened flesh, ribcages, limbs, here a shoulder, maybe a leg, though whether I was seeing it upside down or from the back or front I didn't know. Rising above the pile was the contorted hand of a charred monkey with its fingerprints intact.

As Takam penned a complaint report, the minivan continued into Yaoundé without the woman. A dozen fuel tankers and logging trucks rolled by the checkpoint without inspection, trucks that often carried hundreds of kilograms of meat because they came from the front lines of deforestation. Takam closed the book of law, put down his pen, and smiled at the woman as though he might pour her a drink. They bargained. She bought the meat back from him, then loaded her white sack and boarded the next van.

In hopes of finding people fighting such abuse, I talked to a dozen Cameroonians who directed me, not into the field, but to Bastos, Yaoundé's neighborhood of embassies, consulates, NGOs, and the houses of the expatriates paid to work behind high walls and razor wire. It was a world of Mercedes, swimming pools, servants, and model-thin Cameroonian girls wearing their hair straight in hopes of making boyfriends of white men. I tried to book interviews with wildlife NGOs said to be working to stop the slaughter of endangered species. I called the Cameroon office of the World Conservation Society (WCS), the World Bank, the environmental departments of the EU and the UN, but I couldn't get an appointment to see *anyone*, much less a director or a man or woman down in the trenches fighting to disprove Goodall's dark prophesy.

I visited the massive headquarters of the World Wildlife Fund. A Cameroonian woman met me at the front door, which led into a foyer as luxurious and large as that of a fine hotel. The woman just stared at me.

"I came two weeks before now and last week," I said. "I called the director. I'm working here as a photojournalist."

"There's nobody you can talk to today," she said. "We have a library."

When I finally got inside WCS, a man told me, "We do workshops with government officials and help in management plans. We help the government in the acquisition of materials, like buying jeeps. We build capacity." When I asked him about simply enforcing the law against killing endangered species, he said, "That's the work of the government. We don't tell the government what to do."

An EU official said that Cameroon had never had a single prosecution for wildlife crime. "The one case we know of was over a black rhino," the man told me. "It happened only because a researcher had embedded a transmitter in *that rhino's* horn." A directional antenna had led researchers to the house of the army captain who'd ordered a horn from the bush and paid for the animal to be shot. Western Black Rhinos in Cameroon numbered no more than a dozen at that time.* Nothing came of the trial, and the captain was promoted afterwards. The EU official said to me, "Look, it's difficult to work with the government here."

I was lost in problems far greater than I'd imagined. There was so much to fix in Cameroon that writing an article about apes, even a series of articles, was a meaningless response. I *had* written an article. But it lacked an ending, lacked any hero or hope for solutions. I was frustrated and overwhelmed. The system of NGOs and the expatriates paid to protect wildlife seemed to do little more than put on workshops for corrupt officials. The situation echoed Lokichokio, where million-dollar NGOs couldn't save the Sudanese from humiliation just outside the camp. When I left Old Julius and boarded the bus for Abong-Mbang, I felt that I stood on the rim of a gorge with no way across.

One hundred and forty-five kilometers east of Yaoundé, the paved road ended at Ayos, a truck stop of a town full of idling logging trucks, bars, and women grilling over open fires. Three signed contracts to pave the road beyond Ayos had failed to generate a single kilometer of tarmac, as the officials who'd made the deals had likely divided the money with the contractors. My minivan rattled on, up the narrow clay road, over ridges like those on a beach at low tide. The logging trucks came one after another, truck after truck, the forest slowly making its exit for the port in Douala, some of the trees as big around as my van, most headed to Europe and Asia for a future as furniture.

It was dusk when the bus bounced into Abong-Mbang. A curtain of trees, dark in twilight, rose to the north of the road. Abong-Mbang was bordered by forested swamp whose water had saved some of the area from logging. I squeezed through a line of motorcycle taximen waiting on their bikes for passengers and I sat in a metal chair at a roadside bar where Congolese jazz played on the stereo, the bright

---

* The Western Black Rhinoceros, once widespread in central-west Africa, was tentatively declared extinct on July 7, 2006 by IUCN.

guitar riffs perfect for the tropics. Two men were drinking Guinness, holding their palms over their bottles to keep away the flies. They struggled with my English when I asked about bushmeat in town. A motorcyclist, with a manicured moustache and flip-up sunglasses, had been listening. He stepped off his bike and said, "Bon, of course there is bushmeat, boy. In the market."

"Chimp and gorilla," said one of the men with a beer.

The motorcyclist listened to the two men speak French, then he pointed up the road. He wore one black driving glove, on his left hand. "They say we also have two live ones."

"What live ones?"

"Bon, one small gorilla, one chimp."

I took a long sip of Coke, not wanting to betray my eagerness to know more, though I doubted that finding live apes was as easy as getting off a bus. I scratched my neck and took my time and finally said, "So, it's possible to see them?"

The motorcyclist, who was in his forties, tilted his head to the side and lit a cigarette. "The name's Calabash, boy. We can go tomorrow."

"Do you know a cheap hotel?" I said. "The *cheapest* hotel."

Calabash flashed a smile that said he'd been waiting for me to ask. I climbed onto the back of his bike and we rode off, the wind blowing into my eyes. We stopped at a hotel by the police station, and he ushered me inside to ensure the price of the room was fair. "No," Calabash said to the clerk. "That's too much. Ofi is my friend."

The next morning, Calabash was waiting outside the hotel like a man who knew how the day would end. He flicked aside his cigarette and straddled the engine. "Bon, come. Let's go, boy. We go." He kick-started the motorbike, opened the throttle and flipped down his sunglasses, and we rode through Abong-Mbang, the engine growling under us, the sun shining through the dust as we zipped south from the hotel. I'd barely slept pondering what I'd learned from the men at the bar. If they were right, then we were on our way to save a baby gorilla. I smiled and let the air whistle into my mouth. Back in Yaoundé, I'd volunteered at the Cameroon Wildlife Aid Fund (CWAF), which ran a shelter for orphaned apes, the same place Rachel had volunteered in the time after our split in Ethiopia. While I was pouring concrete one day, the power died in the electric fence of a chimp enclosure, and half a dozen chimps stormed out through the gate, running on their fists. They sprinted forward, jumped and hugged me, clung to my chest, our species linked effortlessly in that moment of shared joy. In the jungle, baby chimps and gorillas were often killed by the bullets that killed their mothers. When infant apes did survive, it was often because they lacked the meat to justify a bullet. Survivors were helpless and clung to their mothers' bodies. Baby chimps were tougher than gorillas. Captured chimps died of dehydration, malnutrition, disease, but some survived in captivity. Orphaned gorillas, though, even with their physical needs met, tended to let themselves go, to break down and die without warning.

Calabash swerved through Abong-Mbang's alleyways. We passed small farms full of papaya trees and cassava. I gripped the rack over the bike's rear wheel. Gnats like drops of water smashed and died against my cheeks. We turned in at a cinderblock house and motored over the red hardpan to the door. A woman appeared, drying her hands on a towel. A man with a bad leg limped around from the trees behind the house. They greeted us warmly. In French, Calabash asked about the gorilla. His mouth opened as he listened, then he shook his head. He sighed before turning to me.

"Boy, they say this gorilla, bon—they say it is dead two months ago."

"What? What did they do? How? Did they eat him?"

Calabash started to ask this last question but frowned and climbed onto the bike, to make clear he hadn't brought me along to interrogate people. "We'll see more, boy."

I just lost a gorilla, I said to myself. I should have come sooner.

Calabash cut the engine as we coasted up to another house. A friendly old man came to the door buttoning his shirt. His living room was full of kitsch: a plastic giraffe, a hologram waterfall hanging near the television. The man left us and returned carrying what I thought at a distance was the skull of a human. But it was gorilla skull. The canines were long, the ridges over the eyes as thick as a child's arm. The back of the skull was smashed. The man said that two years earlier, the silverback had wandered out of the jungle and into Abong-Mbang. Locals had called the old man because he was a retired gendarme and had a rifle. He'd shot the gorilla as it was walking past the hospital.

"I have a picture from that day."

"Bring it," Calabash said.

The man dropped the photograph on the table in front of us. The gorilla was sprawled out on his back, a giant monster of a man who seemed to have been plopped down against the fake backdrop of a staged photograph: a rudimentary brick building and a crowd. In the style of a Western trophy hunter, the retired gendarme posed with his rifle and with his hand on the head of slain ape.

"Take a picture of it," Calabash said to me.

I pulled out my camera. I was staring at the front-page photograph that a week earlier I'd dreamed of getting, the photograph that would have landed my article in a major magazine—if publishing would have done any good.

We said good-bye, and in the road Calabash lit a cigarette and held the smoke in his lungs. He wore a faded red T-shirt and a smudged tan jacket, and his gray pants held many weeks of dirt.

I asked about his motorcycle and his job as a taximan.

He pulled the cigarette from his lips and smiled slyly. "Bon, it's vacation now, boy, so I move people on my engine. I am the head teacher of the school here."

Calabash watched me, to gauge my response; I didn't want him to know I thought he might be joking. He flicked away the cigarette and straddled the engine. "Come, boy, Let's go. The chimp is there, boy. The hunter has him." He flipped down his sunglasses and we rode off. The line of motorcycle taximen near the market swung their heads as we shot by. A girl sweeping out a bar looked up and dropped her broom. The sun was nearly as hot on my skin as the engine block was against my boot. We drove downhill and then climbed to an empty checkpoint just west of town. The rushing wind seemed to take hold of my eyelashes and close my eyes; I was tired enough to doze in the open air at fifty kilometers an hour.

We arrived sooner than I was ready for. Calabash parked his Honda beside a solid house. Children appeared with the engine's roar but did not come to greet us—as they would have in Kenya, Tanzania, Malawi, Mozambique. Men stood back with their arms crossed, all wearing coarse clothes save for one, who had a sleek, colorful shirt of yellow and red. His jaw line was sharp, his face thin. He glanced at me and stepped toward Calabash, who spoke in French, gestured, mentioned the chimp.

"*Oui, oui*," the man said as if welcoming customers to a shop. "We have it."

In the living room sat a thick mahogany table and the plush couches of a man doing well. We exited a door in the rear of the house and crossed the dirt to a cinderblock kitchen. The walls were blackened from old fires, the air sour with oil burned in a thousand dinners. The kitchen's soot seemed to drip with grease. On the ash-coated floor were burned hunks of firewood, and, tied to a log, near banana peels and a beer bottle, was a baby chimpanzee.

The chimp gripped the log as we stepped toward him. He was drooping, staring at the ground, withdrawn, half-dead compared to the chimps at CWAF. His belly was round, bound with sisal rope. His eyes sagged like those of someone who hadn't slept. The hunter untied one end of the rope from the log and dragged the chimp across the filthy floor. The chimp gripped the rope as he slid and got to his feet and walked through the door on his back legs, his right hand touching the ground for balance. The poacher, like a shopkeeper giving me a proper view of his goods, pulled the tiny ape into the sunlight on the front porch. He secured the rope to a table leg. Men threw shreds of cassava at the chimp, held the food close, laughed, yanked it away, making him lunge. The wrinkles of the chimp's face and his short white beard bestowed him with a look of wisdom. One man poked the chimp's stomach, poked him again, and the chimp snapped and bent over until his stomach was on the concrete, arms and legs folded under him, head jerking side to side. Back and forth. Like a rat.

He looked sick.

Calabash leaned against the house, watching the chimp, watching me. I fought the instinct to push the men away.

"How often do you get one?" I said through Calabash.

"I have them all the time," the poacher said. "I sold one to a white man. I can get you more. Two more if you want."

The hunter seemed savvy, though perhaps he was just trying to impress. He was *not* a village hunter, not a man used by bushmeat dealers for his knowledge of the forest or a man who needed a dealer to supply money for guns, bullets, and porters. He was a businessman. The chimp was still with him, though, and not moving toward the international market where he was worth thousands of dollars. That meant the hunter wasn't well-connected. There was no mention of price. Calabash climbed onto the motorcycle, flipped down his glasses and said to the hunter, "We might come back. We might not."

On the western edge of Abong-Mbang, the checkpoint was now manned, and a bamboo pole blocked the road. As we waited for a policeman to pull the pole aside, I said to Calabash, "I'm not going to buy the chimp."

Calabash raised his sunglasses.

"I'm going to take him," I said. "He needs to be in a reserve. Let's go to MINEF."

The corners of Calabash's mouth curled into a smile and he looked at me anew as I'd looked at him. "Okay, boy. Okay. If that's the program, then we go to MINEF. But you know, boy—bon, these people at MINEF are very difficult."

"I don't expect much."

The paint was peeling on both the outer and inner walls of the MINEF station. Two men sat in an open room, one without a uniform, the other sleeping, arms folded on his desk and his head down.

To the man who was awake, I said, "I've just seen a chimpanzee—"

"No no no, boy," Calabash said and led me to the office of the *chef du poste.*

The chief looked up from a stack of papers. He wore an unbuttoned green uniform. On the wall was a poster printed by the German aid agency GTZ, which showed animals grouped by the class of their protection. Chimps were class A.

The man greeted me in French.

"I've just seen a chimpanzee," I said, standing in front of him.

The chief didn't respond to my English. When Calabash began to translate the man raised his hand. "Yes, I understand."

"This chimp needs to arrive to Yaoundé, to the zoo," I told him, "and the poachers need to be arrested."

The chief glanced at Calabash for some indication of the kind of problem that had just arrived in his office.

"The poachers need to be arrested," I repeated.

"No, we can't do it."

I pointed at the poster of protected animals next to his desk. "The law is written *here*: anyone caught with an endangered species is supposed to go to prison. This law needs to be applied. You are the Ministry of Forests." I tapped my finger on the poster atop the word, MINEF.

"That's not our job."

"This chimp needs to move to the zoo of *your* ministry."

"That's not our job and we can't do it."

"So do we need to call the ministry in Yaoundé and tell them you are unable to get the chimp?"

"Look," he said, pretending to browse documents, "we are not just leaving the office to go to the field. If you want us to do this, you need to provide the means. We don't have the means."

I pointed to rips in my trousers, to my arms, which were covered in moot-moot bites from the jungle at CWAF. "You're not going to get anything from me. I'm in Africa now a total of three and a half years. Look at me. I'm not a tourist. I have no money to give you."

The *chef du poste* stared at Calabash and frowned.

"We need money for transport," the chief said.

"What money for transport? The chimp is in Abong-Mbang!"

"For us to go and do this work we need *motivation*."

"I passed three days of arrest in Liberia because I wouldn't pay a bribe. You're not getting any money from me. We need to take this chimp today!"

"We are not the police. We don't have guns. Poachers are dangerous. These people can kill us. The poachers will not just give us this animal."

"But this is your work! To enforce the law. Maybe I should write this to the minister." And Fela's voice sang in my head, *Authority stealing pass arm robbery* . . .

The chief was wholly unfazed. "We cannot do it," he said. "But if you want to have a chimp, you can buy it. Just give us the money."

I pulled Calabash toward the door. "This is useless. The fucking man in charge of protecting animals in this region is trying to sell me a chimp."

In my hotel room that night I paced beside the bed, my notebook on the table, pen in hand, a new Coke open and three empty bottles on the floor. I was anxious and angry and I shoved the table to the center of the room to maximize light from the dim, dirty bulb. I slammed down a chair and wrote and stormed around the table. The chimp will not die in a filthy kitchen. I clenched my teeth and struggled to put into words the grotesqueness of a world turned upside down, where the guardians were the destroyers.

I nearly smashed the Coke bottles lined up by the door.

But how could I be angry at a system?

Then the words flowed. The blockage was kicked free, and I realized how clear the problem was. The obstacle in fighting the bushmeat trade was just corruption. The laws existed and had to be enforced. It was so uncomplicated, it was surprising. The NGOs knew what was happening. Of course they'd seen what I'd seen. And why weren't they shouting? Why did they pretend that they and the government were working together, pretend that if the international community poured more money into conservation, they would provide the solution? Using public funds, NGOs bought jeeps for MINEF and put on workshops, which they paid people like the *chef du poste* to attend. And WWF distributed pamphlets with photographs of gorillas depicted as if they were thriving in the wild, but they were actually orphans at CWAF.

I slapped so hard at a mosquito that pain tore through my chest.

I wrote to get my anger on the page. In Lokichokio, it was the NGOs who'd sent a car of security guards to order me to leave. Then Aya came to berate me. Not only did NGOs fail to stand up to governments and men like the *chef du poste*, they contributed to and reinforced corruption.

Over the next two hours, with my brain firing at the speed of its very best days, I imagined a new kind of organization, staffed by volunteers, activists, fighters. The NGO would run investigations with undercover agents who would locate players in the trade of endangered species.

An operations unit would take MINEF officers and policemen by the hands and carry out arrests with them while fighting corruption *during* the arrests. In the courts, legal experts would track cases through to prosecution to minimize opportunities for lawyers and judges to take bribes. Finally, a media unit would publicize results, help to criminalize the bushmeat trade, begin to steer people toward other businesses, and broadcast that the web of corruption could be beaten.

I gulped down the last of my Coke and it was as sweet as water from a river. I realized I'd just written a blueprint for the kind of organization I'd hoped to find in Cameroon, the project in the field, that longed-for ending of the article. As first light shone through the window, I crawled into bed, satisfied. But there was no article. I had to give the idea to someone.

Where were the people who could undertake it?

Calabash woke me. His glasses were flipped up when I opened the door, the driving glove on his left hand. "It's late, boy," he said, tapping his watch.

I packed my small backpack. It was July 29, 2002.

We returned to MINEF and walked straight to the office of the *chef du poste*.

"Let's save each other's time," I said. "The chimp needs to get to Yaoundé. If you're too afraid to do anything, I'll handle the confiscation. Just give me the book of law. And if you know someone who wants to go to Yaoundé, I'll pay his ride and you give him a document that says we can travel with the ape."

The chief didn't lift his eyes from his newspaper. "Yes, okay."

I was so surprised he hadn't said no that I repeated myself.

"Okay, whatever, go and do it. If you come back, I'll find you someone."

I took the bilingual book of law from his table.

West to the edge of Abong-Mbang, Calabash and I rode over forested hills on his red Honda. When we stopped at the hunter's house, my heart was thrumming. Not too passionate, I said to myself. Don't ruin it with rage. I stepped off the bike and breathed and thought, Here, it begins.

"Hello, you came again," the hunter said from his doorway. "Come inside."

The other men smiled in anticipation, I figured, of money changing hands.

"So you came back to buy it?" the poacher said in French.

A second man entered and stood beside him in the living room.

"What's the price of the chimp?" I said, hearing nervousness in my voice.

Calabash translated. "100,000 francs." $165.

I nodded and closed my mouth to hide that I was breathing hard.

"Sit there," I said, motioning toward the table.

They sat and looked up as if waiting for me to begin the negotiation. I took a piece of paper from my backpack, wrote my name and put the pen and paper on the table. "Write your name here with the price of the chimp," I said to the hunter. He wrote and slid the paper back across the table. I folded the page into my pocket and opened the green book of law.

"Read," I said, pointing.

The men placed their hands on the tabletop and leaned forward. What I'd marked stated that any person caught in possession of a protected species, alive or dead, whole or part, would be liable to a fine of three to ten million CFA and/or one to three years in prison.

The poacher raised his chin and stared at me. The other man was still reading. The poacher looked back at the book as if he'd missed something. Then both men looked at Calabash, who motioned with his hand that they had to deal with me.

Through Calabash I said, "I know very well this article is worth a bribe—of what? Two thousand or three thousand francs? Small money. But that's why I'm here. My job is to get this law enforced. I work for a big international organization and we make sure there is no bribing. Already, they have sent a car from Yaoundé to arrest you."

Calabash smiled and shook his head. "Boy."

The hunter looked shocked, nauseated.

"The car is on its way to your house," I said, hearing a quiver in my voice with this bluff. "It's coming to take you to be on trial in Yaoundé."

The men spoke to each other. The hunter scratched his neck, glanced at the book. The other fidgeted. The hunter raised his hands to his chest and spoke to Calabash, who shrugged and pointed to me.

"It's true you invited me into your house and allowed me to take pictures," I said. "Maybe I can see if there is something I can do. If you agree to remain my informers, I can try to explain this to the men in the vehicle and maybe I can convince them to give you another chance—if you will provide information about other hunters and dealers."

"Of course," said the hunter. "Please talk with them."

"And you'll also give me the chimp."

"Yes yes."

The men stood. The second man smiled briefly, jammed his hands in his pockets.

"Let's take him," I said and moved toward the back door.

In the kitchen, the chimp grabbed a branch jutting from the stack of firewood.

"Ooh ooh," I said softly, trying to console him in the way I'd learned at CWAF, though chimps had more than fifteen different versions of "ooh ooh." I knelt and reached in to untie the rope from his belly, thinking he might bite.

"He'll run," Calabash said.

Still kneeling, I unknotted the rope, put it aside and pulled my hands back. "Come. Come here." I extended my arms and waited for the chimp to reach out to me. He let go of the branch, hesitated, raised his arms and pursed his lips. I wrapped one arm around him and pulled him to me. The chimp locked on to my chest and was transformed.

I could feel his breath on my neck.

Calabash spoke to the men, who looked puzzled by the affection of the chimp: before a rat and now a baby.

"Let's go," I said. "I have to call my associates coming in the van."

We crossed the house and climbed onto the bike. The chimp buried his head in my underarm. Calabash kick-started the engine, and the chimp clamped down on my nipple, swung his head from side to side, the grip of his arms so strong I couldn't have pried him loose. The chimp could live half a century, could outlive me.

Calabash was still talking to the hunter.

"Calabash, let's move."

He flipped down his glasses, hit the throttle, and steered us into the road.

Calabash left me at the empty checkpoint outside Abong-Mbang on the chance a bus would pass. But, save for logging trucks, the road was empty. Through late morning and early afternoon, Calabash rode back and forth between the checkpoint and town, the growl of his engine announcing his approach long before he appeared. Near four o'clock, he arrived again in a cloud of dust, flipped up his glasses, and lit a cigarette. A MINEF official rode on the back of the bike.

"The *chef du poste*," Calabash said, shaking his head, "is a very difficult man. Bon, this time it's working. We have this man going with you to Yaoundé, and he has the letter, boy, so you can carry the chimp." Calabash held the cigarette between his lips as he climbed off the bike and dusted off his pants. "We have no cars going anywhere now, boy. But I think there are missionaries who need to move soon. I'll go back to town to check." He shook his head when he noticed the chimp sucking on my finger. "Boy, I knew, bon, when I saw you that you are very clever."

"I don't know how to thank you, Calabash. We've had a great adventure."

"Boy, the name isn't 'Calabash.' It's Kalebass. Ka–le–bass. Kamdem Charlie Rostrand le bass." He mimed strumming a guitar. "That's how they call me."

"You're a musician!"

He smiled and tilted back his head to blow cigarette smoke. "Boy, some time ago, if you were saying Kalebass in this area, people knew me from the radio."

"I can't believe you didn't tell me!"

"Maybe sometime I can play for you, boy."

I gave Kalebass 15,000 francs, most of the money I had, which would at least reimburse him for the gasoline we'd burned.

"Bon, I need to go and see on the missionaries. It may take some time but I think you can go with them." Kalebass tossed his cigarette butt in the dirt. He glanced at the money I'd just given him and then held out 10,000 francs. "Take it back, boy. You need it more than me."

I didn't reach for the money.

"Boy, don't worry. Take it," Kalebass said and pulled out another cigarette. "I'm a gambler."

DOUBTS

"We don't have space," said the woman at CWAF when I phoned from Yaoundé. "*You* stay with the chimp." And she hung up.

I hadn't considered CWAF would refuse to take him.

It was midnight, and the mosquitoes were screeching. My MINEF escort raised his eyebrows to ask again if he'd be paid for coming. The missionaries had dropped us at the monastery, and we shambled in the dark through Mont Febé, a neighborhood as empty as the end of town. The chimp, clinging to my chest beneath a towel, had defecated all over my clothes, and I needed a hotel equipped with more than bucket baths, a hotel expensive enough to offer anonymity. I called an Israeli friend, Eran, who arrived in a car, checked into a hotel for me and got the key. And I crept up to the room with the chimp concealed.

A tile floor, a television, and stained wood walls made the hotel room the nicest I'd ever rented. I put the chimp down and pivoted toward the window, and he scurried after me. Future, as I'd named him, pulled himself onto the bed and urinated on my pillow. The MINEF official crawled onto the other side of the bed and passed out in his uniform. Bug-covered and wet, Future streaked the sheets wherever he moved, leaving a trail of brown handprints. The banana I peeled for him he dropped on the tile and mashed under his foot as he followed me whining to the sink.

"Ah ah ah," I said and sat with Future on the floor. I set my pillow in the nook of an open closet and he climbed on and curled up, the pillow soon brown, the wall smeared, the room fecund with jungle rot. I inched over to the bed, and the chimp whimpered and wobbled toward me on two legs.

"Ah ah ahhh," I said, shifting back to the floor. Future settled on the pillow, kept his hand on me. I worked my fingers through his hair, grooming him, pinching bugs that I pretended to bring to my mouth. I could feel his heart racing against his fragile ribs. He was as tired as I was, though, and soon asleep. With the sheets in ruin and no change of clothes in my bag, I skipped the shower, lay on the mattress, and shut my eyes.

I woke at dawn, as damp and sluggish as if I'd slept on a Maasai bed in a pool of brown rainwater. The MINEF official was snoring. The skin at my nipple was sore, marked by Future's teeth. The instant I swung around and planted my feet on the floor, Future climbed my legs and wrapped himself around my stomach. Returning to Nigeria was out of the question. I couldn't pass the project off to anyone. In writing the plan to fight against the system that was failing great apes, I'd already laid out my path. Or maybe Future had. In the absence of borders, there was no such thing as a voyeur.

He cried, "Ooh ooh ooh ooh ooh," when I shut him in the room with the MINEF official, Future's voice higher and higher pitched as I bounded downstairs and outside to the payphone and called CWAF. "The chimp and I are in a hotel," I said to the same woman I'd woken in the night. "I need to put him somewhere so I can get things done."

After a long silence, she said, "When you leave Cameroon in a week or two, you know we're the ones who'll have to care for this chimp!"

"I take all responsibility. Just help me with the next step. I can't go around town with a chimp on my back."

"I'll give you the number of the conservator of the zoo."

The MINEF man rode with me to the conservator's house, lingered briefly, and left. With Future's arms hooked over my shoulders, I lugged a welded orange cage into the grass near the monkey exhibit. I tried to pull the chimp off me, to push him into the cage, but he screamed and wouldn't budge. Bananas failed as a lure. Neither milk nor papaya induced Future to loosen his grip. The zoo's curious staff migrated forward as Future and I squeezed together into the small steel cage. The chimp went quiet when he spotted a pair of monkeys sneaking past the fenced pond of the crocodiles; holes in the monkey enclosure made them the lords of the zoo.

When a man wearing an ironed green shirt approached, Future barked, "Ooh! Ooh!" to defend us.

"He loves you too much," said a woman who stood by the cage.

"Excuse me, sir," said the man in green.

"I'm Ofir."

"Sir, might I—"

"Call me Ofir. I'm not a knight."

His name was Ignatius, and in his moustache were shreds of food. He tried to grab Future through the bars so I could slip out, but Future snapped at his fingers. I reclined against the inside of the cramped cage, my head forced downward, and I peeled a banana for myself; in the last forty-eight hours I wasn't sure I'd put anything into my stomach besides Coke. With Future clinging to me, I described my plan for an NGO. Ignatius had founded his own NGO to educate children about the environment using board games. As he spoke, it was hard not to focus on the shreds of fruit snared in his moustache.

"You understand," Ignatius said, "that no one has ever tried to enforce the law."

"I need volunteers. Lots of volunteers," I said. "I can't do this alone."

Ignatius raised a finger. "The wrong people, you understand, would just look at you as a chance to eat money, to chop." Before leaving, he said, "Ofir, we are together."

I tried to escape the cage, but Future stumbled toward me like a toddler and I couldn't risk snapping closed the guillotine door. I propped it open with a stick, kept my legs outside and began a long session of grooming. But I was too slow when I tried to swivel out. A woman with hair extensions, baggy blue overalls, and nice cheek-bones swept the concrete near the cage. She stared, swept, looked up again.

A man walked by, said, "White, it's good place for all of you in that cage."

Future trembled as I used a piece of twine to tie him to the back bars. I tore loose, climbed out and lowered the door. "It's okay. I'm coming back," I said, untying him from the outside, leaving him free within the cage. "I have to buy your shots, boy." Future gripped the bars and screamed, his shrieks louder and faster as I hurried away while he banged his head against the steel.

From the cyber café at Nlongkak, I emailed Duncan Willetts, hoping he knew players involved in the success story of Kenyan wildlife. I needed allies outside Cameroon and help building my case against the wrongs I'd found. I designed a flier, a call for activists and vol-unteers, and emailed it to Lucy to display at Planet Safari and to my father to post in travel shops in Tel Aviv. I asked my father to research how to establish the NGO in Israel and I fired off emails to friends all over Africa. Duncan Willetts responded immediately about a wildlife activist named Karl Ammann. I was two pages into an email to Karl when the power died, erasing my words.

The conservator refused to let me pitch my tent in the grass and sleep beside Future's cage, so I reached the zoo as it opened the next morning. The chimp's nose was scraped, bloody. The hunter's sisal rope had left abrasions on his waist. As I washed him with a rag, he gave me hickies on the neck. I cleaned the cage and hung a rope swing, and a veterinarian administered a tetanus shot, tested him for tuberculosis with an injection in the eyelid, and drew blood for the lab at Centre Pasteur to check for Simian Immunodeficiency Virus and other diseases. I sat on a bench near the cage, mixing water and Guigoz milk powder, then bottle-fed the chimp. The woman with hair extensions and tattered blue overalls smiled as she raked leaves from trees like the Israeli Army's beloved eucalypti, which shed their leaves faster than anyone could rake them. Two monkeys dashed toward the bananas atop Future's cage, and he leaned out from my arms to bark, "Ooh! Ooh!"

Our third morning in Yaoundé, I fed Future and rushed across town because my visa was expiring. I stopped at the cyber café. Karl Ammann had written me back. He was precisely the man whose help I needed; in the late eighties, Karl had *exposed* the bushmeat trade. He wrote, "I can help find a place for the chimp. We need to talk about your ideas. I'll be in Cameroon in three weeks." I banged out responses to urgent emails, made phone calls, and hurried out the door, not stopping to eat before I walked up a hill to Police Frontiere.

In a dirty unlit office jammed with stalagmites of paper sat three officials at three desks. One read a magazine. A fat man was sleeping, head down. The third man had glasses so thick, his eyes looked like tiny black stones. I explained that my tourist visa was about to expire and I said, "I want to stay and help Cameroon protect its wildlife."

The man in glasses motioned for my passport, then held up his hand. "Wait," he said and put the passport on the desk atop a stack of papers. He turned and made small talk with the man who wasn't sleeping. For twenty minutes I stood in front of him. Then he grabbed a plate of rice from the edge of his desk and began to eat.

"Should I go and come back?" I said, anxious to check on Future.

"I told you to wait."

Half an hour later, he opened my passport. "It's not possible," he said. "Take it."

"I just want to stay so that I can help."

"I told you, 'It's not possible.' Now go back to your country, white."

"Is there someone else I should talk to?"

He laughed and said, "Speak French, I don't understand you," and turned away.

Behind barbed wire at the World Bank, my meeting with an official was not in an office but a hallway. Though I wore a white dress shirt

I'd bought at Marché Melen, I was sure the man standing in front of me thought I was just a traveler. "Enforcement is the role of the state," he said. "I don't think you understand. NGOs *advise*. They are engaged in sensitization, capacity building, and workshops." My argument about what NGOs *ought* to do got me interrupted. "What you propose," the man said, "contradicts the nature of Development. Your idea will not work. Sorry."

Ignatius and I sat at the Nlongkak bar outside the cyber café. He was buttoned up perfectly in an ironed shirt and had more food in his whiskers. A meat man roasted beef on a grill. A car honked; I jerked awake and began to rock again in my wobbly metal chair. For three nights, I'd been too stressed to sleep.

"Consider this name," Ignatius said: "The Cameroon Association for the Promotion of Wildlife Law Application." His face puckered as he pronounced the acronym, causing the food finally to fall from his moustache.

"Ignatius, we're about action, not administration."

The man beside us was yelling at the waitress over his bill.

"Cameroon Wildlife Enforcement Organization," Ignatius said.

"What's that when we shorten it?"

He scribbled in his notebook and looked up. "CAWEO."

"No. No CEEWIF or APLOE or anything that sounds like a hand cream."

"Okay. Okay. Cameroon Organization for Wildlife."

"Catchy. But shortened—doesn't work."

"The Last of the Great Apes," Ignatius said without looking up.

I nearly leapt from my chair. "Fantastic! The Last Great Ape Organization."

Ignatius wrote in his notebook and grimaced. "Wait. That would be TLGAO."

"We'll make it LAGA."

"It doesn't work like that! You can't invent rules for initials! What about the O?"

At Police Frontiere, the man in glasses made me wait for an hour and then said, "Let me see if I can do something for you."

"I'm staying because I want to contribute. You can talk to the zoo's conservator. I'm going to work with the government. I *have* to extend the visa."

"Okay, okay. Wait."

He put the passport on the desk precisely where his hand fell on a stack of papers. The fat man, awake today, pointed to the man in glasses and said to me, "He is *hungry.*"

I stood before them for half an hour, completely ignored.

"Maybe I should come in the afternoon?" I said.

"Yes," said the man in glasses. "Come at one o'clock."

When I returned, my passport sat exactly where it had been, and the devil in glasses was gone. The fat man said, "He's out. He's not coming again today."

The woman in overalls swept near the lions, who had the scarred, fly-covered ears of street dogs, and I felt as dejected as they looked; nothing I did could stop Future from bashing his face against the cage. Monkeys charged and made off with one of our pineapples. The woman smiled, then turned away when she found me staring at her. Future intentionally spilled his milk on me, to say I wasn't giving him enough attention. I pulled off my wet shirt, and Future peeled a scab off one of my insect bites. The cleaning lady stepped forward. Future watched, didn't bark. She held out a letter and walked away with her broom.

"I liked you from the moment I saw you," she'd written among sketched flowers. "I really want to be with you. Love, Leocadie."

I walked over to her, with the chimp riding on my back and my shirt in my hand. Leocadie was too shy to lift her gaze from the grass. I said, "You're very nice. I'd really like to be your friend. But there's someone I love."

"You married?"

"No. But I am in love."

I had conversations going in nearly all the countries I'd ever been. Phone calls led to new contacts, which led to emails and meetings and more phone calls, an administrative atom bomb that just made me anxious. Shahar had designed a logo for LAGA, using an image of Future's face. Udi Ran at *Teva Hadvarim* was running an ad for volunteers and he'd offered my father the use of his lawyers for help establishing the organization. At the EU Program for the Environment, a Dutchman named Jaap said, "Your idea *could* be a solution, but it won't work. The government will never allow it."

"I know it's possible to extend the visa," I said to the man in glasses at Police Frontiere. "Who is the person who *signs* the visas? I have one day left."

The man in glasses stared at me with an indifference bordering on hatred.

The fat man cackled.

A beautiful woman arrived, dressed in black, her hair straightened. She was Nigerian. She said, "Do you have the visa for my brother? He came two days ago."

"We didn't look at his dossier," said the man in glasses. "Maybe— next week."

The fat man folded up his newspaper and pushed back his chair, the full measure of his girth revealed when he stepped around the desk toward her. He extended an arm and smiled, and his hand worked down the woman's back. He pressed his stomach against her and they moved up the hall, and I realized her beauty was the reason she'd been sent.

Future's face was oozing blood. I turned and whipped pineapple rind at the monkeys. "He cry cry cry every time when you go," Leocadie said. I told her I wasn't sleeping at all out of worry for him. She said she had a cousin with an empty apartment, and we rode in a taxi to the neighborhood of Mendong. At Carrefour Banane women sat in the grass, selling clusters of bananas and recycled Johnny Walker bottles filled with peanuts. Beyond the end of the paved road, on a hill offering views of jagged, forested mountains, Yaoundé looked like a clearing in the rainforest.

Leocadie climbed a set of stairs leading up from the clay road into a three-room apartment with a green concrete floor. The kitchen was but a counter with a metal sink, and all the windows were barred. "I have to rent it," I said to Leocadie's cousin Antoinette, who lived next door.

It was pitch black with the power out when I returned the next night carrying my backpack and Future. He rushed from room to empty room, his ahs and oohs echoing off the walls, the child in the shack across the road screaming as she was beaten by her mother. I sat on the floor in lantern light. The apartment was an empty concrete shell as cold as the forest floor, as inhospitable as Cameroon. I opened a disposable diaper, a gift from CWAF, and spread Future's legs to wrap him up. Within an hour the diaper was wet and it fell around his ankles like the saddle off Konjo and he jumped free and ran diaper-less into the next room. Then peed on the green floor. I called to Antoinette through the barred window, and she arrived in the darkness to give me a lesson on *cloth* diapers.

I was woken in the night by Future's head jerking, his eyeballs twitching against my chest. He woke and cried and sucked my neck until he fell back asleep on top of me. Ignatius had spoken of gorillas taught sign language, of Michael, an orphan from Cameroon, who'd signed the story of his mother's killing. I woke again when Future's pee seeped from his diaper to my underwear. At five A.M., he bounced on my crotch, sat on my stomach, and squeezed a pimple on my chest. I woke for good when he tried to yank off my nipples. I slogged to the balcony and mixed a cup of Nescafé for myself and a bottle of milk for Future. I felt beaten down and exhausted. With my visa now expired, I might be forced to leave Cameroon, and if I were allowed to stay, I lacked the money to pay for the apartment. Problems were mounting. The NGO application in Israel had been rejected. My first volunteer, Noa, who'd seen the flier at Planet Safari, was turned away at the Yaoundé airport for arriving without a visa, the frustration and stress of everything heightened by a chimp with emotional needs nearly as extreme as those of a child. Who would care for him if I was deported?

Weeks earlier, I'd wandered into a village near the park that CWAF ran, and the villagers hadn't so much as offered me a cup of water. In every village I've ever been to, such an omission would have been unthinkable. The possibility was real here that I would fail to help Future, that saving him from the hunter would amount to nothing, that the supposed ideals that had led me to Cameroon would be crushed by a place both vicious and broken—as I struggled not to drown in the problems I sought to repair.

I was late returning to Mendong. I picked Future up from Antoinette's. Her daughter, off from school, had been babysitting. In the night, the older sister in the shack across the street had died in a failed abortion performed in secret with knitting needles. Antoinette, a nurse, had rushed over when they woke her but she hadn't been able to stop the bleeding.

The power was out and I jammed a candle into an empty bottle, lit it. I pulled off my reeking black shirt, and a knock echoed into the empty house. I turned the key in the metal door, figuring it would be Antoinette, hoping she'd have food. But it was Leocadie. She wore an old-fashioned dress and held out a gift of two plates, a fork, and a big red spoon. She put them in the kitchen. "Did you eat, Ofir? You need to eat." And she inspected the living room. "I need to wash this floor." She picked up a saucepan in the kitchen and scrubbed.

"Stop, it's okay." I took her hand and we sat with Future before us, watching.

"Leocadie, you're a good person."

She lowered her head and looked up at me. She was as kind as Elizabeth, who on the plateau overlooking Lake Turkana had sung to me as she'd sung to her siblings. Leocadie reached out and tucked my hair behind my ear.

"You're tired," she said. "You look too tired."

"Leocadie, I can't. I'm just going to hurt you."

But I didn't say it loud enough to mean anything. We stood and moved toward the bedroom, my hand working down her back. I closed the door and sat beside her on the bed frame. Leocadie looked down. As I reached over and unzipped her dress, she jerked with my touch, giggled, and whispered, "Sorry. Go on." Future whimpered outside the door. I reached out to touch Leocadie again, and the bed frame broke loose at a joint and we crashed half a meter to the floor. As I fixed the bed, my mind went back to young Elizabeth, whom I never considered touching. Leocadie sat down and didn't move. I shimmied her dress above her waist, and she jerked, giggled, and whispered, "Sorry. Continue." It was obvious she was just trying to please me. I couldn't look at Leocadie's eyes. *Man is nobler than the forces that destroy him.* I knew I was ugly when I pulled off her dress and unzipped my pants.

AFRICA'S MOST DANGEROUS JOURNALIST

In Mendong, the pipes were waterless for days and I wouldn't have been dirtier lying in goat dung. The season's first rain pinged on tin roofs and swept over the house, blowing a box of sugar cubes out of the windowsill and into the kitchen sink. I shuttered the windows, grabbed a towel and a bar of soap and stripped to my boxers, and I descended the stairs in the downpour. The steep clay road was soon a raging red river of mud. I held my breath and stepped into the cold cascade pouring out of the gutter, arcing down some eight meters from my roof to the road. I closed my eyes as the water hit my shoulders and back. I was nearly overwhelmed by the gifts I'd received from Africa, gifts for which I was too often unworthy. Africa had left me with the untouchable, irrational hope that no cause worth saving was lost. I'd tried to repay the kindness of villagers on my journeys by dancing in village parties and wielding a hoe in the fields and teaching science at ramshackle schools. In writing about war zones, I'd tried to share the virtue that had arisen from suffering. It was time now for far more. And far more, eventually, than just animals. It was time to reciprocate the generosity of the hundreds of families who'd hosted me, who'd shared their lives and made me a member of their communities, who'd come to me without walls or expectations, who'd given up their beds and fed me from their pots with food they'd grown themselves.

The steam of rainwater washed the soap off my back. I dashed up to the kitchen and carried down the plastic garbage can I'd bought for storing water. Half a minute after the storm passed, the flow from the gutter was just a drip. I lugged the half-full garbage can back to the kitchen, swiveling it up a step at a time and pouring out what I'd been too ambitious to lift. The skepticism I'd heard about my plan and the seeming impossibility of collaborating with the Cameroonian government had strengthened my resolve. I'd stopped looking for signals from the environment that I would succeed and started focusing on targets.

Future was waiting when I opened the door, and he shadowed the heavy trashcan I dragged inside, then determined it wasn't a threat and shuttled through the flat, opening windows. Newly confident, Future no longer needed to be held at all times. He charged a giant beetle and flicked it into the wall. I sat at the coffee table to work on LAGA's budget. Future, more interested in my hair now that it was growing long, combed his fingers through it. He cleaned beneath my fingernails, peeled dry skin from the pads of my feet, put his finger in my mouth when I yawned—an act of trust. Then turned his back to be groomed.

Ignatius brought a retired military adjutant named Christopher to Mendong. He was heavy of breath and as hulking as the Rock Man from *The Never-Ending Story*. One look at Future in the living room and Christopher put his hands over his head, shouted, and backed away through the door. When he finally stepped forward again, he mumbled, "Good morning, sir. Pleased to meet you, sir." He repeated nearly everything I said, which doubled the length of the interview.

"Ignatius, this won't work," I whispered when Christopher descended to the road. "We need *young* men. He's *old*."

"Ofir, that's his advantage. No one will suspect he's working undercover."

At Ignatius's office, a small old man cruised in with his shoulders swinging as though he'd just dined with a king. The office was narrower than the front seat of a car and we had to pull the table out so

Vincent could squeeze through to a chair. Vincent Gudmia Mfonfu, an Anglophone, was the journalist for MINEF. He was nearing retirement but he disdained his boss, who played favorites, who'd adopted Hinduism, and who burned incense in her office and put up an Ohm sign people took to be witchcraft.

"Okay, Vincent," I said, "Ignatius tells me you're talented. But we have to build a team of journalists. We need to get stories into newspapers, onto the radio and TV, so we can broadcast our news after we make arrests."

"You don't need a team. I can do it all."

"Alone? That's not possible."

He shrugged.

"Vincent, we need half a dozen people. I'm talking about getting spots into the press every day!"

"Yes. So I can give you my CV when we're together again. I'll show you some articles I wrote." He leaned back in his chair and flashed the wry smile of a prankster.

"Vincent, I know Ignatius told you, but I want to emphasize that we have *no* money."

He nodded.

It was too hot to close the door of the office, and outside a man was repairing a tape deck playing music at triple speed.

"So explain more about how you want the organization to run," Vincent said.

"Okay. LAGA is focused on results and on measuring them. How many prosecutions. How many media pieces published. How many investigations. The ratio of investigations to arrests. If we fail, let the donors and the public kick us out. If we succeed, we may help more than wildlife. By embarrassing the corrupt development system and setting a new standard for what counts as work, we might help the system to change. NGOs, if they measure anything but the number of jeeps they give away, have been in the business of measuring *the problem*. Whether it's health, poverty, conservation, it's all the same. In the conservation business, they measure how many animals have died, how much bushmeat is moving. When the trend is positive, NGOs take credit for the success and ask for more money. When the trend is negative, they use it as proof that they are even more needed and they ask for more money. They act like the money given to them is theirs. But it's not. Billions of taxpayer dollars and donations from well-meaning people have been thrown into conservation for elephants and apes, but the race to extinction *still* accelerates every year."

Yaoundé had police roadblocks like some towns had traffic lights. With the risk high that my expired visa would be discovered on a random taxi ride, contacts in the Israeli community put me in touch with a Cameroonian military officer; Cameroon's presidential guard was trained by the Israeli Army. The officer told me, "You won't solve your visa problem at Police Frontiere. We'll do something else." We went together to an immigration office in a different part of Yaoundé, where I paid the standard fee for a resident permit that gave me the right to stay in Cameroon for two years.

Nearly every dollar I had I spent on Future's milk powder, leaving me with barely enough money to fry one plantain and an egg for dinner. In town for lunch I ate either a tiny Mambo chocolate bar or *puff-puff* donuts and beans. The NGO's application was approved in Israel, but only after Dad and Udi Ran drafted a letter stating that "human monkey" was the *only* Hebrew translation for ape; the director of charities was an ultra-orthodox Jew and he saw the NGO's name as blasphemous. Karl Ammann wrote his contacts, hoping to build enthusiasm for my project. David, who I'd been emailing almost daily, wrote from Ghana that in a small village he'd met a man who claimed to be 140 years old. David was about to cross Nigeria to come and help.

I ended my first two interviews with policemen the instant they asked about money. The third interview was with a clean-shaven and happy man named Julius, a policeman who lived near Marché Melen. Julius wore an olive green uniform with the sleeves rolled back to the elbows, and he greeted me in the doorway of Ignatius's office with his beautiful wife, Pierra. Though slender, Julius carried himself in a way that made him seem threateningly strong. Here was a man who could lift the Wedding Stone.

"In our country, many policemen use their jobs to harass people," Julius said after we sat at the table. "Most have no values. My education and my faith would never allow me to do such things."

"You know wildlife law is not enforced," I said.

"It's more than wildlife law, Mr. Ofir, let me tell you. I caught a white man in his car with a twelve-year-old Cameroonian girl. He was touching her. In the station, she talked and told everything. She was just a small girl. No question, the man needed to be behind bars. Then there were a few phone calls to my chief. My chief released the man, just let him go."

"Julius, if I say tomorrow that we have to storm a market and arrest two people and get them to the station, are you able to do it?"

He didn't break eye contact. "Yes. No problem."

I woke at dawn and planted my feet on the floor—into two centimeters of water. I sloshed into the bathroom and closed the faucet I'd unwittingly left open while the pipes were dry. Back on the bed, too tired to deal with the flood, I slapped Future's hand away when he tried to peel the scar off my neck. He did a somersault and lay, as I was, hands behind his head. I finally squeegeed the water out through the second bedroom and off the balcony.

I left Future at Antoinette's and skated down the muddy hill to Carrefour Banane and caught a shared taxi. Miles of winding neighborhoods, rattling with cars, led inward to the city center. Outside the post office was a secondary market of magazines stolen from the mail. There was an abandoned tall shell of a building with "Vote Biya" scrawled on its top floor. In power since 1982, Paul Biya moved in Yaoundé under protection of snipers.

I arrived at Ignatius's office. Four days after our first meeting, Vincent strolled in with nothing in his hands but a Cameroonian newspaper. He flipped the paper onto the table, the *Herald*, opened to an article adorned with a photograph of a mandrill. The headline read, "New NGO to Enforce Law."

Vincent tried to conceal a smile.

"An Israel-based organization," said the article, "The Last Great Ape (LAGA), is intensifying law enforcement in the country. The director of LAGA, Ofir Drori, said, 'In Cameroon there has never been a prosecution for wildlife crime. Without decisive action . . .'"

Vincent's laughter poured out of him.

"Shit. I can't believe it. Vincent, I mean, were you interviewing me? You were interviewing me! The NGO is not even registered yet in Cameroon. There's a picture of the minister in the next article." My panic eased, but just slightly. "I have to careful with you, Vincent. I'm impressed. You're the most dangerous journalist in Africa."

THE NEW TEAM

My taxi swung left at Carrefour Banane. Women sat on buckets by the road, hawking peanuts and bananas. Fish ladies grilled mackerel. The field around the elementary school had been cut in my two days away, likely by machete-wielding students. I'd traveled to Abong-Mbang to get Kalebass's advice, to ask him to work as an investigator for LAGA, and to give him back the 10,000 francs he'd gambled on.

A last, lone tree rose like an antenna from the ridge above my house, hinting at the height of the old forest. As I stuck my nose out the window and smelled the wet grass, I wondered whether Kakuya, Isaac's old father, was still alive. Corn was coming up along the tarmac's edge. The belly of my cab scraped through a muddy pothole, and I told the driver, "Move left; that next one's deep." We passed a bar run by a giantess who served soup too spicy to be edible, too spicy to let the mouth know in what week it had been cooked.

"Stop here," I said to the driver at the pavement's end. "You'll get stuck climbing up to my place." I wiggled out of the cab.

"Hey, 'Mr. Follow Follow!' I come with greetings from the land of Fela."

"I can't believe it! David, I was sure you'd be stuck in the mud for a week."

He'd called two mornings prior from Lagos.

"What mud? I took a boat."

"How did you find me? We don't have street numbers. We hardly have streets."

"Finding a *mzungu* in Mendong? Not exactly my toughest mission."

We walked to Carrefour Banane and ordered mackerel from a woman grilling on a metal grate set over a wheel drum. "No *pepe* but lots of green sauce," I told the fish lady. David and I toasted and clinked our Cokes. I said, "Man, I need you here."

"Yesterday I wasn't sure I'd make it. The boat from Oron to Idenau— if we took it a hundred times, we'd die at least once. The Nigerians knew their rowboat was a drowning machine. They were so protective of me, they made me buy and inflate a tire tube. I rode all the way across the Gulf of Guinea with a tire tube around my waist.

"There were storms that were black, end-of-the-world black. The engine of our boat kept stalling. Huge waves. Nigerian patrols kept stopping us in the middle of the ocean. One soldier had an Uzi and a helmet that kept slipping over his face. He put his foot on our boat and stared at me with no hint of anything happening in his brain. I thought, If you could keep a gun away from one man out of a million, here's your guy. His captain said to me, 'Oibo, can you swim?' You know Fela's people—they took care of me and stopped the soldiers from giving me trouble. But they weren't much help to the Cameroonians, who had to empty their pockets paying bribes to boats full of soldiers. 'Pay or turn back.' Once we reached Cameroonian waters, it all evened out and the Cameroonian soldiers emptied the pockets of the Nigerians."

I ripped the fins off my fish.

"So tell me the real stuff," David said. "How is it here?"

"Daud. In Nigeria, you know, a cab driver can invite you to his house for dinner. Dar es Salaam, we walked half a block for bread and got greetings from a dozen people on the way. Here? You say hello to a child and she ignores you. Can you imagine this? Even in Liberia I had fun playing with children. Four days in Cameroon and I knew this place was different from any country I'd ever entered. It's like there's nothing holding the people together. The breakdown feels complete, like we could be in Kenya but fifty years in the future with no tradition left. War or no war, this is the worst place I've been in Africa. Maybe that's why I'm here."

Four volunteers arrived—Dan, Hadar, Ravit, and Tom—Israelis inspired by Future's story to purchase plane tickets and leave their lives behind. I promised myself that I would harness their optimism and ignite in them the urge for action. They'd come hoping to make a difference, and I wanted to help them prove to themselves that they could.

I'd rented Antoinette's house with my father's help, and she'd moved her family into the two-room apartment beneath my flat. The volunteers and I sat for our first morning meeting at the long wood table in Antoinette's living room. Dan's feet were propped on the table, dreadlocks bundled in his hand. Hadar had arrived from the airport wearing knee-high leather boots and dragging suitcases through the mud. Tom, within minutes of first reaching Mendong, had picked up Dan's guitar and started singing. There was a different energy in each one of them.

"Our primary goal is to bring the NGO into existence," I said, "while working toward the first prosecution. We'll move simultaneously on many fronts, developing strategies for investigations and operations, identifying sources of funding, linking up with NGOs and institutions that can help us politically and help us gain legitimacy for what we are about to do. We'll be training personnel as we build our team."

Future, on my back, leaned around and took my finger, sucked it for a second, then tossed it aside.

"Short term," I said, "read all the information in the packets I've given you. Educate yourselves about enforcement. Think about initiatives of your own. As you grow into your roles, I want to become less essential to LAGA's existence." As this last phrase left my mouth, I knew I didn't fully believe it.

"One project we need to begin immediately is to turn this house into our headquarters. We need to organize it, paint the inside, put our name on the outer wall."

"Yeah, man," Dan said. "Maybe we can get plants in here to soften up the house. You know, man, it's totally concrete."

"Good. Write it down."

Tom tapped his pen on the table. "I'll start working on ideas for the legal unit."

"Good. Write it down. I want to stress that you have the space to act on your own, so long as you coordinate your work with the group. You have the space to be yourself within the work. And you have the space to make mistakes—even costly ones—so long as your commitment is total. Understand?"

I met Karl Ammann in Mont Febé. He locked his hotel room door after I stepped inside. "I can't afford to be in Cameroon more than a day or two," Karl said. "I'm not wanted in this country." He was Swiss, in his late forties, and he was squinting at me, his bangs messy on his forehead. "This government is completely dysfunctional. NGOs are dysfunctional. It's all a big joke. I'm just coming from Central African Republic. The shiny NGO 4×4s there are used to *transport* elephant meat. We documented all of this." A too-short moustache gave Karl's mouth the appearance of never being closed. "Ofir, you're an outsider. That's why I want to support what you're doing. But you know the NGOs will never want you to succeed. NGOs diffuse the pressure of actually doing anything to fix a problem by saying they can take care of it. It's feel-good conservation at its best. Band-Aids for cancer patients. These useless NGOs are worse than corrupt governments."

Facing Karl's criticism and seeking to improve its image, CIB, a logging company in northern Congo, had created a partnership with WCS. Karl sent an undercover investigator to measure the progress of the collaboration. The investigator started his fieldwork by filming employees in the logging company workshop who were manufacturing bullets to kill elephants.

"When the crazy war started in DRC," Karl said, "the expats fled and flew away. The NGOs were the first to disappear, leaving behind all the people they were paid to help. As long as they can play in their swimming pools, everything is great. The only ones left are the missionaries. At least those people care about what they're doing." Karl was nearly out of breath. "Ofir, I don't have a solution for your chimp. I hope at some point one of the shelters here will take it. If it were a gorilla, everyone would jump for it; it's all about the politics of their funding. There's an Israeli named Bill Clark who does a lot for wildlife law enforcement. He works with Interpol and he can help you." Karl scanned a draft of the program I'd written. "You need to give me a clearer budget so I can get you funding. There's so much money in conservation—millions completely wasted. You'd expect there'd be a small amount to get the bloody law enforced."

So thrilled was I after the meeting that I ran the two kilometers to Bastos.

A few days later, I was sick with malaria for perhaps the fortieth time. Future counter-attacked the toilet, barking "Ooh! Ooh!" as I vomited into it. I wiped my mouth and stepped to the sink, spit. Future scaled my leg to my shoulder and continued his oral assault on the toilet, as if it had caused my illness.

"You all right?" David said and handed me a Coke.

I shrugged, lowered a tied tie over my head. A friend at the British High Commission had loaned me a suit, and at an outdoor market I'd bartered for loafers that felt as flimsy as ballet shoes after years of stomping around in hiking boots. We were following Vincent's roadmap for building a relationship with the government. "Shine your shoes," he'd said. "It's the first thing they'll look at when we enter MINEF. And shave very well. It's all part of the French way."

I left Future with the Chadian houseworker of Antoinette, whom I'd hired to be his caretaker. I trudged through the heat to Carrefour Banane and scraped galoshes of red mud off my loafers before climbing into a shared taxi. My nausea swelled with the swerves of the cab as we motored through Yaoundé. Fearing my fever was about to spike, I wrote thoughts in a notebook to distract myself, and the driver spun around and pointed at my pen. He said, "Are you spying on me?"

Across from the Hilton was MINEF's modern headquarters, eighteen stories of metal and glass that dwarfed nearby government buildings with proof of the importance of logging in the national economy. Vincent stood at the entrance of the monolith with a newspaper under his arm. "Ofi, you have to take out the earrings," he said. "Remember to address the Minister as 'Your Excellency' and say it at the beginning of any response to him. First, we pass through the protocol."

"What's the protocol?" I said, shivering from the malaria.

"No. The protocol is the man who *manages* the meetings of the minister. It's quite French. You'll see."

We rode the elevator up into the nerve center that had sired all the MINEF outposts with empty beer bottles and sleeping men. Vincent led me into a luxurious air-conditioned office where a man in a dark suit greeted us and said, "The minister will be with you shortly." Vincent led me to a couch and whispered, "Ofi, our main goal with the government is not to make mistakes. At all costs we must avoid a *total no* from the minister. That would be a very quick ending for us." My aching stomach felt like it was digesting flakes off a rusted pipe.

"The minister will receive you now," the protocol said. "You will wait until I announce you. You will shake the hand of the minister, you first, he second. Do not speak to His Excellency unless he addresses you. Be brief. His Excellency is very busy, and still has to appear in the National Assembly later today. You enter first, he second."

Sylvester Naah Ondoa, MINEF's minister, oversaw the largest stream of revenue in Cameroon after petroleum. He waved us to his fine couches as he might shoo flies.

"Thank you, Your Excellency," I said in English.

"Yes." He nodded, looked at the ceiling and yawned.

I leaned forward and spoke loudly to break his indifference.

The minister folded his hands together. He said, "Collaboration is very important. My ministry regards the protection of wildlife as an extremely important ingredient in the protection of the environment and forests." He looked over his shoulder for five seconds. "As you well know, in 1999 I convened an international meeting resulting in the Yaoundé Declaration. The international community lauded us for our commitment to biodiversity, conservation, and the sustainable management of forest ecosystems. My twelve points are well known to have advanced the entire sub-region, and we have seen tremendous improvement in building up the protection of our forests.

"Concerning this collaboration," the minister said, "you can meet with the director of wildlife on the needs of the ministry."

Future hunted shoes under the table at the morning meeting, then climbed up behind Hadar to eat her hair. A video camera was running; I was documenting the experience of the volunteers. I said, "It's now ten after seven. We meet at seven o'clock sharp. Understand?"

"We came to Cameroon because we want to help," said Hadar, who wore a black turtleneck. "It's okay if we don't wake up at seven."

Her knee-high leather boots sat against the living room wall.

"This is not summer camp," I said. "Conditions in this country demand that we work day and night. In the procedures of work—waking up, meeting each morning, creating and completing missions and meeting again at the end of each day—there is only *my* way. In the *work*, you have room to find your own way."

Ever so slightly Hadar shook her head. Before her arrival, she'd met my father in Tel Aviv, designed our letterhead, and organized a meeting for the incoming volunteers. Tom was tapping his pencil on the table. Ravit sat slumped in her chair. Arms wheeling, Future skated across the floor on his diapered ass.

"Shouldn't we use disposable diapers for Future?" Hadar said. "They're cleaner."

"What? Who cares if they're cleaner?" I said. "We're not buying expensive diapers for a chimpanzee when our neighbors have to use cloth diapers for their *babies*."

"Future has a rash the way it is now," she said. "The diapers don't cost so much. We may even get them for free; Ravit thinks she can get them donated."

"Future is not wearing disposable diapers. End of discussion."

Vincent and I rode the elevator up into MINEF's tower a few days after our meeting with the minister. I thought of the street boys I'd once taken to the roof of Planet Safari. When the elevator shook loose from the ground floor, the boys had lunged for the walls. Then laughed as we'd climbed.

The seventeenth floor of MINEF gave views of the Hilton and part of the prime minister's office in the Stars Building, which was shaped like an hourglass. Off to the left was the other world, the rusted tin roofs of markets and poor neighborhoods.

"Ahh, this is great," said Denis Koulagna, director of wildlife.

Vincent sat beside me and crossed his legs.

"The ministry welcomes collaboration with NGOs. We really lack the capacity to carry out all the activities of the ministry. Partnerships are very important to us. You need to bring all your files to me so we can start the process of passing through different departments. It will be better if you concentrate on giving us the information you gather so that we, here in MINEF, can use it to carry out operations in the field."

I looked at Vincent and swallowed against the reality that Koulagna had just announced his intention to minimize our role. I was about to state that in the current environment information was plentiful but enforcement was nonexistent when Vincent's hand rose from his lap. He said, "Director, we will return with a full program."

Vincent stood, shook Koulagna's hand and ushered me out.

"Ofi, of course he's trying to minimize us," Vincent said in the hallway. "When the minister sent us here, Koulagna probably assumed he had a free hand to block us. Remember, no mistakes. If he won't approve our program, we go back to the minister."

Future darted out of the kitchen of Antoinette's house and tried to stick his finger into an electrical socket. "Future, no!" He'd been stealing the toys of Antoinette's children. "Tom, with the legal unit, do you have comments on improving procedures?"

"I didn't read the packet."

Dan was inspecting his dreadlocks, Ravit gazing at the wall.

"Listen," I said, checking my anger, "we're not here to do normal work."

"Hey, man, it's cool," Dan said. "We'll get up to speed. All of us, man."

The day Dan told me he was going to get paint for the house, I'd found him near Carrefour Banane playing checkers in a bar.

"Okay. Another question," I said. "We're going to save more orphaned apes, and the shelters don't have space for them. Do you think we should consider eventually having our own shelter? Thoughts?"

Silence. No one even moved.

"Hadar," I said, "I'd like you to stay here this morning and teach Future's caretaker more of what you know about chimps. Ravit and Tom can continue to work on the Internet, searching for sister NGOs, finding African countries with functional enforcement. Let's gather background material from the government on processes concerning the law. And all of you should start writing about your experiences."

Silence.

Tom cleaned a fingernail. Hadar yawned. They reacted as if I'd been speaking broken Amharic or said nothing at all. Had I insulted them by working on my own during the day, by keeping to myself at night? In the blank stares of the team was a taste of the old doubt I'd felt each time I returned to Israel, that I wasn't as special as I believed. They didn't like me; that was clear. I couldn't believe it had happened in just ten days.

The next evening when I returned from town, Dan was lounging in one of the crescent moon curves of the outer wall of Antoinette's house, strumming his guitar. Tom was drinking beer. And Future was sucking on a lollipop.

"I don't want you to pay people to wash your clothes," I said at a meeting.

"But we help them by giving them money," Tom said.

"It creates a gap between you and everyone else who lives here."

"You're too strict," Hadar said in a soft voice. "We don't have to wash our own clothes to save apes."

"Does someone in Israel wash your clothes for you when you're twenty-two?"

"My mom," Tom said and laughed.

"Maybe you forgot," said Hadar, "but in Israel we have washing machines."

FUTURE NEAR DEATH

"Come quick, boy, it's a chimp," Kalebass said. "You have to take him fast."

David and I caught the next van to Abong-Mbang and arrived after dark. My frustration that Kalebass had given to the hunter a symbolic amount of $10 was overwhelmed by how the chimp was actually a baby gorilla. I snuck him into our hotel room under a towel, and we waited as Kalebass searched for transport back to Yaoundé. The gorilla's black face shined in the light of the overhead bulb. He watched us as we watched him. To sit with the tiny ape was to be in the presence of a mind that knew another world. He carried within him the quiet of forest life, a calmness that made Future seem epileptic.

David walked to the bathroom. He'd doctored the torn elbows of his blue dress shirt with electrical tape. He'd told me that when he returned to the U.S. he might move to an Indian reservation to write and teach.

The gorilla whimpered and moved off after David on his fists.

"Come here, Life," I said and grabbed a milk-filled Coke bottle.

David sighed. "We don't have to call him 'Life.' We're saving an orphan gorilla, for Christ's sake. Let's call him Jack like Kalebass does."

Twenty-four hours later, we found a vehicle and stuffed the ape, screaming, into a box, then taped it closed. David dumped one of Jack's turds out of his boot and followed me downstairs. In the front seat of a battered sedan sat the driver and a man in a coat. Jack screeched in the box inside the closed trunk. The dented *clandeau* was of a kind that plied the dirt tracks between villages, often carrying a bushmeat buyer who returned to town with a trunk full of smoked animals.

The *chef du poste* at MINEF had refused to provide us documentation to transport the gorilla. He'd said, "What's in it for me?" So David and I were committing the same crime LAGA was meant to stop: possession of an endangered species. With a dozen roadblocks separating us from Yaoundé, we were vulnerable to all the policemen and MINEF officials who knew that badgering foreigners, especially those dumb enough to move contraband, was a lucrative trade. Worse, if we were caught, the ministry might use it as an excuse to end my ever-tenuous project in Cameroon.

The taxi couldn't idle, and the engine stalled a few meters from the hotel. The screams of the baby gorilla filled the silence.

"Don't let the engine die," David said in French. "Keep it running."

The driver revved the engine, revved it again.

Half an hour into the darkness outside town, the road was blocked by a jackknifed rig. Three dozen logging trucks idled in smoky light along one side of the road, all loaded with massive trees. Silhouetted drivers prowled between trucks with flashlights, a seedy scene of industry on a clay road through the forest. Our driver revved the engine again and again to keep it from stalling and to mask Jack's screams. The man in the passenger seat in the coat shifted anxiously, glanced over his shoulder at us, his nervousness that of someone contemplating a crime.

"Should we head back to town and try to move in the morning?" David said.

I didn't respond.

"I'm covered in Jack's scabies," he said, itching his face.

After an hour we were moving again and ahead of the logging trucks, our dim headlights barely able to tunnel into the darkness as we rattled and rocked like a horse-drawn cart pushed down a mountainside. My head wobbled with exhaustion. I fell asleep, woke; David was the only friend I would have allowed myself to drift off beside in such a moment. I shot awake. The man in the passenger seat swung around to look at us.

"Don't fight sleep," David said. "I can stay awake all night. But I'm afraid if we both pass out we'll end up getting robbed and left somewhere in the trees."

The driver revved the engine and held two cigarettes out the window as we rolled up to a roadblock. The policeman grabbed the cigarettes and waved us through, and a boy dragged nail-studded boards from the road. My head snapped back, and I woke. The men in the front seat were speaking their tribal language. The driver handed cigarettes to the policeman at the next roadblock so there would be no questions. I pulled my camera into my lap, and the man in the passenger seat spun around with a flashlight and shined it on my hands.

"Damn," David whispered. "I should have known; *he* is the one afraid of *us*." *

Jack was no longer screaming when the lights of the dashboard and the headlights died. The car coasted to a stop. We opened the doors and stood in the road, the silence like that of a world missing electricity. I could just see David's profile in the starlight as we pushed the taxi through the mud. We laughed, because there was little else to do.

"Amen," I said, when the driver got the engine started.

"Are you a Christian?" said the passenger in English.

The car was shaking.

"Are you a Christian?" he said a second time.

David sang, "*It is a known fact that for many thousand years . . .*"

We stalled again, got stuck in the mud, stalled a third time. A flat tire, added to battery failure, made plain we weren't reaching Yaoundé in the *clandeau*. Marooned in the dark, we waited until the logging trucks blocked by the jackknifed rig finally caught up. A

---

* David learned the next year that the man had a crowbar hidden up the sleeve of his coat.

public minivan appeared, which we had little choice but to join. David loaded the box into the rear hatchback, and we squeezed into the van, jammed with twenty-two passengers. The mass of bodies was a moving universe of potential bribes and the very reason we'd avoided public transport. A cry rose over the rumble of the van—one of the goats roped to the bus roof, I hoped, and not Jack struggling for air.

Policemen at roadblocks stopped us throughout the night. No one opened the hatchback or inspected the box. Jack had gone silent.

Near the Nkoabang checkpoint on Yaoundé's eastern edge, a stout middle-aged policeman snatched the documents of the driver and said, "You're from Central African Republic? You don't have proper ID. Go into the station." He checked the ID of the next man and said, "This isn't even you. Follow the driver. I'll deal with you later."

"Where's your vaccination card?" he said to me.

"I don't have it."

"10,000 francs."

"I'm not paying you anything."

"Fine. Go into the station."

I walked around the van and stopped and remembered Jack. I pulled 10,000 francs from my pocket and handed it over, amazed that I had. David walked to the rear of the van to fetch his vaccination card from his backpack, which sat beside Jack's box. David got his card and closed the hatchback, but it banged against the broken latch, inches from the gorilla, and the door flew open. A man slammed it down three times, then left it up with the box in view, grabbed a wrench and went at the latch like a man chopping wood. The officer walked around holding a flashlight, the box with its large holes a meter from his hand. I thought, If you're still alive, Jack, please, don't scream now.

David stepped in front of the policeman and said, "My friend, you're working too late. This is no time to be in your shoes when you should be in bed with your wife."

The policeman thumbed through David's passport. "It can be difficult."

The driver was back from the station, slamming the hatchback, the box visible, then not, then visible again. The policeman scoped the vaccination card, and David said, "You can see I've had so many shots I've been emptying my pockets to keep too many doctors in business."

The policeman traced his finger over a page, shined his light at the truck.

"Too many shots," David said.

The policeman handed him the documents, and the driver got the door closed.

Near sunrise, we reached Mendong and climbed on foot to the house. We were dragging, our faces gritty with dust. Jack was still warm but hadn't moved when David touched him through a hole in the box. The gorilla had been closed up more than eight hours when we unlocked my front door.

I set the box on my coffee table, pulled at the tape, yanked it.

"I'm actually stalling a bit," I said and then looked up. "If something is wrong, just remember, we tried our best."

I pulled back the cardboard flaps and found Jack looking up at me. I lifted him, took him in my hands, and his head fell backwards. When I got him to my chest, he turned and looked at David, and our relief escaped as laughter.

Just after dawn, David and I walked next door to Antoinette's house to wait for the volunteers to wake. At the foot of the long wood table, David snapped a video camera to a tripod. I was excited to reenergize the team with the surprise of Jack, to connect the volunteers again to the reason they'd come to Central Africa. Two new volunteers had joined before Kalebass' call: Natalie, an Israeli, and her German boy-friend, Jens. Dan was still sleeping; I'd told him he could not continue to work with LAGA.

I sat at the head of the table. Hidden under a blanket and holding me was the baby gorilla. Tom woke and took a chair, his notebook in front of him. Hadar sat to my left, her fingernails painted black. I said, "In Abong-Mbang I thought I was going to save a baby chimp, but I got a surprise." I pulled back the blanket to reveal Jack.

The sublime animal turned his head and measured the faces around him. Natalie, chin in hand, looked away. Tom didn't react. No one spoke or lifted a hand.

"We had some checkpoints," I said, filling the silence. "It was a bit scary. Our driver didn't have the correct identity card. The policeman took him aside and told him, '60,000.' He gave the price. That's how it is."

Jens, who looked like an Amish carpenter, said, "fifty thousand is fifty dollars?"

"It's one hundred dollars," I said.

Only Hadar reached out to touch Jack. The other volunteers sat frozen.

The silence at the table was the sound of failure.

I glanced at David, whose expression told me what I didn't want to admit: when it came to the volunteers, there was no team at all.

"The gorilla will need vaccinations," I said to say something. "His belly is very swollen. I think he has worms. But generally I think he's okay. His stool is fine."

"He has worms?" Hadar said. "That means that he needs to have the same surgery Michelle did?"

"What?"

"In the zoo, remember?"

"That was not worms. That was a tumor."

"Oh, okay."

David turned off the camera and walked out of the house.

I closed my eyes and thought of Mom reading to me as a child the only book about a boy with my name. It was called *Hot Corn*. In the story, Ofir rallied neighborhood kids while beating a drum and shouting "Hot corn! Hot corn!" As the crowd followed him and grew, kids sang, "Hot corn! We're going to have hot corn." But Ofir had no hot corn to give; he'd just thought it was a great idea. "Boo, Ofir, bad boy! Where is the corn?" And the children ostracized him. Each time my mother read me the story, she skipped the part where Ofir had no hot corn. She even crossed through those pages with a pen to ensure no babysitters read them to me.

"The volunteers have completely disengaged," I said to David. "With Jack, they weren't connected to him or me. We're gone two days and it's so obvious. They think I'm an asshole."

"No. To see this magnificent creature and not move their elbows off the table—"

"Had I brought him on the second day, it would have been different."

"They had Future on the second day," David said. "A gorilla—Jack is majestic. He's sitting at the breakfast table and how do they respond? They don't."

"Listen, they're in a country they don't like. Jens doesn't even know the currency—"

"Ofir, I'm just talking about passion."

"But if their passion for working with me was destroyed—"

"They just got here. And no offense, but I'm sure that if they really had passion, you couldn't just crush it in two weeks."

"David, you're looking at it as proof they were never LAGA material, that they shouldn't have been here to begin with."

"While you're building things, the theoretical volunteer isn't very valuable."

"I told you I've been battling the anger I felt for them," I said. "Anger they didn't share my commitment. But listening to you now, I realize how it's completely my fault. Their emails made me so optimistic. One story of a baby chimp led to six plane tickets, six people sponsoring themselves. I thought they were already connected to the cause. But I didn't connect them to anything, like when I traveled to Kenya with Ofer. I never should have brought six volunteers at once. I didn't give positive feedback. I wasn't sensitive. Natalie and Jens just shut down; I overwhelmed them in forty-eight hours."

"You're making this about you, and it's not," he said. "I don't agree they're activists in non-activists' clothes. Dan's a great guy but he was never going to fight at your side. When you said you didn't want him smoking pot, he said okay, he'd just do it elsewhere. Hadar got out of the taxi with a suitcase full of designer shoes! Jens, a fighter? Are you kidding?"

"Look, poor soldiers are a reflection of their officer. I could have sent any one of them to a village and given them a small challenge, told them to teach something to kids for a week. To work in the fields. Sleep in a hut. They would have come back changed; you know the power this continent has to do that to people. I don't care how lost someone is, how closed off. It may sound irrational and I haven't figured out exactly how, but you just have to find a way to put a match in someone's hand."

Sheri Speede, an American veterinarian who ran a small sanctuary near Belabo, had been telling me that by keeping Future I risked his being unable to re-assimilate into a family of chimps. I'd tried my best to keep him wild, as my mother would have done. But Sheri didn't like that he often imitated me by walking on two legs. I said, "Sheri, so you have a spot for him now. Okay. But there are so many chimps in shelters. Future is important as an ambassador. Look how many volunteers he brought here. We can rescue other apes to fill the space you have. I want his life to mean something."

"We've all been through this, Ofir," she said. "I know he's your baby. But think about it: if you love him, he needs to be with chimps, not humans. And in a few years we may even be able to integrate him back into the forest."

Sheri had a black belt in karate and she'd married a Cameroonian man. Their daughter, who'd grown up at the shelter, had greeted her classmates on the first day of kindergarten with her wrist outstretched and her hand curled downward, a chimp gesture.

It was the possibility that Future might live again in the rain-forest that spurred me to travel to Belabo in mid-November. Four other chimps and their caretakers had come, four chimps who, with Future, were to form a new family. At the shelter, we learned that Sheri was away; she'd been caring for a sick adult chimp who'd fallen from a tree and been attacked by ants. Future jumped from my arms and tumbled into the grass with the baby apes but kept looking back. He climbed a banana tree and swung from a long leaf that tore and set him on the ground again. One chimp discovered papayas, bananas, pineapples, the stockpile for all the chimps of the shelter, and Future and his mates charged the food like the monkeys at the Yaoundé zoo.

Under the direction of a French woman, the caretakers and I stepped into the quarantine cage. Fresh sawdust covered the ground. The smallest chimp, Moon, entered the enclosure holding his caretaker's leg, then scampered up the bars. Future lay in my lap and I tickled his feet, his laughter like that of someone who couldn't get the sound out of his mouth. I pushed his hand away when he tried to pick my ear, and he climbed up after Moon. Then hung upside down and looked at me. An hour later, when all five chimps were climbing on the cage, the French woman said, "Go!" The caretakers and I scrambled out. She slammed the door, said, "Please don't look back. Move quickly." The chimps shrieked. Adult chimps watching from other enclosures held the bars and jumped up and down like prisoners inciting a riot. The screams of the young chimps were commensurate with the sound of children being stripped from parents.

"Keep moving!" the French woman called out.

Future's cries found me within the hysteria.

Moon's caretaker was sobbing. I wiped my own tears.

"I'm never going to care for a chimp again," the man said. "It's too tough."

I stopped to catch my breath when I was beyond view of the cage. My body shook. Future screamed and I fought the instinct to turn back to hug him and let him bury his face against my neck.

Ravit had cared for Jack in the first week of his quarantine; Jack was to be paired with a young CWAF gorilla once the veterinarian determined he was healthy. Ravit walked up the stairs to my Mendong apartment. I'd told the volunteers I was ending our relationship. But Ravit still wanted to work with me. She had the will to continue and was giving me another chance. The right choice was to honor her effort to reach Cameroon. But I said, "Ravit, I need a clean slate." So she left, and after she was gone I realized I hadn't even thanked her.

A week later, Sheri Speede called. "Future has an infection. There's another antibiotic that may be more helpful than what we've given him. You'll have to pick some up. Ofir, his condition is critical. I can't imagine anything but emotional shock made him deteriorate like this."

I raced to Belabo, traveling in the night along Cameroon's lone train line and then hiring a motorcycle for the hundred minute ride to the shelter. I tried to imagine what Future remembered of the time when I'd taken him from the hunter's house, whether he saw me as his rescuer, his father, or just the safest warm chest.

Future lay motionless on a table in the office of the shelter. His eyelids were barely open, but I got him to drink. Three seconds after he swallowed, the liquid passed out his rear. He lacked the strength even to hook his finger over the collar of my shirt. Sheri administered the antibiotics through an IV, and I lay with a hand on Future to ensure he didn't rip the IV from his leg; there was a chance we wouldn't be able to get it back in. I spent two full days and four nights in his cage. Anxious listening to the jungle, swarmed by mosquitoes and unable to sleep, I tried to laugh at what David would have said: *So much drama; even your chimp is the most dramatic.*

When Future was walking and strong enough to hang from my arm, I left the sanctuary, both of us too exhausted for dramatic goodbyes. In Yaoundé, my house and the giant headquarters were empty, the apes in shelters, David back in the U.S., the volunteers gone and their anger with them. The world that had formed around me so quickly had crumbled away.

HUNTING THE HUNTERS

Girls swept the ground outside Ignatius's office, the door open as always because of the heat. Temgoua, a MINEF official in his forties, shook out his green beret and snapped it down. Julius, the policeman with rope-like veins in his arms, was focused, leaning forward. I said, "We're going to collect Officer Eric on the way. He's ready and he is on uniform."

"Mmm," Julius and Temgoua hummed in accord.

"Now. What we have: we have two ladies in Mvog Mbi. Okay. Both of them are selling elephant meat. One is selling elephant and gorilla in large quantities."

"Mmm," said Julius.

Temgoua adjusted his beret and smiled. He was a quiet man, passionate about the protection of wildlife, and in the years of his assignment by MINEF in the North he'd chased elephants away from crops so conflict wouldn't lead to their killing. Temgoua spent much of his salary on cable television so he could watch nature films. He'd told me he felt trapped in the Yaoundé office with his MINEF coworkers who didn't care about wildlife.

"The sellers are there in Mvog Mbi, in the junction," I said. "There is a small roundabout fence with an MTN sign. Okay." I drew a diagram. "There are three ladies. One two three. On two ladies, we already have the evidence. We have the film. These are the two ladies on the left."

John, an investigator, had just bought elephant meat from both women and filmed it with a hidden camera hooked up to a motorcycle battery and fitted into a shoulder bag. John's high-pitched voice and stutter made a lousy first impression and made it easy for him to win the trust of dealers.

"Now, you'll see the footage and you'll recognize the faces of the women. Twenty minutes ago, my man called from the field to tell me exactly what they're wearing. Both of them are now there. The one on the right is wearing a black headscarf. The other one is not wearing any headscarf and she's wearing a blue dress."

A sewing machine whirred beyond the office door.

"We are going to take two special taxis. Okay. One after the other. We arrive. We stop near to that roundabout. We drop. You approach those ladies, you ask to see what they are selling and you find the elephant. It's inside a bucket. I'm filming the whole thing. We arrest them and we go. No delays."

The air over Yaoundé was silvery with smoke, stinking from plastic bags tangled in fields that farmers were burning in preparation for planting. Old Julius, the village man who cooked at the Abong-Mbang bus stand, had warned me against carrying out operations at Mvog Mbi; the market was full of bushmeat vendors who had never been challenged. Though illegal, the trade in protected species was not considered criminal behavior. With the police routinely abusive and MINEF officials *involved* in the bushmeat trade, market vendors might become enraged at the sight of uniformed men acting in a way most would assume was just bullying for a bribe.

The taxis stopped at the roundabout, and I opened the cab door. Six months in Cameroon had been building to this moment, and I had no idea how the operation would unfold. Julius led three armed policemen toward the vendors. People swirled in the commotion of green uniforms. Temgoua and I hurried out of our cab. The women, shaded by umbrellas, sat with piles of greasy black meat. But between us and them was a stomach-high iron fence, far more of an obstacle than the hidden footage had revealed. Julius and Temgoua squeezed through the crowd to find their way to the vendors. People flocked to the circular fence to watch. The gathering mob wedged between me and the officers, and by the time Julius reached the fat woman in the black headscarf we'd lost the element of surprise. Temgoua bent down to inspect her bushmeat and stood silently, as though pondering something.

"Fast, fast, put it all together!" Julius said.

People murmured, began to shout.

"Move out!" Julius said to the crowd. "You have nothing to see here. Just go."

Julius ordered his timid officers to climb over the fence toward him and he pulled the fat seller up by the arm.

"Don't go with them!" a man said to her.

Julius whipped around and said, "This is not concerning you!"

Temgoua bent down before a random seller, picked up a hunk of meat and showed it to one of the policemen as if giving a workshop. "This is elephant. Do you see, it's gray? The skin on this side is wrinkled. These spots are where the hairs used to be. That's how it is."

One bushmeat seller stood and walked off. The crowd was thickening, growing louder. I leaned over the roundabout fence and said to Temgoua, "Just take it. It's fine. We can identify it at the station."

The second seller, the skinny woman in a blue dress, sat unbothered.

"Julius! Deal with her."

He walked past the cairns of black flesh and picked up a piece of meat.

"*Elle est parti*," said the skinny woman, as if the owner of the meat had left.

The shouting mob blocked my view of the policemen. The crowd was finding its voice. There was one face in front of me, then three. Temgoua stood in a sea of market-goers as the flashpoint neared.

"Just take it! It's fine," I said to Julius. "Take it in a plastic bag. Julius, *c'est fini*."

A man bowed his chest and said, "You can't chase us away!"

Julius seized both women by the arms and led them through the crowd to the cabs. One policeman loaded meat into the trunk, and we departed, lucky—no coordination, no communication, no leadership.

At the MINEF station, both women admitted to trading elephant meat, one of them chimpanzee, and they signed their complaint reports. If the minister channeled the cases to court, the state council would decide whether the women would stand trial. Julius and Temgoua received 10,000-franc bonuses, the junior officers 5,000, all of it financed by me and my father. The bushmeat was fed to hyenas, crocodiles, and lions at the zoo. And the operation and follow-up were filmed for accountability.

Vincent said, "The radio news is singing and singing the operation."

Old Julius advised me to return to Mvog Mbi in the morning on the assumption that the women, released after signing their statements, would sell off their stockpiles. And the next day they were back at the market. Christopher fitted his disguise onto his head—the top hat. He repeated my instructions back to me and left with the hidden camera. But when he returned with the footage, I saw that in buying elephant meat from the woman in the blue dress, he'd passed the money to her through a small girl—a mistake rookie investigators would make when too focused on completing a sale.

The team returned to the market in two cabs. Julius slammed his door and stormed toward the sellers with three policemen in tow. Temgoua and I followed. The fat woman in the black headscarf was there, the skinny woman gone. The shouting began as people swarmed to the railing to watch the fight.

"Faster, Temgoua," Julius said. "Not like yesterday." Julius stood over the fat woman and said to her, "Do you have it now? Where is it?"

She stuttered.

"Where is your sister? You are doing it again without shame? Just to cry later?"

"That's elephant there," I said.

"There's nothing," Temgoua said. "There's just a pangolin. Alive."

Then he found and held up a piece of elephant meat.

"No, I don't have," the fat woman pleaded. "No, I didn't know."

While Temgoua lectured her, Julius disappeared into the crowd. He returned with the skinny woman. A market vendor stepped forward, said, "Leave it to the biggest man." The skinny woman raised her arms, slapped her hands, shouted in her tribal language—to rally support.

"She is resisting," I said.

The market was with her. The policemen were scattered, people swarming. One policeman stood like a bystander, smiling, as clueless as Jens. Temgoua was nowhere in sight. A seller shoved one of our men. We were easy prey.

The skinny woman was furious.

"It's okay, mama," I said to her. "Stay here."

"Stay here," Julius repeated. "When we'll engage more people—"

"What will you engage?" a man yelled.

"We'll engage whoever we want."

Men pushed between Julius and me. Two policemen raised their guns. Horns blared. Julius gripped the fat woman's arm. A man yelled, "Was she hunting the animals? Bring any *man* you want." In rough French, so everyone would hear, I said, "Selling elephant meat. That's one. That's two. It's fine like that. The pangolin also. And all the elephant. Wrap it and let's go." People seemed to be forming a wall around us.

"No. She doesn't go!"

"Get out of our market!"

Where the hell was Temgoua? "Julius, we wrap it up," I said and turned to the skinny woman. "You can stay here. You're only making things worse for yourself."

Temgoua appeared holding a monitor lizard the size of a small crocodile. Steps from the taxi, a man smacked Temgoua's arm and swiped the lizard. Julius guided the fat woman into the cab along with an old female seller. Someone swiped a bag of bushmeat from the hatchback before the policemen could get it closed. Peopled were blocking our way, slapping and banging the sides of the taxis. Julius climbed out and swelled in his uniform as he roared, "Move!"

And they did; Julius was not a man to ignore.

We rode away from the market. I rewound in my mind the events of the reckless, amateurish operation that would prove I was a risk to myself and to everyone. The video footage I vowed to erase. At the station, the fat woman confessed again and signed a second complaint report. To the old woman I said, "You are my grandmother. Out of respect to you, you'll go free. But please don't sell these endangered species again."

The pangolin, a long scaly mammal, unrolled from her protective ball and moved off with the ancient dignity of a dinosaur when I released her by the river behind Mendong. On Monday, Christopher confirmed that the skinny woman was back at the market, and Julius took five armed men and arrested her without a struggle. She'd worn the colors of the flag and an arm band streaked with the flames of Cameroon's ruling party.

Two weeks earlier, I'd gone to Belabo. Future, Moon, and the other young chimps were out of quarantine, acting like a family, making daily trips into the forest with older chimps and a caretaker. Future climbed in the trees. He came to me but not at first, and I sensed that one day he wouldn't remember me at all. I tried not to see his growing indifference as rejection, tried to see it as a closing of the circle that meant he was returning to the life he was supposed to live.

On the ride back to Yaoundé, two live crocodiles—threatened animals in Cameroon—were lifted onto my bus roof in a crate, and a woman and a young man boarded. With the bus in motion and the woman eyeing me, I called Koulagna, director of wildlife, on my very first cell phone. When the *Alliance Voyages* bus stopped in Ayos for a food break, I got the license plate number, phoned Takam at the Nkoabang checkpoint and insisted he stop the van. After midnight, just before we reached Nkoabang, I beeped Takam with my cell phone, and he stepped into the road waving a flashlight. I ducked behind my seat to avoid any eye contact that might reveal Takam and I knew each other. He confiscated the crate and led the young man but not the woman into the MINEF cabin. I continued into Yaoundé and approached her at the end of the line.

"I saw you're traveling with crocodiles," I said. "Did they take them away?"

"This is nothing. I'm going to recover them. My husband is a government official. I'll give them a small gift and that's all."

"Well, I need pets. I was hoping to get your crocodiles to have for my garden and my swimming pool."

She looked me up and down and shook her head. "These two animals were ordered."

I gave her my number. "Call me if you get more."

When I asked for her number, she said, "I have to move."

I returned to the checkpoint not long after dawn. Takam was sleeping, his uniform unbuttoned. He said, "You came too late. Someone came just now with a letter from the sub-director of human resources of MINEF. This letter says, 'These crocodiles belong to me. Release them.' The official arrived in his car and took them. That boy who we got down from the bus—he just went and ran away."

I rode to the ministry and took the elevator up to Koulagna's office. Waving the sub-director's hand-written letter in the air, I said to Koulagna, "We need to open an investigation into this right now."

A staff member of the wildlife department, Nango, stood beside me.

"This is really outrageous," Koulagna said. "We'll write a letter to the minister."

"No. The sub-director of human resources is here in the building," I said. "We're going to his office now to do an investigation."

Koulagna shrugged. "Okay."

The staff member followed me to the sub-director's office. Outside it, he approached the secretary and said, "Please, do you think the sub-director can receive us now?" I was already knocking on the door. Staff member Nango tried to step around me as the door opened. Over my shoulder, he said, "Mr. Director—"

The sub-director motioned for us to sit on the leather couches in his carpeted office. He wore a pinstriped suit and wore his stylish hair an inch thick. He was in charge of the river of money running through payroll in MINEF.

"How can I help you?" he said.

Though filming inside the ministry was prohibited, I shoved my video camera into his face, put the letter in front of him and said, "Did you write this letter?"

He looked away.

The staff member was shocked. He stuttered, "Mr. Director, excuse me, but the director of wildlife told me to accompany this man—"

"Did you write this letter?" I said again to the sub-director.

He showed his crooked bottom teeth. "Ah, I don't know."

"But it carries your signature. Is it your signature? Are those croco-diles with you?"

The man looked to the staff officer for help, as the poacher in Abong-Mbang had looked to Kalebass.

I said, "You sabotaged an operation of my organization and the depart-ment of wildlife of this ministry—by taking those crocodiles."

"Yes. I took them."

He looked at me, then at the camera, as if realizing he'd just made a mistake.

"This is what we're going to do," I said. "We're going to take your car, go to your house right now and move your crocodiles to the zoo."

The ride in the sub-director's new sedan wouldn't have been more awkward had he caught me with his wife. In the sealed, air-conditioned car, I could smell that I hadn't washed in days—the smell of Future, bananas, sawdust, sweat. The sub-director's house was a palace, and around the back was an open crate. One crocodile had been set on the concrete. Its legs were contorted and bent back over its spine, bound with strips of rubber.

"I didn't know about the crocodiles," the sub-director said after we arrived with the animals at the zoo. "I received them as a gift. A man said I had a package at the checkpoint and I needed to come and pick it up. I didn't know what was inside."

"So who is the person? He gave you a gift without knowing you? You usually receive gifts from people you don't know?" I moved the camera up to his nose.

"No, it's the *chef du poste* of Kagnol."

Kagnol was a MINEF station at a logging operation in the East.

"So where is the chief now?"

"I don't know. I don't know him."

I grabbed the sub-director's cell phone from his hand. On the chance he'd last spoken to the *chef du poste*, I hit "last dialed calls" then "talk." I was just trying to shake him up when I handed the phone back and said, "Why don't you talk to him?"

The sub-director looked at me, exhaled, swallowed and then, to my surprise, actually began speaking to the *chef du poste* in French. Unable to hide a smile, I had to turn my head. I understood from the conversation that the *chef du poste* was in Yaoundé.

THE LAST GREAT APE • 227

"Tell him to meet us in your office in thirty minutes," I said.

Back at MINEF headquarters, I managed to get both men to confess and write statements. Had the minister entered and seen me bullying two of his officials, I would have been driven to the airport and expelled from Cameroon. I folded the signed statements into my bag. And at the zoo I untied the crocodiles. The first slid into the water. The mangled legs of the second were paralyzed, and the other crocodiles killed him.

After the arrest of the elephant-meat dealers, Karl Ammann wrote, "This is only markets; you'll never get the big people." After the case of the sub-director and the chief of Kagnol, he wrote, "This will never arrive in court. You can make arrests, but the people will just go home. There's no use in waiting to release the footage of the sub-director admitting to ordering the crocodiles." In no email had Karl given feedback about my proposal or news about funding for LAGA. I wrote back, "Karl, we're just starting. The prosecutions will come. I'm going to give the minister a chance to do something about the case of the crocodiles."

Vincent and I sat before a television at the Nlongkak bar. He was wearing tribal clothes. We'd edited film of Future with moments from the arrests at Mvog Mbi that I hadn't erased, and the piece was broadcast on the evening news, with Vincent narrating. Vincent sipped his third Castel beer and watched, not the television, but my face. "Vincent," I said, "you are a magician."

We recruited Barrister Ntolo to work our case against the elephant-meat dealers. She had handled the failed case of the army captain and the rhino horn, and, in theory, the ministry paid her an honorarium for each case. Delayed and often nonexistent payments made a system rife with corruption only more vulnerable. When the skinny elephant-meat dealer arrived to Barrister Ntolo's office with a bribe, the barrister refused her. The skinny woman said, "If you don't want the money, someone else will take it."

Karl wrote finally that he had a man ready to make a $10,000 donation, the first to LAGA. I hammered out emails to Ofer, David, and Dad from the Nlongkak cyber café and bounded up and outside, feeling the urge to hug the meat man cooking beef over a metal drum. I breathed in the sweet cloud drifting off his grill. People were drinking in the bar. Music was playing. But I found I wanted to be home in Mendong. As I stopped a shared taxi, I was struck with the realization that I was sad, again—my old companion. But why? It wasn't until the cab reached Carrefour Banane and I slogged and slipped up the muddy hill to my house, that I understood the melancholy was entangled with loneliness. I unlocked my front door, cringing as the mother in the shack across the road shouted at little Mattou. How could I share the relief and pride I felt in landing the first donor, in making LAGA self-sufficient, when the people I loved seemed so far off, when they lacked the language even to discuss my life in Cameroon? And each day I didn't share it, the bridge between us became harder to rebuild. How was it possible, anyway, to share experiences like speaking with the Womo or sensing changes in the way my mouth had reacted to food along the Gibe River? Wasn't story a poor imitation?

We live, as we dream—alone.

The money from Karl's donor brought the sting of responsibility, perhaps a completion of the shift from absolute freedom to its loss. I had no choice but to continue building LAGA, but in doing so I was losing control of time, drifting away from so much of what I was. I missed the days of pure fun, dancing with Ofer and Shahar until exhaustion peeled away all but the love of being together. I put on music in the living room in Mendong, Peter Murphy's "Strange Kind of Love," and I danced alone in the darkness.

I strolled into Agora, an expensive restaurant in Nlongkak. I had just enough energy for an easy operation; earlier in the day, through the obstacle course of a crowded market, Julius and I had sprinted after a man cradling a crocodile like a football.

At Agora, people dined at half a dozen tables. The menu, full of protected species, was painted on the wall: crocodile, viper, boa, giant pangolin.

"Give me one Coke," I said when the waiter came. "Very cold. And for dinner, please, do you have crocodile today?" I pointed at the wall.

He nodded.

"Then I'll have the crocodile."

The dish came. The meat was covered with bumps. I took a bite and called Julius, who was on standby at the Nlongkak bar. Julius arrived, tipsy, with Temgoua and two policemen to my table. I turned on the video camera and began to film. Julius called to the waiters and said, "Where is the woman who owns this restaurant?"

"I don't know if she can come," said one of the waiters. "What exactly do you want? She has no problems with the police."

Temgoua started in on a wordy explanation of wildlife law, and Julius interrupted him. "Please bring her."

A waiter disappeared into the kitchen. For several minutes, we stood around the plate of crocodile, listening to slow soft music playing on the restaurant's stereo.

A large woman burst through the kitchen door, screaming as she staggered between tables and rushed us. I grabbed the camera. Silverware flew into the air as Julius and Temgoua fled. The woman's shaved head was colored orange. She grabbed a chair and chased me around tables where people were eating. And she yelled, "I want the head of the white man on a plate! On a plate! You're going to pay for this." She lunged for the camera in my hands. Temgoua tried to reason with her about the plight of animals. The woman and I circled the same table three times, knocked into a couple eating a meal. "Get out of my restaurant! You don't know who you're messing with. I will talk to your minister and you'll see what will happen!" I dodged her fist. "You're going to die. I will kill you! Kill you!"

I woke in a terrible mood with no ongoing operations. The anti-poaching chief, Etoga, was trying to bury all our cases. Thoughts of Rachel arrived and I remembered her saying I was like a rock. "Yeah," I said, "like a rock submerged in a river." And she said, "What you want to be requires that you feel nothing." I'd made a ceremony of playing guitar before I went to sleep each night, the same songs I always played when I thought of Rachel, songs to help me hold on to the feeling of what it was like to love her.

I attached a small microphone to my shirt with Scotch tape and went to town, determined by day's end to make an arrest. The artisana was a curio market controlled by Muslims. Elephants in ebony, carvings from Kenya of Maasai and hordes of bronze statues made me wonder how all the sellers stayed in business in a country with no tourists. Hanging from a post was a mask made from the shell of a sea turtle. On one side was a mosaic of tin and bronze. The backside looked like the ribs of a skeleton.

Men in robes—Hausa men—watched me from behind the fortress of statues and masks. I'd seen ivory for sale on another visit to the artisana—rings, necklaces, tiny carvings. Today, I was looking for what was concealed, a door behind the stalls, a closed shop. I bartered and paid for a bracelet adorned with a carved nutshell, so as not to seem suspicious for coming to a market and buying nothing.

I descended stairs through a narrow passage, ducked through a tiny doorway, and found myself in a room filled with curios. Two men passed a calculator back and forth, the taller man wearing a light blue gown. The basement was so crammed with objects, I feared I would knock into them: carvings the size of small boys, ebony chairs embedded with cowry shells, a mask with five red horns and devilish eyes—the artifacts of a hundred cultures collecting dust in a window-less room.

On two wooden bases stood long elephant tusks. I closed my eyes. Then stepped back and pointed at the five-horned mask. "Where is it from?" I said.

"Congo," said the man in the blue gown.

I nearly tripped into a foot-high wooden man holding a spear for attack, his body stuck with hundreds of rusted nails like a fetish of black magic.

"This is nice," I said of one of the polished tusks. "Do you have more?"

"Yes, of course," he said in a deep voice.

The dark Hausa man had a fat face and a round stomach, a gold watch on his wrist and prayer beads in one hand. Next to him was an elephant foot with three giant toenails that looked less like an object that could be sold than a hacked-off limb. The skin was cracked and wrinkled, the top adorned with leather and the fur of what looked like a Colobus monkey.

"How much for the tusks?" I said.

"150,000 each."

"This isn't the first time I'm buying ivory. I'm not a tourist. I'll give 200,000 for both."

He didn't answer. He picked up a pencil and glanced at the door as if another customer might walk in. His hand entered his hip pocket, probably to check on his cash.

"And what about the elephant stool?" I said. The foot was surprisingly light, likely hollowed out and dried with sawdust.

The Hausa man said nothing.

"If you have more ivory, bring it," I said. "I'll buy it all."

He looked up with the smile of a man pleasantly surprised, then scribbled on a piece of paper and punched the calculator. "I have two more pairs here," he said and sent the other man out of the shop. "And I have two pairs at my house."

"If those are smaller, I'll pay less for them."

"No, they're big, the same. Polished. Everything."

"It's possible to ship these to my country? I have a big business in the U.S."

"Yes. No problem."

"I won't get any trouble from the Cameroon side?"

"No, it's easy. We do it all the time."

The young man returned with two tusks and then two more. Temgoua said ivory in Yaoundé was worth $30-40 a kilogram, and the stash of tusks was probably worth $1,500. But I agreed to a price of $2,000.

"I'm John," I said and wrote down my cell number for him.

He handed me his card, which was glossy with images that changed in the light. "Adamou Ndjidda," it said. "Trader in gold and ivory."

"I'm not carrying all this out of here," I told him. "Can you deliver it to my house?"

He worked the prayer beads through his fingers. "If you're paying for everything, we can deliver it."

"I'm in Bastos."

We shook hands and I climbed the stairs, and I couldn't believe what I'd stumbled into. Once out of the market, I turned off the hidden microphone and called Julius and then ran to Bastos to search for a place to serve as my home. A one-story house with an open gate was under construction, mostly finished, the workers absent. All we had to do was get Adamou through the gate, and we could block him inside.

I returned to Nlongkak to brief Julius and Temgoua.

Then I called Adamou Ndjidda. I said, "Can you deliver it now?"

"Yes."

"When you arrive to Bastos and you're near the Chinese embassy, call me."

Julius, Temgoua, and I rode in two taxis to the house. And we found that the gates had been *locked*. I ran up the street, frantic, searching for another place and hoping Adamou wasn't about to phone to say he was near. I scanned both sides of the road. Bougainvillea grew atop high walls. Razor wire. A Mercedes passed. A driveway: it led to a closed orange gate. The driveway was blocked on two sides by tall shrubs and deep enough for two cars to park end to end. Whether people were inside the house, I didn't have time to care. I called Julius. We talked strategy. I hid my bag in the shrubs. Adamou phoned, and I directed him toward me. When the taxi appeared up the street, I waved it into the driveway.

Adamou wore his the light blue gown. He and another man climbed out of the cab, chewing gum. I pointed to the gates and said, "I don't understand why my guard is keeping my gate closed." I pulled out my cell phone. "I'll give him another minute to open it. Adamou, you have everything?"

His prayer beads swung in his hand when he motioned toward the car. The cabdriver unlocked the trunk. The ivory was there, the elephant foot and twelve tusks, more even than we'd agreed on—six elephants, the size of the herd in Kenya that had flattened acacia trees chasing me after I'd tied up Lapa.

"I'll call this stupid guard," I said.

I dialed Julius's number.

"Why do I pay you to keep me locked out of my own house?" I said. "Are you coming to open this gate or not?"

Julius and Temgoua arrived in our two cabs, blocking Adamou's exit from the driveway. I pulled the video camera from my bag. Adamou and the second man stood, unresponsive, chomping their gum. Julius inspected the ivory.

"You think this is normal?" Adamou said.

Both men held their arms out and hands up in a perfect gesture of guilt as Temgoua recited the wildlife law.

"What law?" Adamou said. He took two steps toward me and raised his chin. "You say the law. Are you the law?"

Adamou told us that the ivory belonged to him and three others. The next day, the three men, figuring they would get the ivory back, came to the station with falsified documents claiming they had the legal right to possess ivory. We arrested them all. The ivory went into a storage room on the seventeenth floor at MINEF, and Koulagna signed a letter to transmit the case to court.

Karl Ammann's donor, Hans, sent two wires of $3,000 each. Then Hans wrote, "I wouldn't mind if you bought a watch for the anti-poaching chief so he stops being an obstacle to moving your cases to the courts." Livid, I responded that he should keep the rest of his donation and I would gladly refund the $6,000 he'd sent, for it was this casual culture of bribes that kept anything from functioning.

Vincent published an article about our operations at Agora and at two other restaurants. He wrote, with the usual theatrics, that a government crackdown on restaurants was sweeping the nation. Reuters picked up the story. A few days later, Elad was on the Underground in London, listening to music and reading *Metro* magazine, when he spotted a small headline on the back page: "Gorilla Stew Coming off Cameroon's Menu."

At MINEF's zoo in Yaoundé, animals were disappearing—boas, parrots, tortoises—along with building materials. The thefts had become a publicity problem for MINEF's minister. On the hunch that the night watchmen was involved, I worked up a plan and sent John to investigate. After loitering for two days, John approached the night watchman and said, "Can you supply chimps?"

"Yes."

"How do I get one?"

"For small animals we cut the fence. For big ones we need to unlock the cage."

"Don't worry about the keys," said John, in whose pocket was a cheap walkman on RECORD mode. "I can ge ge get keys from the veterinarian."

"It will cost you 100,000 francs for me and 25,000 that I give to the other guard."

At ten minutes to midnight, the police captain of Quartier Melen and I sneaked through the darkness to the zoo's outer wall, near the lion enclosure. I joined my hands. The captain put his foot into my locked fingers and held my shoulder, and I hoisted him up. He got balanced, his stomach atop the wall, legs hanging inside the zoo. He reached down and pulled me up after him. As we crept through the zoo together, the shadow of my gaunt face and my frizzy hair looked like a skull following me along the ground. In a market, an investigator had recorded a bushmeat vendor claiming I had traditional powers; the only people in Cameroon who wore nothing but black, as I did, were witch doctors.

John beeped me. He was outside, waiting for the guard to open the gate. Frogs croaked in the crocodile pond. Monkeys cried out. I got a whiff of urine. The night watchman passed the reptile room holding a flashlight. John was with him. I could hear keys jingling in the darkness as John took them from his pocket and handed them to the guard. We crept closer. The guard set a sack on the concrete that rattled with metal tools. He struggled to work one of the keys into the lock. He tried a second key. With intent to break in and steal proven, the captain jumped out and rushed the guard, grabbed him, and put him in handcuffs. He radioed his people and said, "Wait for us at the gate." Two of the minister's aides were also waiting nearby in a Mercedes, and when I called they were pleased with my report. Before leaving the zoo, I made sure to grab the keys John had given to the watchman to open the cage, because without them I wouldn't be able to open my front door; they were just my house keys.

Eunice was a short young Cameroonian working as a maid for the director of Global Witness. A nature photographer told her about our work and she came to me, wanting to join LAGA. On her first mission as an investigator, Eunice called from Bertoua in the East. "I haven't seen anything, Ofir."

"Eunice, if you open your eyes very well, you will see something."

"How long do I need to stay in this place to see it? And how much money are you giving me for myself? Enough not even for two meals!"

Within a few days, though, Eunice located men with two live apes.

"These people are powerful," she said. "Ofir, I'm afraid. They can kill me and bury me without anybody knowing. They can do it physically but also mystically."

"I'm worried, Eunice," I said. "Is there something traditional you can do from your own village to combat their powers?"

At MINEF, I entered the office of the anti-poaching chief, Etoga. Though LAGA had prosecution dates set for five cases, Etoga was trying to bury at least as many more, including the case against Agora's owner. Etoga had received money at various times from seven projects funded by the international community and he had his own NGO, a governmental-non-governmental organization.

I leaned over his desk and said, "I verified with the minister's office that you have delivered no complaint reports to him. The cases should already be in court. Some are more than a month old."

"The files are with me," Etoga said. "I am seeking advice from the minister."

"It's illegal for you to keep the files."

"Don't tell us what to do."

"The *law* tells you what to do."

The following day, Vincent and I wrote a letter to the minister.

Samuel Nguiffo of Center for Environment and Development (CED) offered his advice, "For now the ministry will let you play because no one here believes you can win. Cameroon is Cameroon. You can fight corruption in the field, but then it has to come to the courts, and in the courts corruption can be even worse. They believe you don't know this. They probably think it's easier to wait until you give up. That explains why, besides blocking some cases, they don't stop your activities. But all this will change when—if—you get the first prosecution. Then you will see the system fighting back. Use all your time now to prepare yourself for this moment."

Etoga moved two of our seized elephant tusks from MINEF's storage room to his office. Like a man with a kingdom, he stood one on either side of his leather chair.

Eunice called. "My phone is sick, so I'm calling from a callbox. Ofir, I told these people I need help to deliver the apes to my buyer in Yaoundé. But they are strong in wanting to do the deal in the village. So I said, 'Could you buy a chicken in a bag? Not even a white man could do such a thing.' After that, they agreed to come. A lady said we cannot travel without her performing a magical act. She said it is to prevent us from danger. Then before my eyes she is disappearing along with the gorillas."

"Eunice, take good care of those magicians not to enter any traps," I said, still confused about what bags had to do with chickens.

Eunice said, "Death has a hundred hands and a thousand ways."

She called the next night en route to Yaoundé. Then called again. "There's a change, Ofir, a different vehicle. The number of the car is CE 4535. A white minibus, *Alliance Voyages*. The man wears a red cap and squared shirt. Did you get it? A red cap and—"

The line died.

Julius, Temgoua, and I headed to Nkoabang. There were three MINEF officers in the station. We brought two more policemen. Out of seven men, only Julius and Temgoua knew Eunice was undercover. She beeped me at two in the morning just before her bus appeared in the cold night, the moment of conflict coming, as always, sooner than I was ready for. Julius strolled into the road and shined a flashlight at the driver's face. The bus stopped and Julius stepped onboard and searched it. I stood near the front fender with Temgoua as Julius climbed back down and whispered, "I don't know where the animals are. I don't see them inside."

We could make no arrest without connecting the red-capped man directly to the apes. I moved to the bus's open door and pretended to talk on my phone. "Yes, we got the small one. Yes. The small woman, right? Like a pygmy. And there's a man with her?"

Julius then pulled tiny Eunice off the bus and into the road.

"Take this pygmy to the station," I yelled at another policeman. Then I turned to Eunice. "You're a thief. You're going to prison with your husband!"

While Julius was checking luggage in the hatchback, Eunice whispered to Temgoua that the gorillas were in a box between the man's feet, a broken wet box so small that Julius hadn't considered that two gorillas could fit inside it. He pulled the red-capped man down to the road, and I sent the bus on.

"Separate these two," I said to Julius in the two-room MINEF cabin. "I want to talk to the pygmy alone." I closed the door. Eunice, seated in front of me, looked traumatized. I whispered, "We're going to arrest you now and release you later." I shouted, "If you don't want to admit, don't admit." I opened the door. "Julius, this one needs to be behind bars!" I mixed in a few French words to ensure that everyone understood. "I'm finished with her. Now bring the man in. I want to see how he helped her."

The baby gorillas were hugging each other in the tiny mashed box.

Michelle, a MINEF officer, escorted Eunice to a waiting taxi.

We finished interrogating the man and sent him and Eunice to the police station in town. As Julius put them into a jail cell, Eunice said to the red-capped man, "Don't worry. I'm soon calling my boss. He's a big man and has money to get us out of this trouble."

"Please do something," the man said. "I'm counting on you."

Eunice stayed in the cell without food or water for half a day. She told me later that Michelle, the MINEF officer charged with guarding her in the taxi outside the checkpoint, had said, "Run! Run fast now! Don't be stupid. It's dark. The white man won't catch you."

Eunice said, "Ofir, I'm never doing this again."

The media was humming with Vincent's work, with radio, television, and print pieces placed, on average, every other day in the national media. Christopher met me around the back of Hotel Azur in Bastos with footage he'd just shot, and I watched, on the tiny screen of the video camera, as Christopher said to the dealer, "You call her how? Kita, eh?" Christopher was at the gate when the dealer arrived and he signaled for us to charge. Julius and I sprinted out to arrest Tonye

Nken. Kita, the mustard-eyed chimp, was now living with me, another overgrown child in constant need of attention.

I was interviewed over the phone by an Israeli journalist. And I did a radio interview in Yaoundé, which was heard by my Israeli friend Eran. He said, "You talked too loud and too fast. Important people don't speak like that here. To be respected, lower your volume. The lower the volume, the more powerful the person." And I thought of Foday Sankoh's quiet, chilling voice when he'd spoken on the radio in Freetown.

The gown-wearing ivory dealer Adamou Ndjidda and his three associates appeared at the court. Outside, several men approached our legal adviser, Marius, and squeezed him into a corner. One of them said, "We're going to get you for doing this to our brother."

As we left the hearing, Marius said to me, "These are people who can kill me—all of their friends from Briqueterie. This is a dangerous neighborhood they come from."

"Marius, this is what we do," I said. "Of course, we are taking risks. But I'm sure if they try to kill someone it will be me."

Marius was not easily intimidated and he'd dreamed of opening an NGO to prove to his family that he could succeed on his own. "You know what?" he said. "I'll study wrestling."

"Fantastic. LAGA will sponsor it."

Bill Clark, an Israeli involved in wildlife law enforcement, had met with Koulagna in Geneva at a UN conference. Bill declared that he and the International Fund for Animal Welfare (IFAW) were ready to donate to projects in Cameroon. I could only imagine Koulagna's glee when Bill told him he'd personally delivered five Cessnas to Mali for wildlife surveying. "If Ofir's plan can work, then it's proof of political will," Clark had told Koulagna, "and it would mean we could *invest* in Cameroon." IFAW was ready to give $35,000 to LAGA, a year's funding, as soon as they received a written endorsement from the government, the kind of regulatory step meant to prevent conflict between governments and NGOs. I brought Koulagna my project proposal, our budget, and the letter Bill had drafted for him to sign.

"Director, Bill told me he talked with you."

"Yes, yes, there's no problem."

I returned a few days later. Instead of handing me the signed endorsement, Koulagna gave me a piece of paper titled "Budget for IFAW Proposition." My detailed budget had been reduced to half a dozen lines. For the wildlife department and the anti-poaching unit, both under Koulagna's control, he'd allocated $10,000. Protected areas, also under his control, $17,000. Sensitization campaign, $3,000. Of the $35,000 meant for LAGA there was but one budget line: LAGA intelligence operations, $5,000.

Half my blood rushed to my head. I said, "What field equipment do you want to buy for the wildlife department, which sits in offices? It says '$7,000—equipment.'"

"Just equipment," Koulagna said. "We haven't decided."

"$1,000 for office consumables for your office: is that for law enforcement?"

I was angry enough to burst. I'd heard stories of envelopes passing between NGO directors and high-level officials, but this did not lessen my shock.

Koulagna, ever calm and respectful, said, "Negotiate this with my collaborator." He meant Etoga, the anti-poaching chief.

"Director, this isn't a market. I'm not negotiating anything."

I went straight to the cyber café, scanned the document, and emailed it to IFAW. I wrote, "This is exactly the reason I'm here. If you are able to get me the funding without a letter from the government, I would be very happy. If you can't, it means you are probably not ready to be our donor."

"This is the game," Karl wrote. "The government wants to give LAGA a 15% commission for bringing them free pocket money."

IFAW neither responded nor sent the donation.

THE PROSECUTION

Yaoundé's court complex was as neglected as the law. Rusty front gates slumped on their hinges. Umbrella-shaded women sold plantains and peanuts next to policemen lounging at the entrance. A broken sidewalk led into a courtyard of dirt and weeds. Marius and I climbed stairs stained at the edges with algae. He was wearing an ill-fitting suit bought with money I'd loaned him, and sight of him in the baggy suit conjured thoughts of the army, the rookies and I stepping on the hems of our first uniforms, rolling back the sleeves to find our hands. Marius had a masters in law and would have already been a lawyer had the Cameroon Bar Association not frozen all exams in order to prohibit the accreditation of new lawyers.

The Court of First Instance had a milk-thin coat of paint that was half-peeled and washing away. Policemen at a table waved us up a damp staircase. The massive wood doors guarding the courtroom were open. Light shone through patterned slits in the concrete walls, compensating for the unlit fluorescent bulbs in the ceiling. Beneath the thin soles of my five-dollar loafers I could feel sand on the floor.

We sat. In the next aisle was Temgoua, wearing his beret, leaning forward and listening to the court clerk. Ntolo, our lawyer, sat near the female judge, who wore a black robe and the colonial relic of a curly white wig. In the packed gallery was Tonye Nken's son, the boy who'd ridden to Mendong with Kita and me after the arrest of his father outside Hotel Azur. I'd tried to approach the boy at other court hearings, but he'd waved me off.

The case against *Alliance Voyages* over Eunice's gorillas was blocked by the anti-poaching chief, who then reported that the file had been "lost." The owner of Agora restaurant was said to have contacts in President Biya's office; the case never arrived to court. The two elephant-meat dealers from Mvog Mbi had received negligible fines and suspended sentences. The skinny woman had emphasized poverty and her single motherhood in her defense, mitigating circumstances that made it too easy for a bribable judge to let someone off. In the case against the sub-director of human resources, there were *aggravating* circumstances, but the ministry buried the case. We had eighteen other cases now pending in the courts.

Marius was sweating. He wiped a tissue across his cheek and forehead, and the tissue tore, leaving bits of paper stuck to his face. All those accused in the day's trials entered, their lawyers wearing black gowns and ornamental ruffles. The state counsel wore a sash of red, yellow and green, the colors of the flag. The judge pulled a file from the stack of papers beside her, and the clerk called a new case.

I'd spent many days in different courts. Once, in the High Court, a poorly dressed boy no older than fifteen had approached the bench. A policeman removed his handcuffs.

"I'm sorry," the boy said. "I stole just one shoe."

"So you have only one foot to steal just one shoe?" said the judge.

The courtroom burst into laughter. But the laughter ceased when the judge ruled that he was delaying the case for a month. Back in handcuffs, the boy was returned to jail. Ten minutes later that same day, three men were ushered in. The clerk read that they were accused of being members of a criminal gang who'd robbed room after room at Yaoundé University. They'd been arrested in the act, and a judicial police officer approached the judge and placed stolen cell phones and a pistol on the bench. The judge asked no questions and delayed the case for a month but this time granted provisional liberty, allowing the men to go free. The gallery murmured in protest as the men walked out of the courtroom, but the judge silenced them with the gavel.

On the hot July afternoon, with Marius sweating beside me, the court clerk finally said, "*Ministere publique contre* Tonye Nken."

I tapped Marius's hand. "Listen well. Listen well."

Temgoua turned and nodded.

The accused walked forward and faced the judge, slumped over, wearing glasses.

"Tonye Nken, you are found guilty of the illegal detention of a protected animal. You are sentenced to a one month imprisonment, 500,000 francs in damages to the government, and a 100,000 franc fine."

Tonye Nken lowered his head.

"Marius, did she say what I think she said?"

"I'm not sure."

Temgoua was smiling.

"Let's go," I said. "Let's go!"

Outside, Temgoua laughed, slapped my hand and straightened his beret. I looked up at the sky and thought of Father Albert dancing in a sea of Turkana grandmothers. Indeed, a tree had grown.

"You see now?" said Barrister Ntolo. "I told you we'd get a prosecution."

Vincent arrived with Tansa Musa from Reuters and a camera crew from Cameroon Radio Television Corporation (CRTV). Vincent said, "Tansa, you can start by interviewing Ofir, the director of LAGA. He is here." Vincent turned to me. "Ofir, I briefed Tansa on the significance of this first prosecution and on our *collaboration with the government*. I'm sure he has some good questions to ask you about our *collaboration with the government*."

Vincent led the CRTV crew to interview Barrister Ntolo.

I called Julius and the Jane Goodall Institute and a Cameroonian judge named Magistrate Tejiozem who'd advised us on methods for fighting corruption in the legal system. I called contacts at the World Bank and the EU, requested that they send letters of congratulations to the ministry as fast as possible. Media attention now was sure to highlight a decade of non-application of the law and the workshop business that had masqueraded as progress. The government had to be credited for change, not criticized for the past.

The next morning, the smile fixed on my face was a detriment to drinking coffee. I felt such contentment—that a minor, improvised effort by a handful of people had accomplished what the government and a professional industry of NGOs and millions of dollars had not. And it had been captured, in articles by Reuters and the BBC.

I met Vincent at the Nlongkak bar that night. He sipped from a Castel beer bottle thicker than his arm. "Up to now," Vincent said and frowned, "the minister has granted no interviews."

"But that's what we expected. Who do we have now at the ministry?"

"Cameroon *Tribune* is still waiting there," he said. "BBC called twice. The *Herald* called. Reuters was with me. We'll keep the story in the air as long as we can, Ofi. As we've said, if the ministry wants to kick us out of the country, they have to ignore this. They *can't* denounce it. If they comment at all on the prosecution, they have to endorse it because it's in line with their policy. And if they do endorse it, it will be more difficult to put you on a plane next week."

The Reuters article quoted a man outside the courthouse who'd said, "If we are killing animals, they're our animals. I don't know why a white man should be so concerned when our own government is not disturbing us."

"The minister *has* to speak," I told Vincent. "He has congratulations from the EU, NGOs, the World Bank. We have articles in the international press . . ."

Four days after the prosecution, the minister had still given no interviews. Vincent was hounding MINEF, "like the rainy season." He said, "Ofi, we'll eventually find our way in." We were on the phone for hours, directing waves of reporters to the ministry, giving interviews, sending video footage to any news outlet who might run a piece, trying to show that what we'd started was too strong to be stopped. *Voice of America* was calling the ministry over and over again, and Francis Ngwa, the Cameroonian correspondent for BBC, was as tenacious as Vincent. "The government needs to change," Francis said. "I want to see the minister take a stand on this. What you're doing is a very brave thing. I've never seen anything like this—pulling tricks on the government!"

My mother rang my cell phone while I stood in Ignatius's office.

She was so enthusiastic about the prosecution that I had to hold the phone away from my head. "But Mom," I said, "it's possible I'll be sent out of the country."

I'd reached acceptance, though. LAGA had earned the first prosecution under wildlife law for all of Central and West Africa. If there had been a wildlife case somewhere, it was not known to us. Small-time poachers had been jailed, but for possession of illegal arms and threatening security, not for killing endangered species. Still, both the prosecution and the thrust of LAGA were less about conservation than about fighting corruption. Every major problem I'd seen in Africa had been linked to corruption, from soldiers abusing refugees to broken education systems where teachers' salaries and funds for building schools were stolen. LAGA had taken an ineffective legal system and gotten it to function and thus exposed the failure of the workshop NGOs, by proving they had not done what they could have. I'd been in Cameroon one year. And the joy of the success was as much my own as the memory of walking all those months in Turkana.

The fifth day after the prosecution, Vincent appeared at the door of Ignatius' office. He shuffled in, two quick steps, and tossed a Cameroon *Tribune* on the table. Vincent opened the newspaper to the centerfold and leaned back against the wall with his arms crossed, his attempt to conceal a smile failing as his teeth appeared above the curve of his bottom lip. I put my hands on the table and leaned over the paper. On the right side was an interview I'd given the day of the verdict. On the left was a picture of the minister, Clarkson Tanyi Mbianyor, with an interview praising LAGA, the prosecution, and the law enforcement process.

"Vincent! This is incredible. I can't believe we pulled it off."

"Ofi, it's a convention," Vincent said softly, touching one page and then the other. "Our informal convention with the government."

IN THE PACK, IN THE POT, IN MY STOMACH

Tsetse flies swarmed the canoe.

"Ofi, you really ought to put on a shirt," David said from the bow.

The armored insects cruised out from the banks of the Boumba River to crawl up David's sleeves, to bite him through two pairs of pants, to burrow into his boots and suck blood from his ankles. He slapped his neck and said, "I'm not saying clothes are perfect, but this Tarzan underwear thing is absurd; you have so many welts on your body, you look like you've been whipped."

Old-growth forest rose from the banks of the winding Boumba. Vines hung down to the water. Monkeys clattered in the canopy, the red and green leaves fluttering around them like a massive colony of butterflies. In two days on the river, floating just faster than we might have walked, we'd seen no one. David had spent nearly a year in Texas mediating a dispute between family members, then returned to Cameroon to rent the two-room apartment beneath my flat in Mendong. He'd found the canoe, bought it from a man living in isolation on the river, and gotten word to me that he was waiting back in Lomié. I met him on Christmas Day after learning that my grandfather Moshe had died on Hanukkah Eve and been buried in Israel.

Downriver, though how many days ahead we didn't know, was a waterfall, the *Chutes de Medoum*. David had been making himself dizzy trying to match the river's curves with the topographic maps he'd bought off the wall of a government office. The maps dated to the year of his birth, 1972, and I'd offered to burn them for him. North of the river was a logging concession owned by Frank Biya, eldest son of the president. The jungle's original inhabitants, the Baka Pygmies, had been forced to abandon their way of life as hunter-gatherers and settle in destitute roadside villages—to prepare the jungle for logging. Under Cameroon's two presidents since independence in 1960, Ahmadou Ahidjo and Biya, more than eighty percent of Cameroon's forest had been logged or allocated for logging.

Yellow and purple butterflies swirled over the canoe. Rapids hissed up ahead with the threat of fast or falling water. We powered to the banks in a burst of half-panicked strokes, our brittle, waterlogged boat so heavy that we had to paddle for ten seconds before it began to respond.

The days on the Boumba were the first I'd taken off from LAGA since I'd moved Future to the Belabo shelter more than a year earlier. LAGA was growing, and Galit Zangwill, a pistol of a woman, had joined. Inspired by the prosecution, she'd sold her car, emptied her Tel Aviv apartment, and flown to Cameroon. Within two days of arriving, Galit corrected me on directions I gave to a taximan. She matched my intensity and thirst for action, and our conversations sounded to others like fighting. Galit coached Eunice, now our office manager, in administration. She trained a legal adviser named Horline who was working alongside Marius. And she went undercover as an ivory buyer.

Modernization was coming to Mendong in the form of motorcycle taximen who shuttled passengers from Carrefour Banane up the hill past my house. Yaoundé was pushing ever outward, a frenzy of building colored the gray of cinderblocks and sheet metal, the forest reverberating with hammering and chainsaws. One evening when Galit and I were walking home from Carrefour Banane, a motorcyclist zipped past and while staring at Galit said, "*Cherie*," and made a kissing sound. The motorcyclist U-turned and buzzed us a second time, saying to Galit, "*Cherie! Cherie!*" The driver motored up the road and turned. As he shifted gears and roared toward us again, Galit reached into her bag for a canister of teargas and sprayed it over her shoulder into the air. The motorcyclist drove into the cloud and spun off his bike.

I tried regularly to ask Galit whether her missions were satisfactory and challenging, whether she was enjoying our work. After a meeting at the British High Commission, I asked her what I'd done well and what I'd done poorly. Galit looked at me and shook her head. "You kept on saying 'I I I,' and we are two people."

Gray parrots whistled their surreal language as they flew in flocks above the canopy. How invigorating it was to enjoy the pull of the Boumba, to reconnect to the bush in a way that LAGA made difficult. We paddled ashore and hacked down brush on the riverbank to make room for the tent. Then David struggled with damp kindling to light a fire.

"Just pour kerosene on it," I said.

He looked up. "You're a man of contradictions, nature boy. If it were minus-twenty and you'd gone through the ice, *then* I'd use kerosene."

The armada of tsetse flies had mostly disappeared with dusk.

"So tell me," David said, chopping garlic after his fire caught, "what kind of self-respecting adventurer starts a fire with kerosene? Your whole code needs tweaking. The meal I'm cooking, like all the others I've cooked, is my refutation that you have to live on untreated river water and seaweed to prove you're having an adventure. Your story in Ethiopia just kills me. You had a *horse*! And you took just four days of food! You could've taken 20kg of rice."

"Daud, listen. If you're in a village and you have a giant can of peanut butter that you eat in the dark so you're not hungry, you haven't cut the safety rope. You're either participating fully or you're not. Keep a foot in your own world, and it changes your interaction with everyone and everything. Once you connect your fate to the bush—that's when you become open."

"But you don't know the environment of the bush you're traveling in, what plants to eat if you're hungry, where to get water—"

"So you learn. Either you have a safety net or you don't."

David added sardines to the garlic, onions, and boiling oil. He said, "Then should we not carry malaria medication because villagers don't have it?"

"Had I kept traveling, I would have stopped carrying medicine. I'm sure. And probably, eventually, everything else. Just a *shuka* and a knife."

"In terms of dinner tonight, Ofi, I'm happy to eat your half of the safety net."

Back in August, Vincent met me in Mendong, put down his old-school tape recorder, and said, "There's a conference coming in Cameroon, AFLEG (African Forest Law Enforcement and Governance). We need to be in it." We then began what Vincent called "Another long game of chess." We wrote a letter to the minister asking to participate. We met with the director of wildlife. We met with the minister's technical adviser to learn who was organizing the event and began a dialogue with him. We called the EU and the World Bank and asked them to push for our inclusion. The multi-front effort—our model for mere survival in Cameroon—led not just to an invitation to the conference but to inclusion *on* the Cameroonian delegation.

"International legitimacy and political stability," Vincent said over a beer at Nlongkak. "These are our goals. Everyone must know that the Cameroonian government made the brave decision to go forward with the LAGA experiment."

AFLEG convened at the Congress Palace in Yaoundé, on a hill that gave views of thunderheads darkening the jungle beyond Mendong. The palace was full of meeting halls, garish in décor and adorned with portraits of Paul Biya. There were simultaneous translations of the meetings, for participants who'd come from across Africa, the U.S., Germany, France. Wearing a tie tied by Vincent's wife, I lobbied for independent monitoring of all protected bushmeat, even in logging concessions. I handed out media kits that were the work of Galit and the team: a description of our court case tracking system, methods for achieving total transparency, and a detailed proposal of LAGA's future plans that David and I had hammered out during many long nights of argument.

"CED and Greenpeace," said Cameroon's minister to his Congolese counterpart, "these are nothing but liars and bandits!"

I brought two letters to AFLEG, one naming LAGA to the government's delegation, the other, written to me after Tonye Nken's prosecution, titled "A Call For Order." It said, "I would like to remind you that wildlife law enforcement is an activity that falls within the sovereignty of the state . . . We urge you to restrict all of your activities to the collection of information and to communicating it to MINEF for its exploitation." The letter had originated in Koulagna's office.

I sat down with World Bank forest adviser Giuseppe Topa, set both letters in front of him, and said, "If you think what LAGA has done is what is needed, then we have two options—two letters. Who makes the difference between one course and the other is the international community. Without you I have no power."

Topa said, "The Bank will do what it can to ensure that LAGA continues its work. I would ignore this second letter."

David and I were on foot, scouting the *Chutes de Medoum*.

"Ofir, there's no way I'm letting you run this."

"We take everything out of the canoe and I ride it over the falls."

"You're looking at two kilometers of rapids! In a canoe too heavy to steer."

"But we can't just leave the *Moshe* behind," I said.

The canoe we'd named after my grandfather. It was so waterlogged, it would have taken ten men to carry it around the falls.

"If you run this," David said, "you and the *Moshe* will be in pieces. Do you hear that sound of water crashing into rocks? I'm not keen on sharing the story of your last minutes with your mother."

"But you know what she would say."

"What *I* say is that the sanctity of Drori family passion and personal choice is invalidated when the chance is greater than ninety percent that you'll smash in your face."

A small viper slithered across the trail.

"Remember," David said, "I've had my own problems in the bush: the bog, brush fires, the tropical storm atop that volcano. But I do owe my mother not to risk my life in any way greater than I already have by traveling through the jungle with *you*."

I hadn't given up on riding over the falls, but we fetched our gear from the boat and followed a trail inland. We came upon two thatched huts where men lounged in air thick with flies and bees. One man said he was the son of the chief of Pana, a nearby village. A woman sat on a stool in front of a small pot filled with an uncooked stew holding some twenty species of fish and crustaceans that David counted. He said, "Here in one pot is proof of what it means for a river to have never been fished."

There was food already cooked, and we had to ask for a bite.

Nestor, a suspicious old man, spoke of the people who'd last tried to run the *Chutes de Medoum*. "Three Germans. Fifty years ago. They didn't make it."

David laughed and looked at me, knowing it only made the challenge more appealing.

Two hunters appeared from the trees, one with an eye so misaligned it seemed to be turned inward toward his brain. Both men wore large backpacks made of bamboo. Jutting through the gaps in one pack were hands and hooves of antelope and monkeys—more than the sum of the animals we'd seen along the Boumba, now mashed together, entangled and turned almost into charcoal. The meat smelled of burnt hair. The second pack held pieces of a dismembered mama gorilla and her baby.

It was impossible to escape the reasons I'd come to Cameroon.

Two more pack-carrying hunters arrived. In one of the packs rode half the mama gorilla, her head split down the middle by a machete, both halves of her face pressed against the bamboo. The skin was dried and shrunken around her eyes, as if the heat of the fire had affixed to her an expression of horror. My mind flashed to the Freetown street girl whose eyes had told the story of the war. I didn't want this. Not now, not when I'd come to rest, not with the LAGA team hundreds of kilometers away and Julius beyond reach. The feeling of impotence amplified my anger.

The main hunter appeared, swinging a double-barreled shotgun. His name was Kelgy Djep, and he wore a new pair of rubber boots. He wiped sweat from his brow and laughed a nervous, quiet laugh. An old man walked beside him.

David asked to see the gun and then read the barrel, "'Made in the USSR.'"

"I'm from Yokadouma," the old man said. "These are my hunters."

He was a dealer. He activated hunters to slaughter all the animals they could find. Poaching did not originate in the forest; it was driven by the commercial trade. The old man had likely come into the bush—a rarity for a dealer—because it was New Year's Eve; and the hunters might be tempted to sell meat on the sly to fund a celebration.

The hunter with the owl eye removed hunks of gorilla from his pack. Then he pulled out a gorilla hand twice the size of his. The son of the chief of Pana bartered with the dealer, then stuffed the hand and a piece of meat into his bag.

We have to do something, I thought.

In the caravan of hunters, we headed for Pana.

Earlier that month, Born Free and the British High Commission sponsored my trip to London for a conference—Bushmeat and Livelihood—and I rode the Underground to the meeting hall. Intimidated by all the Brits, I pretended to have a reason to make a phone call and just rang Elad, on whose couch I was sleeping.* I spotted our delegation in the crowd, Koulagna among them, his arms wrapped around his shivering body. We shook hands and laughed that we were together here.

"Can you believe how cold it is in London?" I said.

"The only thing worse is the food," Koulagna said and laughed.

A stream of conference-goers approached me when they saw I was part of the delegation, which was headed by the minister. Koulagna and I stood shoulder to shoulder and together we emphasized the importance of law enforcement. Koulagna was from Cameroon's Muslim north but he was a Christian. He'd been my best teacher in the art of politics, and even when I'd left his office feeling out-maneuvered, I'd never failed to appreciate his craft.

A Ghanaian king in native dress, flanked by spear-bearing guards, stepped up to the microphone to address the delegates. Though the weather outside was near freezing, half his chest remained uncovered. Conservation is already African, the king said in words reminding me of Isaac. Nature is a gift we were given to preserve.

---

* In 2008, Elad released his fifth album of experimental music, which was described by a critic as a "laid-back, evilly-humming introverted rattlesnake of electric drone."

On the advice of Francis Ngwa, I went to Bushhouse London to record an interview with the BBC, which was broadcast internationally. Vincent called when he heard me on the radio in Cameroon. "You're terrorizing people here with your powers! All our enemies in the ministry are shaking." Galit, who was running LAGA in my absence, called to say that the ivory dealer Adamou Ndjidda had received a month in jail.

In my backpack was a video camera, and David and I concluded that the only meaningful outlet for our anger was filming the hunters on a hunt. If we had footage of Kelgy Djep splitting open the head of the next mama gorilla he killed, we could bring the world down on Cameroon. To gain the trust of the hunters, we needed to be who we weren't, and David was posing as a man enthusiastic about hunting and working to convince Kelgy Djep to take him on his next trip into the jungle; whites did come to the forests of eastern Cameroon to hunt elephants and leopards. But getting any indication from Kelgy about his plans was nearly impossible, because he and the hunters, since returning to their villages, had been drunk to the point of incoherence.

In Pana, we sat around the night fire, which burned to keep away moot-moots. The son of the chief pointed at what I assumed was Venus and said, "Is that a U.S .satellite? I know they're spying on our village." He went into his hut. He'd been feeding us, though he'd already mentioned he wanted the canoe as a gift. When he returned to the fire, he was carrying two pots that he set on the ground at our feet.

He said, "*Ca c'est la gorille.*"

Chills washed over me. I shook my head. David and I glanced at each other. There wasn't a chance he would eat it. He tore away a hunk of couscous manioc and faked dipping it into the molasses-black gorilla stew. "Ofi," he whispered, "it's too dark for them to see and it's okay if we give it all back to them."

He was wrong, I thought, if we were going to get revenge. For if they were to believe we were hunters, we couldn't refuse the spoils of the hunt.

I stared at the chunks of gorilla meat in the pot and pulled my legs to my chest. Here it was, almost by accident, the confrontation I hadn't come looking for, that I hadn't known to look for, but that was so eerily perfect I might have. Every instinct in my body screamed to run, to back away, to take shelter. A *moran* of the Maasai searched for the lion, not to prove to others who he was, but to determine who he was for himself. The confrontation sitting before me on the ground didn't put my life at risk. But whether I had the tools to cope with the emotional fallout of eating the meat of an ape, I had no way of knowing. That I didn't know this and that I might easily push the pot away were *precisely* the reasons why my heart was thumping against my knees. The true journey was the one from which you *chose* not to return. I thought of Future, Jack, and Kita as I forced the first bite of flesh into my mouth. Then a second bite. A third.

I felt sick.

"Thanks," David said, handing the pots back. "We already ate in the other village."

No one would understand this. No one would understand but David, and part of me wished even he weren't here so I might be able to forget. Though it was too deep a cut to leave any hope of forgetting. I entered the house of the son of the chief of Pana and fed sugar cubes into my mouth.

SUIT ADVENTURES AND THE COCKROACHES OF THE SEA

The high-rise hotel of the Japanese delegation stood on the far side of Sukhumvit Road, a giant obstacle of access lanes, overpasses, tracks of the Bangkok sky train and cars zipping by at 100km an hour. Takang Ebai and Francis Tarla, both Cameroonian officials, looked at me, then back at the massive road, and we laughed as if it were our first time out of the bush.

"We can't cross here!" Takang said. "Let's move down. Maybe there's a way."

We strolled up Sukhumvit, chatting like men scouting for a bar, unconcerned with whether we were late for dinner with the Japanese delegation. We walked a kilometer along the highway and U-turned and found a small gap in the fence. And we sprinted across traffic in our suits.

We'd come to Thailand, along with 1,200 delegates from some 150 countries, for the United Nations Convention on International Trade in Endangered Species (CITES). Vincent's never-ending chess match had succeeded in getting LAGA onto Cameroon's delegation, a rare feat at CITES for an NGO. In Bangkok, countries would debate and vote on proposals related to increasing or decreasing protection under international law for dozens of species, including elephants and whales. On the eve of the conference, the Japanese invited the Cameroonian delegation and me to dinner.

The marble lobby of the hotel and then the mirrored elevator put an end to conversation. I looked at Takang and Takang looked at Francis. All of us were nervous about what was waiting high up in the luxury hotel. CITES proposals and laws protecting wildlife were in direct conflict with Japanese economic interests, and, in the days leading up to the conference, the Japanese ambassador to Cameroon had been aggressive in working the halls of MINEF.

Takang, the new director of wildlife, was a forthright and honest man so overwhelmed by the breakfast buffet at our hotel that he'd insisted we not waste the abundance on breakfast alone and try to eat enough to stay full until dinner. Francis, the director of the Wildlife School of Garoua, was short, round, and full of laughter.

The elevator opened, and a Thai bellhop directed us through a restaurant to a private dining room. Two young Japanese men stood by the door. The head Japanese delegate, Kiyoshi Koinuma, was seated at a circular wood table with four other Japanese men, the head Norwegian delegate, and a Tunisian.

"Did you have a hard time finding the hotel?" said the elder Japanese.

"No, no," Takang said, glancing at Francis. "No problem at all."

Takang sat and shifted uncomfortably.

"So Bangkok is a beautiful city, right?" Kiyoshi said. "You should take your time and enjoy yourselves. You know there are many things to do in Bangkok."

"Yes, of course," Takang said, waving his hand. "We are sure to enjoy everything. Oh, yes."

Takang had great flaring ears.

The waiters descended and loaded tiny bowls onto the table and began spinning a built-in carousel, wheeling bowls around the table's curve with such precision it seemed rehearsed. A bowl stopped in front of me. I picked up a spoon and stared down at a piece of meat floating in colorless broth.

A younger Japanese man at the table began speaking: "Have you had a chance—"

"If you want explore the city," Kiyoshi said, interrupting the younger Japanese, "we can take you around. You don't only need to work; you need to enjoy."

Francis was squeezing his napkin.

We emptied our small white bowls and placed them on the giant carousel. They were whisked around the curve of the table and replaced by more small white bowls. I stared down at another piece of meat floating in colorless broth. Takang smiled at me and let out a little laugh as he sipped from his spoon, no doubt thinking as I was that it wasn't food.

"What you had first was shark fin soup," Kiyoshi said. "And this is another shark fin soup, which is better."

The Norwegian, Oystein Storkersen, leaned toward Takang and said, "How was the ivory dialogue?"

"Tiring," Takang said. "Too tiring."

"To me it seems to be a simple issue," Storkersen said, setting his elbows on the table. "They just have to sell that ivory and that's it."

CITES had relaxed the ban on the international trade in ivory and approved the sale of the Southern African ivory stockpiles to the Japanese. But Japan had not met the conditions to become a buyer, and the heated debate between countries before the conference concerned whether to allow the sale to proceed. There were two camps: pro-use and pro-conservation. The pro-use side, supported by most everyone, including Cameroon, claimed that in order to preserve wildlife it had to be used—hunted and traded. *Kill them to save them.* On the conservation side, in the entire convention, only the Israelis, because of Bill Clark, the Indians; and the Kenyans, led by Patrick Omondi, were strong voices for conservation. The EU and the U.S. were conspicuously quiet on the ivory issue.

"Selling the stockpile is not as simple as you present," I said to the Norwegian, though it occurred to me that I shouldn't reveal my position. "The issue is what will happen with elephants, not with the existing ivory. Selling any ivory will likely lead to a surge in poaching and will open a bigger window for illegal dealing, with CITES permits used for laundering it. This is a major problem in Cameroon. Our elephants are being killed off."

Kiyoshi began to speak in a loud voice. He moved the subject from the savannah to the ocean and criticized NGOs for acting irrationally and claimed they were harming the fishing industry. "They don't understand the importance of fisheries."

Takang and Francis seemed relieved that they didn't have to talk.

"We have a full scientific program studying whales," said another Japanese. "There are too many of them." *I o.O*

"Every time people interfere in our industry and stop us from whaling, it's contrary to science," Kiyoshi said. "What are the whales?" He paused and looked around the table. "They are the cockroaches of the sea."

Kiyoshi laughed, and his laughter spread to the Japanese on either side of him, to the Norwegian and then to the young Japanese still standing at the door. Outnumbered, Takang and Francis also laughed.

More bowls of soup were spun in front of us, emptied, and ushered off.

Kiyoshi became quiet, then said, "We are very disappointed that our chair was not chosen for Committee I. We proposed a very competent man and he was not considered." The chairman of Committee I oversaw species proposals, including those concerning elephants and whales.

I looked down at the worn knees of my old loaned suit.

Kiyoshi put a sheet of paper on the table in front of him and with two fingers spun the carousel. The paper rode past the younger Japanese and the Tunisian and stopped in front of Takang. I was close enough to read, "Cameroon: Thank you, chairman, Cameroon would like to express its disappointment that the candidate proposed by Japan to chair Committee I was not considered and to protest that no explanation has been given as to why such a competent man . . ."

Takang looked up.

Kiyoshi said, "Read this tomorrow at the conference."

The meeting ended.

We took the elevator down and walked up the road looking for a place to eat.

"Director," I said to Takang, "what are you going to do?"

"What can I do?" he said. "They are the Japanese."

LAGA was running simultaneous investigations and making arrests in provinces across Cameroon. Many potential donors commended our work, but the risk scared them away. They said, "What happens if someone gets killed in the field? How will it reflect on us?" In spite of the worries, the World Bank and others had provided funding. And IFAW had sponsored my flight to Thailand.

But many moneyless months meant our team often worked without pay. Eunice and Julius had contributed their own resources to fund operations. I'd sold a guitar so we could eat. The constant struggle for funding had benefits, though, by weeding out those seeking comfortable jobs and by selecting a class of people driven by principle, pride, and the need to belong to a team. Every new LAGA member had to eat the proverbial shit by proving he or she could go to the field without funding and produce an operation. Those who couldn't invent solutions, we did not want.

LAGA's first investigator, Christopher, had died. His family thought it was from lung cancer, as he was a heavy smoker and had been coughing for months. The whole LAGA team attended his funeral.

With trust beginning to break between players in the animal trade in Cameroon and with the ability to complete transactions growing more difficult, dealers were evolving their methods, demanding that sales occur inside their homes or inside corrupt police stations, moving their contraband, arriving to sales without it, randomly switching meeting places and times. Dealers were cautioning our undercover agents to stay away from wildlife trading, warning them about the very sting operations we were setting up to arrest them in. We'd mapped the flow of ivory and endangered species along international trade routes through Central and West Africa. And we were arresting the major criminals of the trade—a police commissioner, wealthy ivory dealers who'd spent lifetimes building international relationships, foreign nationals, a man who admitted to killing 278 elephants, and a drug dealer who activated poachers.

In the first attempt to replicate the LAGA model elsewhere in Africa, Galit had traveled to Kinshasa. She was thrilled when the minister of environment agreed to our terms and welcomed us to start law enforcement in DRC. But her excitement vanished as the meeting ended when the warlord-turned-minister sent the translator out and asked her in English how she could help him get weapons from Israel.

The prime minister of Thailand opened CITES. With his face projected on screens said to be the largest in Southeast Asia, he declared, "The queen

of Thailand is a conservationist." The man who'd planned the whole conference, Thailand's director of wildlife, was absent; he'd been sacked for
approving the illegal export of one hundred tigers to China.

I participated in the Export Quotas Working Group, which was
charged with setting limits on sports hunting for endangered and
threatened species, including elephants, leopards, and lions. The obese
American delegate chairing the group seemed to open the meeting
by closing it. Though we had two weeks to work, she said, "Since we
don't have enough time in Thailand, I think we should work by email.
I can do most of the work for you and send you a draft decision. My
friend here is my neighbor in Washington, so we will do it together."
She pointed to her friend. He was the head of Safari Club International,
the largest hunting organization in the world. Takang recognized the
man as the sponsor of annual trips of African delegates to Las Vegas
where they discussed the benefits of hunting in strip clubs.

Delegates sat in endless rows of tables, listening to translations of
speeches on their headphones. The head delegate of each country had
an electronic card used for casting the vote. The sixty-second voting
period began on whether to increase protection for the Irrawaddy dol-
phin, against the wishes of the Japanese.* The hall went quiet. Then I
looked up. Two men at the Cambodian table were arguing in front of
me. They stood, faced each other, and began to shout.

"It is my decision and I cast the vote!" said one Cambodian delegate.

"This is *not* the position," said the other.

They grappled over the voting button in a scene straight from *Dr.
Strangelove*.

Later, I described the fight to a colleague, and she said, "I know
that guy. He's not from Cambodia. The Japanese forced him onto that
delegation. The guy's from Singapore and he's been a front man for the
fisheries industry for other delegations in the past."**

The gorge with no way across that I'd found on first arriving in
Cameroon seemed to stretch to everywhere.

---

* June 2009, WWF determined that there were no more than 76 Irrawaddy dol-
phins left, all in their native Mekong River, which was a long way from Japan.
** See: *The Straits Times*, 1/12/2006, "Shark Finning: Shark's fin soup—eat
without guilt" by Giam Choo Hoo.

LOVE, ANGER, & ACTIVISM

I gripped the concrete railing and began up the stairs to the family flat in Tel Aviv, stairs I'd climbed dozens of times oozing blood after flying off skateboards and ramps with Mor. I was in Israel for a week, en route to a meeting in Marrakech on environmental crime. The front door was uneven along the bottom, because Elad and I had once raced to hide the damage of a wrecked hinge by planing off a few centimeters of wood. I turned the key and pushed inside. The flat was now rented to an Arab man who lived elsewhere and who'd left little more in the living room than a mattress.

My parents had divorced, my parents who'd folk-danced three times a week in all the years they'd been together. Before the end, Mor had moved away from Tel Aviv to study sociology, left, as a friend had said, "like a rat fleeing a sinking ship." Mom moved to a kibbutz near the Sea of Galilee, and Dad lived now in Pattaya, Thailand, with a woman with whom he shared no language. He was also the rabbi in the city of sin.

Below the window of my parents' room was the overgrown yard where Mor and I had caught bugs for our lizards, the place we'd pretended we were flowers withering and Mom had sprayed us with water to bring us back to life. The kitchen was foodless, the sink dry and specked with flakes of paint. My room was cluttered, unused, my things still scattered about—letters Mor had written from South America, a projector from my teaching days, and a photograph of Kakuya. I opened my desk and found one of the rings I'd bought for Rachel in Addis Ababa, a woven ring made from the silver of melted coins.

I'd been picking at old wounds.

In Yaoundé, I'd written letters to Rachel as soon as I woke, letters I never sent, and I'd played songs on the guitar for her in the dark. What distress there was in struggling to recall the details—her nose, smile, voice. A memory from Uganda came back to me like a relief, and I remembered her subtle lisp when she said, *"Ani rotsa otkhah."* I want you. The pieces were vanishing, though, memory a creature that aged no matter the care it received.

I'd realized something about myself I didn't like. I'd moved away from, rather than toward, love, not just with Rachel but in ways that hindered my ability to see things like kindness in faces, that hindered my desire to dance in villages and to honor old men. Photography had morphed from a way of sharing the wonder of scenes into a tool, using hidden cameras, aimed at documenting crime. The Sudanese refugee in Lokichokio had been a symbol infused with a motivation that spurred me to fight for change, but I was not driven by love for him as much as by hatred for those who'd wronged him. It was hatred and anger that gave me the energy to act, that then led to the search for more causes and to an awareness of more injustice, which led to more anger. And I found myself in a place far from where I'd imagined I'd be.

I slid the ring onto my finger and unfolded one of Rachel's poems, written in Hebrew, which I still kept in my wallet, though I hadn't heard from her in the three years since she'd pushed me out of our apartment.

> I wait for an alien wind
> to summon me into a hollow refuge
> where I clutch good earth until
> memory carves a tear through stone.

Resting among mounds of ash
I seal my eyes
and on my lips will wither a question.

I locked the flat and boarded a bus to Jerusalem, with music pouring from my headphones. Hope began to reach and curl through my thoughts like a plant finally put in the sun. When I arrived in Jerusalem, with the ring on my finger and old stone walls passing outside the windows of the bus, I was lit up by the urge to share my life with Rachel, to watch her invite neighbors for dinner, to have her encourage me to visit Future in Belabo again, to roam together in search of street boys, as in Nairobi, in hopes of persuading them to abandon their sniffing glue. I'd expected that my long search for purpose would fill me to the point of forgetting her. That my feelings were undiminished made clear the rightness of our time together in the past and the rightness of our being together again—and in marriage.

Dry-mouthed, I put down my bag at a public phone, feeling the pulse in my cheek as I dialed the number of Einat, the only friend Rachel and I shared. I spun the ring on my finger and recited my opening lines so Einat wouldn't stop me before I began.

She answered.

"Hey, Einat, it's me. It's Ofir. Listen, I know I promised never to talk to you about this. I know. But it's important. I've been thinking a lot about this, of Rachel, and you know—I still love her. I love her and I have something to—"

"Ofir!" Einat said.

"Yes but listen to what I'm saying. I want—"

"Ofir!"

"Yes."

"Ofir. Rachel gets married next week."

The moon shone on Marrakech with a light I would have once tried to capture. Off from the conference for an evening, I was finally out of my worn suit, roaming the markets where traders had once sold slaves. Moroccans wandered past fortune-tellers, acrobats, boxing children. The air was spiced with incense. I looked from side to side, trying to take it all in, the fabrics for sale, the peacock feathers, leather lamps, lizards in a wooden cage, painted camel bones, turtles, and a fire blower. The market was so frenetic and disorienting, I felt like Grandpa Moshe in the days my sister and I had forced him to play computer games.

An old blind man held out his hand to the stream of indifferent passersby. He sang, but too softly to gain any measure over the low roar of the market. I joined a crowd around a drum circle. As the beat vibrated into my chest, I understood that years of fighting in Cameroon had left me more fulfilled than I'd ever been but also emotionally depleted, as though what I'd accomplished had been as exhausting as screaming at someone I loved or was struggling to love. As I strolled through the market, past Moroccans ringing a storyteller, I doubted I would be able to hold on to the thought, but for a moment I understood that my ceremonies for Rachel were rituals for a ghost, the desperate urge to correct an imbalance in myself.

I was flooded then with so many moments of happiness with her—of flying in Uganda and our first kiss at the Monkey Park—wild happiness, the happiness of storms. The old stone walls of Marrakech reminded me of Jerusalem and for an instant I was there, in the Old City with Rachel's hand on my leg and the full moon so low it seemed to be touching the town, as the moon was now low over Marrakech. I thought, If I stop giving what I have to memories, perhaps I can give to someone new and relearn to see more of what isn't harsh. Or perhaps the strength for this is beyond me.

I returned to the singing blind man, pulled the silver ring off my finger and placed it in his outstretched hand. Then I turned and walked on through the market.

APPRENTICE SORCERERS IN THE SHADOWS

Paul Biya, in power since 1982, declared that he wanted Cameroon's constitution amended to remove term limits. The president had long been accused by the opposition of being a dictator who'd left the country crippled by corruption and poverty despite its vast natural wealth. Media outlets discussed whether the move to change the constitution was undemocratic. Biya had said that the constitutional limit on his ability to run for another term in 2011 "sits badly with the very idea of democratic choice." Then he closed three radio stations and a television station. In the city of Douala, motorcycle taximen protested, and a riot broke out.

Three days earlier, I'd sent Barrister Mbuan to Douala, a lawyer working LAGA's cases for the ministry. Trapped in his Douala hotel room because of the rioting, shouting into the phone, he described the scene below his window, of motorcyclists wrestling policemen, bloodied faces, guns fired in the air, burning cars. Julius was scrambling to find officers to evacuate him when a cloud of teargas seeped in around the windows and doors of his hotel room, and Barrister Mbuan had to flee.

Deaths that day in Douala sparked student riots in the southwest and northwest provinces. The opposition party called for a rally, which Biya prohibited. As riots spread across Cameroon, I tried to maintain the routine of the office, for, as the army had taught, *the routine protects you.*

I'd moved LAGA and myself from Mendong to Vallée Nlongkak, within Yaoundé proper, and we worked out of a large flat that doubled as my home. For three years, LAGA had averaged one arrest per week of a major dealer for wildlife crime. Depending on the year, 87% to 97% of offenders had been behind bars from the day of the arrest, which was essential when the accused could disappear into a remote village or cross a border out of Cameroon. Vincent, the publishing titan, was running media pieces every day of every year. The LAGA family had grown to a dozen members, all on salary.

When taxi drivers in Yaoundé went on strike, I arranged for a man in a rented car to pick up the staff from their homes and bring them to the office. I was storing food—sacks of rice, sardines, onions, spaghetti, bottled water. The office balcony gave views of smoke rising from nearby streets. Some radio stations were broadcasting nothing but music. Others were silent.

I tried to maintain contact with our investigators, who were stuck in towns across the country. The government was attributing the riots to rising food and fuel prices. "We can already say there are more than one hundred dead," said Madeleine Afite of *Maison des Droits de L'Homme*. "I've been told that I've become a target since I've talked in public about the casualty toll. My car was smashed up last night." No one knew whether Cameroon stood at the edge of revolution, a spontaneous uprising against the president. As rioting intensified, CRTV announced that Biya would give a speech.

"He has to acknowledge why people are in the streets," Julius told me on the phone. He was helping to maintain order in west province.

When Paul Biya appeared on state television, he said, ". . . The apprentice sorcerers in the shadows who have handled these youths were not concerned about the risk they were running . . . To those responsible for manipulating the young for their own aims, I say that their attempts are doomed to failure. All legal means available to the government will be brought into play to ensure the rule of law."

The next morning, though the opposition party had called on people to walk through Yaoundé wearing black, the streets were eerily empty. Kiosks were shuttered, most Cameroonians out of sight. Anxious on empty streets but wanting a hot meal, I went left toward the junction of Vallée Nlongkak. Military vehicles roared by, carrying soldiers. Armed men patrolled on foot. In the spot where a fish lady and meat man usually sold their food was a new army post fortified with sandbags. A soldier of Cameroon's presidential guard gripped a mounted machinegun. And he wore an olive green uniform bearing in Hebrew the initials of the Israel Defense Forces.[*]

---

[*] Biya's Presidential Guard was trained by an Israeli Colonel and was supplied military equipment by Israel.

FELA SAID,
"I HAVE DEATH IN MY POUCH."

"His name is Ikama. He's an ivory dealer. But he's the big one, the big fish," the French investigator told me at a hotel in Brazzaville. "I'm not sure you can go after him. His carving skills are renowned. He's well connected. He mentioned he supplies ministers and a colonel. He trades with West Africans. Chinese nationals visit his workshop every week. But if we can take him down, it will have a real impact on the ivory trade."

A year earlier, the investigator and I had bumped into each other at random in Kinshasa and taken a drink in a dark bar among Israeli diamond merchants. He'd been working undercover for TRAFFIC, the wildlife trade monitoring network, cataloguing ivory for sale in African markets. In Cameroon he'd found that the ivory trade was feeling intense pressure from law enforcement and he'd even been *chased* out of a market for inquiring about ivory when in all the other countries he'd been welcomed. The data he'd collected he didn't want dying in reports, so I'd given him a hidden camera.

"I've just come from Ikama's workshop," the investigator told me in his hotel room in Brazzaville. "Carvers there are using the usual dentistry tools. It smells of burned ivory. The workshop is at his house in the Ouenzé quarter. It's a popular area, maybe not the safest place for an operation. You have a high wall around the compound, newly painted. It looks like a small fortress. Inside you're trapped with no possibility to call anybody in the street."

He drew me a diagram.

"Is he willing to supply the ivory somewhere else?" I said. "Outside the shop?"

"Ikama seems suspicious because I haven't bought anything. VIPs and big dealers from Kinshasa usually come to collect their orders at his house. But if I can buy something, I know I can lure him out."

"I'll get you some Euros," I said, "and you count them in front of him and calculate how much money is missing to complete the deal. We call it *flashing*. Then say you'll meet him later today."

The illegal trade of ivory was escalating under the umbrella of organized crime. At the Hong Kong port, a mobile x-ray scanner had revealed a hidden compartment in a shipping container holding 3.9 tons of ivory, ivory from more than three hundred elephants. The ship had sailed for Hong Kong from Douala, and the shell company that owned the container, Norkis Sarl, operated out of a private house in Yaoundé, in Bastos, not far from WWF. During our investigation, we discovered two more containers with false compartments, which I combed with a tiny brush. The DNA of the ivory chips, Dr. Samuel Wasser of the University of Washington matched with DNA in his database and traced to the rainforest in Gabon near the Congolese border. One container every three months had been sailing for Hong Kong with a hidden compartment packed with ivory. Three suspects, two of them Taiwanese nationals, fled Cameroon when the shipment was seized in Hong Kong. We arrested a Cameroonian accomplice whose testimony led to an indictment of the Taiwanese. But then the police commissioner released the man suddenly, and he disappeared. Later, in a house search, we found a receipt for funds sent by the Taiwanese to their Cameroonian workers who'd "managed" the situation with bribes. The receipt said, "Release Jean Claude in Douala, 500,000 CFA." Cameroon received an Interpol Award for its investigation with LAGA, and our team was now seeking international arrest warrants.

Empowered by press in Europe, by an award received from CITES' secretary general and by the continued enthusiasm of the international community, we'd decided it was time to replicate LAGA in the Republic of Congo. Luc Mathot, a Belgian and the coordinator of the Aspinall Foundation, had contacted me months earlier, enthusiastic about bringing wildlife law enforcement to the country. I'd traveled to Brazzaville with a plan to squeeze the building of a new organization into a month, by fostering relationships with the ministry, the police force, and the courts and by beginning recruitment. The U.S. Fish and Wildlife Service and The United Nations Environment Programme were ready with financial support, and WCS, once closed to the idea of LAGA, had agreed to take part.

In the operation to arrest Ikama, I chose the restaurant inside the Hotel Hippocampe, which was shielded from the street and onlookers. The investigator had picked out more than $2,000 of worked ivory and persuaded Ikama to deliver it in town. Four officers on standby waited in a taxi outside the restaurant, which was deserted. I walked across a terrace toward the Chinese food buffet and took a table. A few meters away, just off the patio, was a broken swing set. At another table sat four men including two undercover gendarmes and Bonaventure, a ministry officer with jurisdiction in all of Congo. Wearing glasses and a fine gray suit, Bonaventure had the look of a statesman. We'd gotten to know each other at conferences where we'd often been the only participants involved with enforcement. He was on the Lusaka Agreement Taskforce.

I focused on the entrance and waited for Ikama.

A man in a blue cap appeared by the terrace. In his hand was a brownish bag as old and ripped as our undercover camera bags. He was a stout man, sweating, wearing tattered clothes, and he surveyed the tables, turned, walked a few meters, then stopped again. Something was wrong. According to the investigator, Ikama had been wearing a blue dress shirt earlier in the day, and I doubted he would have changed into old clothes for a sale. Maybe this man had been sent as a decoy. Or maybe it *was* Ikama. I called the investigator on my cell phone, fearing our target was about to slip away.

"Call him and find out where he is," I said while watching the jittery gendarmes who seemed on the verge of leaping from their chairs to make an arrest—of potentially the wrong man. I hung up, waited. When he rang me back, the investigator said, "I called Ikama. He's leaving his workshop. He'll reach the restaurant in half an hour."

I walked to Bonaventure's table where each man was eyeing the entrance.

"It's delayed," I said.

"But it's him with the brown bag, the heavy bag," said a gendarme. "We go for him."

"No," I said, trying not to shout, "he's *not* the one. Our target is coming."

"You're sure?"

Restless, I crossed the terrace to the parking lot and scanned for anyone loitering. A driver sat inside a car. He glanced over his shoulder at me, and I watched him, worried. When a Congolese man walked out of the restaurant to talk to him, I returned to Bonaventure's table, unable to shake the feeling that something was off. Why was Ikama so late? Maybe someone had entered and talked to the waiters. I missed having Julius here, someone I could trust to act fast and improvise if things spun out of control.

"If the information is bad," said a gendarme, "we can't stay forever."

I clenched my teeth. "Hang on. It won't be long."

I sat and looked at my phone and was about to get up again when I realized I was broadcasting nervousness. I refocused. A man entered in a blue dress shirt. He was distinguished and looked to be in his sixties. He carried a black plastic bag, the woven kind that always cut my hand when I filled them with too many plantains. I called the investigator and whispered, "Call him now. Say you just left the Hippocampe because you were waiting too long. Tell him you can return."

I hung up, held my breath and watched. The phone chimed in Ikama's hand.

I rang Bonaventure across the restaurant. "He's the one."

The men sprang from their chairs and strode toward Ikama, who didn't move. Bonaventure seized the bag and pulled out a carving of a woman.

"That's ivory," a gendarme said.

"You need to come with us to the station," said Bonaventure.

I circled Ikama as the taxi pulled up outside. The gendarmes put Ikama into the back seat with a pair of armed men, and Bonaventure and I followed them to the station.

I'd encouraged LAGA's people to make our NGO a stopping point on the way to their own fights as independent activists. Arrey, an aspiring writer who I'd recruited for our management team, was working on books to educate children about AIDS and the environment. Eric, Vincent's assistant, had registered an NGO with the intent of observing the coming election. Eric argued that efforts to promote democracy around election day ignored that Cameroonians participated in pseudo-democratic activities in everything from village women's meetings to youth groups, where coerced voting was rampant, along with money influence and a lack of freedom of speech; and until these everyday practices were eliminated, election day efforts were doomed. Anna, a linguist, was working on a project to document newspeak in the development and aid business. Saturday afternoons we reserved for debate, films, and presentations. And Cameroon's Peace Corps decided to use our model for activism in their education program. Eunice was now studying in Europe. Galit was back in Israel, pursuing a masters in International Conflicts Resolution. And Marius had gotten a Ph.D. in France in environmental law, earning highest honors.

I faced Bonaventure at Congo's central *gendarmerie*. I said, "From my investigator, I know the man has far more ivory at his house. We have to go and search there."

"First," Bonaventure said, "we need to interrogate him."

"We cannot afford to lose time."

I rallied the gendarmes. The operation with Ikama had been professional, and the men listened to me. "In Cameroon we do this every week. What we do now is continue with the information we have and search his house."

Bonaventure began the interrogation, but then stopped and pulled me aside. "Ofir, I know this man. And *everybody* knows his son. I don't know if you realize we've arrested a well-known man." Bonaventure removed his glasses. "His son was a rebel leader in the war."

"Then we can go to his house with a larger force," I said.

"Ofir, his son could come here to the station with his own people, you understand? If we go to the house, he could meet us there. It could be a disaster."

"There is ivory in his compound, and we need to apply the law."

"Don't push it, Ofir."

Word spread through the station of the identity of the man in the corner wearing a fine blue shirt. His son, Marien Ikama, had been a rebel leader in the Forces Armées Congolaises or the Cobra militia. An officer told me that at war's end, the president had executed many Cobra leaders. Other Cobras had been brought into the government, but questions remained about how many had disarmed.

The men in the station were stalling.

"Let's wait," a gendarme said. "Let's wait."

"This area where Ikama lives is a difficult place," said a man in a blue army jacket. "These old rebels are there. We can't enter with just five men."

The gendarmes were pacing with their rifles when the captain arrived wearing Adidas warm-ups. A lean man with a shaved head, he did not break my gaze when I briefed him on the situation. "We go now," I said. "Now. Before word is out he's arrested. There's no other option, and it's better we do it quick."

The captain looked at my boots and then back at my face, and I imagined he was wondering why I was talking like his commander.

"So we'll take more men," the captain said.

Fifteen gendarmes loaded into two open-backed vehicles and a private car. Over Bonaventure's protestations that I shouldn't go because of the risk, I climbed into the back of one vehicle, and we headed out. The men gripped rifles as we raced through Brazzaville, everyone quiet and many staring at their shoes. Daylight was fading, and we zipped in and out of traffic, our drivers honking, flashing their lights. I was the only man without a gun.

"Maybe we don't have enough people," one officer said.

"You know if they come we'll have a fight."

Ikama's neighborhood, the 5th district of Brazzaville, was dirty, potholed, and full of mud-brick houses. We turned, turned again, through alleys narrow enough to be blocked by a single car. And I lost all sense of where we were. I flashed to Sierra Leone and tried to call on old moments I'd been able to pass with a little determination and heavy doses of luck—when I'd dragged myself bleeding up to the road in Nigeria and stormed markets with Julius. Cameroonians had told me I was making bigger and bigger enemies. LAGA had uncovered high-level corruption in Cameroon's ministry; the number two man, the secretary general, had been suspected of involvement in a CITES fraud scheme and the illegal export of thousands of African gray parrots. I'd been threatened, told my days were numbered, and I slept with the lights on and a Maasai knife beside my bed. As our trucks raced through the alleyways, I knew the risks I was taking were pushing me closer to a violent end. The life of every man heading toward Ikama's house was on the line. But for me it was okay to die doing what I was meant to do on the continent I loved. I leaned back and opened my eyes and looked up at the sky darkening over Brazzaville.

I'm too fond of stars to be fearful of the night.

We stopped at a metal gate. I gripped my teargas and jumped down with the gendarmes, legs shaking, the men gripping rifles with both hands. Stay close to the guns, I told myself. A soldier pounded the gate as gendarmes flared out around the house. A young man opened the gate and backpedalled with his hands in the air. The captain and I crossed the courtyard to a workbench fitted with clamps. There were grinders, a saw. "This is where he cuts the ivory," I shouted. "Look at the dust." I grabbed a sack from the ground and yanked out three chunks of cut ivory, dropped one. "You see? There *is* more here at the house."

We sprinted to the living room. Three leopard skins lay on the floor. The ceiling was festooned with a fancy pattern of stained wood, this one room twice the size of many huts along the road. We bounded into a bedroom. Against the wall stood an old man with a small boy, and they swung their heads to watch the captain and me dash through a doorway. Two gendarmes ran in with guns raised. The captain shouted through a window to those at the perimeter.

"Where's the ivory?" yelled a gendarme at the old man. "Show it to us."

"I didn't do anything," the old man said. "I'll collaborate."

I sprinted outside to search. There had to be more ivory. Men shouted orders back and forth. We were taking too long. We needed to be gone. Behind the workbench in the front was a small window blocked by blue curtains. Through the gap I could see into a room filled with carvings. "Captain!" He ran out and looked to where I pointed. Five seconds later we were back in the living room, and he was staring down the young man who'd opened the gate.

"Get us into that room!" the captain said.

"I don't have the key. I don't have it."

The captain looked at the door. Scratched his neck. He was thinking it was better to leave. I stepped around him and kicked it. "This door can be broken," I said. "Let's do it together."

The captain took one step back and rammed his shoulder into the door, which splintered open at the hinges. There were two exhibit rooms full of worked ivory, statues, jewelry, a long finely carved tusk, necklaces on the walls. Unprocessed ivory lay on the floor. Everywhere we looked was ivory. The rooms were like temples.

"We have to move," the captain said to the men. "Fill up those sacks. Let's go."

The soldiers spun their rifles onto their backs, and the four of us tossed pieces of ivory into the grain sacks like men in a bank vault. The soldiers kept glancing toward the door, yelling to men beyond the room.

"Wrap it up," we heard from outside.

The captain said, "We have enough. Let's move out."

I picked up a few last pieces, tucked the leopard skins under my arm and raced through the compound. Troops at the gate turned and yelled to those beyond.

"We can move! Start the trucks!"

A man was standing in the back of one vehicle, rifle ready. Men hopped in around him. "Come come come," they said to us. The drivers gunned the engines as we tore away from Ikama's house through muddy alleys, the men watching behind us, everyone breathing hard, our heads wobbling with the potholes. I watched ahead of us, as far as the headlights allowed, fearing we would find our path out the neighborhood blocked.

When Marius returned from France with his Ph.D., we began building a new NGO, Anti-Corruption Cameroon (AC), with the aim of establishing anti-corruption law enforcement built on the same model as LAGA. The international community had long framed corruption as a technical problem and not a problem of accountability; the fight against corruption ignored *people*, and in Cameroon people died in hospitals because they couldn't pay bribes to doctors.

In the ministries in Yaoundé, at the court, in immigration and Police Frontiere, we pasted up posters that read, "If you are a victim of corruption, call this number and we will help you fight back." An investigator searched for victims. He approached people on the steps of different ministries to ask if they'd been refused services. Marius, working without salary, began taking calls on a dedicated cell phone. Wildlife could never fight for itself, but a single prosecution over corruption, we believed, might unleash a surge of emotion and all at once re-empower a people. AC was to give Cameroonians the option to launch cost-free court cases against corrupt officials using our legal team, which had documented and overcome bribing attempts in eighty percent of our court cases.

Marius and I sent an undercover investigator to the media school at Yaoundé University along with a bailiff who, being sworn in by the court, could give admissible testimony of an act of corruption. A presidential decree had fixed a low price for higher education, but the director of the media school had forced students to pay an amount more than ten times that price. The assistant university director pointed to a piece of paper and said to our investigator and the bailiff, "If you want to register to study, you need to deposit this amount into this bank account."

We drafted a complaint. The students' association registered the complaint with the court and signed it as an organization, because students feared that signing the complaint as individuals would endanger their lives. They were demanding damages on behalf of all students who'd paid bribes and the poorer students who'd lost the opportunity to study because they could not pay. Marius was working to ensure that the case wasn't bribed into oblivion. And I was allocating more and more time to new initiatives related to democracy and human rights, hoping to build and nurture a community of activists and thus focus not just on enemies but allies.

At the station, the mood was tense with the reality we'd forced our way into the house of the father of a rebel leader. Men clutching guns watched the door for Ikama's son. Bonaventure and those who'd stayed behind couldn't believe how much ivory we spread across the tables. The smiling captain praised us for our work, photographed the leopard skins and the ivory necklaces, chopsticks, a small horse, tusks carved with village scenes, statues of bare-breasted women. Ikama stood in the corner, his bottom lip jutting out, arms wrapped around his ribs. A soldier paced, cell phone in one hand, rifle with a banana clip in the other.

Ikama had collaborated with a long-time Japanese mistress in trading ivory.

The room went quiet.

Bonaventure turned his head toward the entrance. Every man in the station was focused on the door. The rebel leader Marien Ikama wore a khaki suit with a short-sleeved top. He was a large man with broad shoulders and a French moustache, and he spoke to the officer nearest the door, in a voice so soft it was nearly inaudible.

The captain stepped forward and extended his hand. Everyone stared as the captain said, "Your father was caught with this merchandise, which is illegal by the authorities of the Ministry of Forest Economy. The wildlife authorities have taken his statement. The state counsel is aware he is being held. We are instructed to keep him in the station until his case arrives to court."

The rebel leader stood quietly, hands at his sides. Anxious officers seemed to be wondering, as I was, whether he had men waiting on the other side of the door.

"You can talk to your father now," the captain said, "and I advise you to speak to the state counsel."

I doubted there was an officer in the room who didn't respect the captain for how he composed himself, defusing much of the tension without being apologetic.

Marien Ikama walked over to his father, spoke briefly with him, and exited.

Several days later, I waited at the Brazzaville courthouse. It was Friday. The court was closing early. Bonaventure was late bringing the complaint report and the transmission letter signed by the director general of the ministry. He was also bringing Ikama, who the state counsel had decided would be moved from the holding cell at the police station to jail.

A skinny old man in glasses worked the desk at the registrar's office.

"Don't close, please," I told him. "We need just a few minutes more."

He smiled from behind a mountain range of files.

The court's corridors were covered but open to the air. The concrete was swept clean, the paint fresh, the shade as cool as if it had just rained. I leaned against the railing and thought of the team back in Cameroon. The guilt and stress I figured I'd feel being away so long from LAGA was absent. I felt relief, actually; LAGA functioned even without my calling to check in. Mostly gone from the time of the first volunteers, when I'd struggled with my ego, was the feeling and fear that I'd couldn't minimize myself for the cause. There was joy in this new freedom. I could cross borders to spread the fight and to find new ones. But it was less and less likely I would ever have the space in my life to let one day on the savannah stretch into a hundred.

Bonaventure arrived in a fine suit. Ikama, not handcuffed, was ringed by family members. His daughters or nieces were talking to him, one woman crying, pleading. The rebel leader followed in khaki, moving with the slow heavy steps of a man who knew he was a presence. Bonaventure led the elder Ikama into the registrar's office. Everyone followed except Marien. Five meters from where I stood, the rebel leader leaned against the concrete railing of the corridor and stared at my face.

I stared back, arms crossed to stop them from trembling. Whatever he might do, he could not do it at the courthouse.

Bonaventure and Ikama exited the registrar's office and moved off toward the jail, trailed by the family. The rebel leader joined the entourage for a few paces and stopped. With no choice but to walk past him to exit the court, I moved forward, my heart thrashing. The rebel stepped away from the railing and stopped in front of me.

"This is not your country," he said in a quiet, chilling voice. "Be careful. You don't know this country."

I reached into my suit pocket and pulled out a business card. I put it in his hand.

"This is my work," I said. "My name is there. You can find me at that address."

I walked down the corridor and swallowed. The road was but a few steps beyond the edge of the court but it might have been all of Central Africa. As I stopped a rattling taxicab and climbed inside, I fought the urge and did not look back.

POSTSCRIPT

Ofir and I began writing at Tel Qazir in July 2008, the kibbutz where his mother moved after she and Azaria divorced. At that time, we were already best friends. The technique we developed in working together was half therapy, half interrogation, as I pushed Ofir to reach into the past and look at himself in new ways. The rush of neurotransmitters released throughout a life of intense experience has preserved his memory down to staggeringly small details, like the colors of chairs. Some days as we worked, the conversation was akin to friends telling stories, as when we planned scenes of his time with Leo in Nigeria and reminisced about walking between villages. Other times we argued for hours, as when we tried to capture the feeling of being charged by hyenas. Then there was Rachel—Rachel and Ofir's quixotic, eternal devotion to all things concerning her that I tried and failed to free him from. To tell Ofir there was no space for scenes of counting her freckles was to invite the risk he might lunge across the table with a knife.

In Israel, as I got to know his mother, Keti, I understood that her son's story could only have arisen from the rare household where courage, individualism, and compassion had been emphasized. "My energy and my children's energy were like wood and fire," Keti told me. I watched her wash random cars at dawn, give falafel to strangers, scoop up a weak fledgling egret on the banks of the Sea of Galilee. So affected was I by Keti, who fits nearly all her possessions into a single small bag, that I returned to the U.S. and gave away much of what I owned. It was my attempt to erase some of what I'd inherited: the distinction between what is mine and what is not.

Since we met in 2000 on the rundown rooftop of Planet Safari in Nairobi, Ofir has nurtured in me the courage to live by my own rules and then to break them, and I hope in writing together I have helped him to know and love more fully who he is. Ofir can be difficult and argumentative and, like all of us, he is often far from the man he was walking the shores of Lake Turkana. But our friendship is a brotherhood, intense and yet full of laughter, forged in the common voice of this story.

Throughout our writing, Ofir insisted we break all illusions of heroism, his belief that it is the stories and details no one wants told that are the truest. It was essential, also, to reject the myth that to aspire to do beautiful things requires nothing more than a motivation of love. We worried, also, that if the book ended merely to encapsulate Ofir's life and work, that our message might die on the page. Even if we did succeed in inspiring anyone, was inspiration without a resulting action too fleeting to have value?

So we close with a conversation from Thailand, where we went to write for a month and visit his father. "Daud," Ofir said, "when I was with you in Texas, remember I did that French radio interview on the phone, with *my* French, my really horrible French? I got emails from people saying they were inspired. Some people wrote, 'Where can I give a small donation?' It's really gratifying to hear this. But giving money is the way out. It's a way of releasing the pressure to do something positive. So I wrote back, 'If you're inspired, there are better things you can do with this feeling. Use this energy to do things in the same spirit. It doesn't have to be in Africa. It doesn't have to be big. There are so many things that are waiting for you to come and change.

"The difference between an activist and a non-activist is understanding you have the ability to make a change. Most people are not participating in shaping the communities they live in. They minimize it to voting. Everybody is pissed off about something: a billboard put up in front of their house, a park in their neighborhood that was bulldozed, something they heard about on television. But they move on. Activism is understanding that you're able to do something as an individual. It doesn't feel like altruism. It feels natural. You recognize your right and your responsibility to participate."

DAVID MCDANNALD is an American writer, who lives on a ranch in the West Texas mountains. He splits his time between caring for the cattle herd and traveling in Africa and South America. He has published fiction and nonfiction in various magazines and journals. He and Ofir met in Kenya in 2000 and they became best friends.

OFIR DRORI is an Israeli activist based in Central Africa. A former army officer, educator, journalist, photographer, and adventurer, he has spent the past decade in two dozen different African countries. He founded LAGA in 2003 and leads various efforts against corruption for conservation, democracy, and the rule of law.